OVERVIEW OF EARLY CUSTOMARY LAWS ACROSS THE WORLD

OVERVIEW OF EARLY CUSTOMARY LAWS ACROSS THE WORLD

Marko Nikolić

SOCIETY Publishing

www.societypublishing.com

Overview of Early Customary Laws Across the World

Marko Nikolić

Society Publishing
224 Shoreacres Road
Burlington, ON L7L 2H2
Canada
www.societypublishing.com
Email: orders@arclereducation.com

ISBN: 978-1-77469-853-2 (Hardcover)

ABOUT THE AUTHOR

Marko obtained his Master's degree from the University of Belgrade - Faculty of Law in 2014. He specialized in Criminal Law, Family Law, and Environmental Law. He spent his Master's year studying international child abduction in the modern world. He was employed in the Ministry of Defense's Legal Department and was also working as a legal secretary in numerous educational institutions. His freelance engagements are including more than 40 long-term clients and he also established a consulting agency in 2021. He is the head of the sector in a company specializing in intellectual property and his focus is in trademarking. In addition to professional literature editing, he published a novel on the subject of history and mythology in 2020. Out of office his main focus are environmental and ecological issues.

TABLE OF CONTENTS

LIST OF FIGURES

LIST OF ABBREVIATIONS

AI	Artificial Intelligence
CAB	Citizens Advice Bureau
CDT	Cognitive Dissonance Theory
CEDAW	Convention on the Elimination of All Forms of Discrimination against Women
EEZ	Exclusive Economic Zone
EU	European Union
GC12	Global Challenge 12
HCD	Human-Centered Design
ICC	International Criminal Court
ICJ	International Court of Justice
ILO	International Labor Organization
MP	Member of Parliament
SDT	Self-Determination Theory
SLT	Social Learning Theory
UDHR	Universal Declaration of Human Rights
UN	United Nations
UNCLOS	United Nations Convention on the Law of the Sea
UNODC	United Nations Office on Drugs and Crime

PREFACE

Customary law is an ancient legal system that has been used for hundreds of years to regulate civil disputes and behavior within a specific community. While it may not have the same power or reach as modern laws, customary law still provides an understanding of the many aspects of past societies around the world while offering guidance on contemporary issues today.

This book considers what customary law is, its origins in various cultures throughout history, and how these laws continue to be reflected in countries all over the globe, even today. The book will also discuss some potential challenges when implementing such legislation and why there are increasing calls for a more unified approach towards customarily sourced norms. We will examine ways in which studying customary law can help shape our view of society's values, including both current and historical perspectives.

Customary law encompasses procedures and practices that are handed down orally or passed on through generations. It is, therefore, an ancient form of legal system that exists in virtually every civilized society and culture across the world. This type of law is based primarily upon local customs and traditions and is generally enforced by a community rather than being imposed from above. It could be argued, therefore, that customary law is the egalitarian version of other forms of ordinary law.

Customary laws are highly influential in modern societies because they function as protective mechanisms to ensure justice among members within a particular community or culture. Such laws are deeply rooted in the history and realities of people. Therefore, they can help to embed justice and order within communities in ways that would be impossible under conventional law. Customary laws also help protect important cultural values from becoming eroded when external forces such as globalization try to impact them negatively. This is particularly important for those communities attempting to escape the ravages of coloniality.

The core principles of customary law include recognizing past relationships (customs between families, for example), mediating disputes (particularly those without established written processes), and providing fair reparation if needed. These rules can often be found encoded in unwritten codes known as "sharia's." These are notable for describing complex social systems for regulating behavior, including marriage ceremonies, divorce decrees, land management matters, and other important facets of life.

This book considers the ways in which we are governed by customary laws around the world today in much the same way as it was centuries ago. Customary law existed before any civil code was developed or installed. We will also explore the processes of officially turning customary law into two sources of law. These include formal codified and non-codified sources. The comprises customs or traditions representing our societal values. In doing so, this book makes the case that customary law is what we want our citizens to adhere to. This ought to be done willingly within communities at large where internal consensus remains paramount.

CHAPTER 1

Introduction to Customary Law

Contents

This introductory chapter begins to explore the basic tenets of customary law. We will explore what customary law is and is not. The chapter will discuss the implications of legal customs as well as their relation to patterns of human behavior. In doing so, we will consider whether objectivity can be achieved in the practices of law. The chapter will then contextualize customary law into societies and communities. To begin this discussion, we must first develop a clear understanding of what customary law is.

1.1. WHAT IS CUSTOMARY LAW?

Customary laws continue to shape many aspects of our lives even though formalized national legislation (Polanski, 2017; Pratiwi et al., 2020; Qerimi, 2020; Quane, 2013; Rautenbach, 2020; Rose, 1989; Rubin, 1990; Russo, 1988). Such legislation will have been signed off over time. Indeed, these laws will be directly or indirectly influencing decisions made by the state and its agencies. They are considered legitimate whether related to family dispute cases or settled via arbitration. Reform is an important agenda item due to any existing deficits in family law.

There are several advantages that are associated with customary law (Dahlitz, 1991; Damato, 1973; Damato et al., 1993; Dancer, 2017; Danilenko, 1988; Davis & Klare, 2010; De ruysscher, 2008; de Vries, 2021). For example, disputes under this regime are settled more quickly than going through expensive court proceedings. Moreover, customary law is associated with quicker decisions taking place with few jurists appointed there ruled only applying certain statutory regulations. Such a regime is advantageous in not covering all areas of law so that only pressing matters are address.

The organization of customary law is based on community consensus (Sheleff, 1994, 2013; Shingleton, 1983; Sibisi, 2020; Siegel, 2015; Sierra, 1995; Singer, 1972; Skomerska-Muchowska, 2017). This means that it is not necessarily an adversarial system thereby allowing some flexibility in the management of cases. Customary law is designed so that people associate on a much deeper level. Supporters of this approach believe it respects what is always acceptable according to traditional views accepted.

It is notable that until now, many disputes were successfully settled using customary law instead forcing decisions on people that disagree with them (Bennett, 2008, 2009, 2015; Benson & Siddiqui, 2014; Bianchi, 2009; Bond, 2009, 2010; Botha & Bekink, 2018). This is a legal system that avoids suddenly and harshly imposing rules on a reluctant society. Indeed, one of the enduring criticisms of conventional law is the possibility that most citizens disagree with them. The failure to gain consensus in conventional legislation can lead to political strife, potentially resulting chaos.

Different contexts will have a range of adaptations and facilitations that support customary law (Maiorescu, 2015; McAuslan, 2015; McCarthy, 1971; McLachlan, 1988; Menski, 1988; Meron, 1987, 1991). The extent to which this type of law is decisive will also vary. For instance, some societies are highly reliant on custom while others merely utilize it as an alternative when conventional law has proved unsatisfactory in some way. The law will fall within a system and structures. Figure 1.1 is an example of a legislative and judicial system that has some limited space for customary laws as part of the heritage of the community.

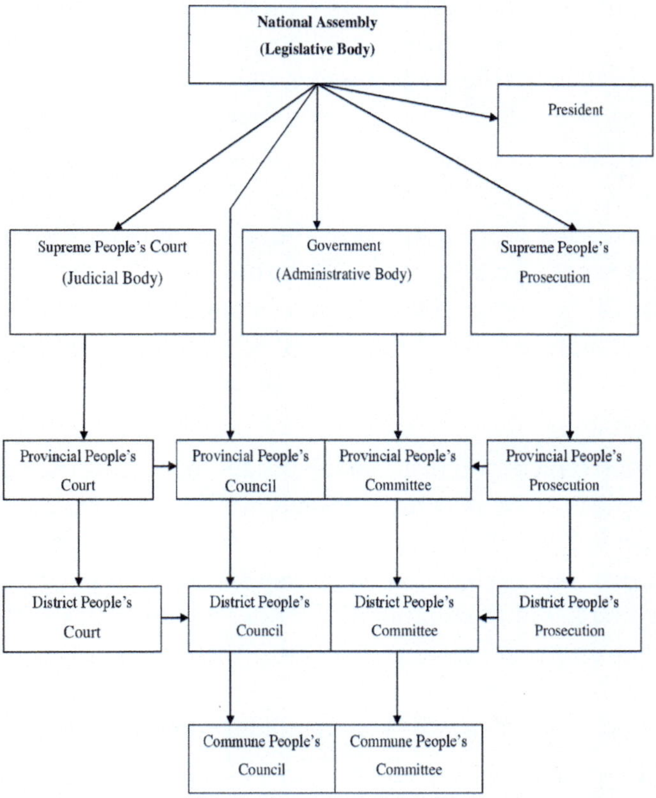

Figure 1.1. Legal pluralism and recognition of customary law in Vietnam.

Source: Nhat Thanh Phan (2011).

Some think of the legal system as a system that is living and must be refreshed by perspectives from the communities that are led under that system (Bourgon, 2020; Budlender et al., 2011; Buss, 2010; Buxbaum, 1968;

Cannizzaro & Bonafe, 2005; Carrillo-Santarelli, 2017; Castillo & Bian, 2014). Customary law is under constant review through societal interactions thus avoiding the effects of closed systems that eventually die. Of course, society can never be satisfied entirely. Nevertheless, customary law attempts to address some of the pressing issues for members of communities. It is notable for following the norms and values of the community. This avoids a conventional path that has been critiqued for furthering entropy within the legal framework.

Settlements under customary law are greatly appreciated all parties involved (Morudu & Maimela, 2021; Murphy, 2014; Mwalimu, 1988; Mwambene, 2012; Mwangi, 2022; Ndulo, 2011). This is because they have the effect of enabling debates. Moreover, it could be argued that customary law rulings are driven by naturally resilient models which reflect the norms, values, and practices of the context under which they are implemented. This means that customary law ties us closer to our communities and traditions.

Customary law is an important part of legal systems around the world (Kim, 2020; Kingwill, 2016; Koskenniemi, 1990; Kreso, 2010; Krieger, 2006; Kumar, 2020; Lagji, 2019; Lavalle, 2014; Laylin, 1976). However, it is often informally overlapping with written legislation. In this section, discuss some of the key components and implications of customary law as they apply to countries today. The concept of customary law encompasses a body of traditional beliefs backed by usage or customs practiced over time in certain regions.

These rules typically reflect social values that are consistent with the norms and values of that context (Kane, 1972; Kassoti, 2017; Kelly & Windia, 2019; Kilian, 2019; Kim, 2009, 2020; Kingwill, 2016). Examples of these norms and values include respect for elders and reciprocity between members within communities. Other communities will emphasize environmental norms regulating land use. Then there are norms that are address dispute resolution procedures. These latter are conceived, designed, and implemented in such a way as to maintain communal peace.

All these achievements of customary law are contextualized (Snyder, 1984; Sprankling, 2014; Sun, 2010; Syaufi & Zahra, 2021; Tan, 1993, 2018; Tegnan, 2015). This type of law relies on consensus and mutuality. Customary law, for example, allows for settling contentious disputes without depending on external judicial machinery. Some systems even include moral codes governing personal behavior. Customary law is owned collectively by a people. That means that the community will harness strategies for ensuring that the law is broadly and specifically protected from undue external influence.

Despite the extreme variations of customary law from one region, it is mainly founded on the same broad principles of community engagement (Petersen, 2017; Pocar, 2016; Poespasari, 2020; Polanski, 2017; Pratiwi et al., 2020; Qerimi, 2020; Quane, 2013; Rautenbach, 2020). The variations in its specific practice reflect local tastes and preferences. Customary laws vary from one place to another due to cultural differences across geographic borders. These issues have the potential for creating even more conflict when dealing with cases that have cross-cultural and cross-border implications. A case in point is land ownership and management which can vastly vary among neighbors who are in a common regional union. As Figure 1.2 shows, the issues may be historical, contemporary, or even looking towards a more sustainable future.

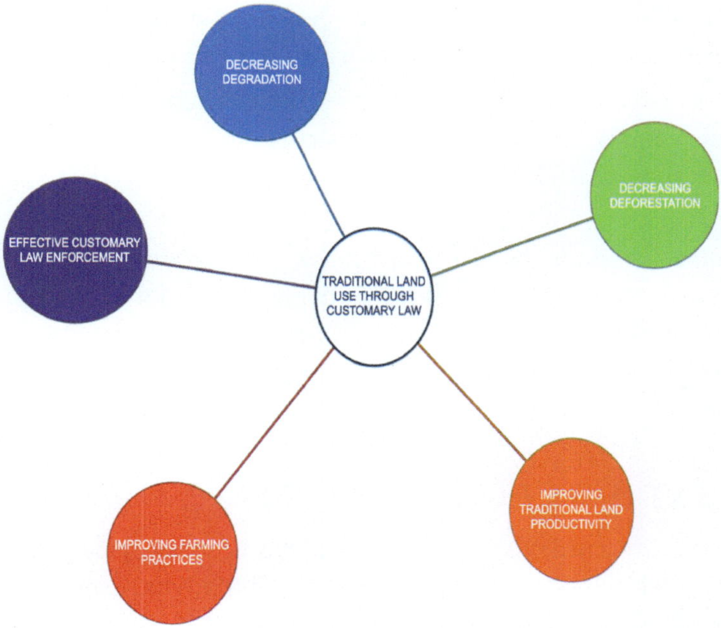

Figure 1.2. Forest management based on local culture of Dayak Kotabaru.

Source: Ifrani, et al., (2019).

Customary law has been described as comprising generalized attitudes toward life (Johnson, 1986; Joireman, 2008; Jonas & Gunda, 2015; Kadens, 2012; Kammerhofer, 2012; Kane, 1972; Kassoti, 2017; Kelly & Windia,

2019). Others speak of custom when enrolled into legalese frameworks. These frameworks comprise present-day laws which are recorded on paper. Those laws are responsible for specifying ways in which things should be handled.

For example, they set the foundation for respecting disciplinary proceedings. Such proceedings are derived from local traditions which have been operationalized and witnessed for many generations.

One characteristic feature uniting customary laws is their emphasis on human relationships rather than rights (Sierra, 1995; Singer, 1972; Skomerska-Muchowska, 2017; Snyder, 1984; Sprankling, 2014; Sun, 2010; Syaufi & Zahra, 2021).

Such an approach can make customary law enforcement difficult, if not impossible, under modern criminal justice systems. In modern judicial systems, penalties are mainly conceived prohibitively as punishments. To this effect, indigenous penalties based solely upon principles like restitution have sometimes served complementarily within nation-states.

This is because the basic intention of conventional laws followed retribution modes and ensuring ordinary civil order through powerful deterrence strategies (Mnisi & Claassens, 2009; Moore, 1986; Morrison, 2016;

Morudu & Maimela, 2021; Murphy, 2014; Mwalimu, 1988). The strategies of contemporary judicial systems are rooted more directly in societal fearfulness as opposed to consensus. To further analyze the implications of customary laws, it is necessary to have a good conceptualization of what a legal custom is and what it is not.

1.2. WHAT IS A LEGAL CUSTOM?

A legal custom is a practice or tradition that has been accepted by a particular society as having the force of law (O'Neill, 2002; Oba, 2002, 2008, 2011; Obatusin, 2018; Olaf & Markus, 2018; Omidire, 1990; Orebech et al., 2005). It is an unwritten rule, based on long-standing practices and beliefs, which may be enforced by courts in certain circumstances.

Legal customs are often seen as part of the common law system, where they can supplement written laws to provide additional guidance for judges when making decisions. Figure 1.3 represents a typological diagram of customs.

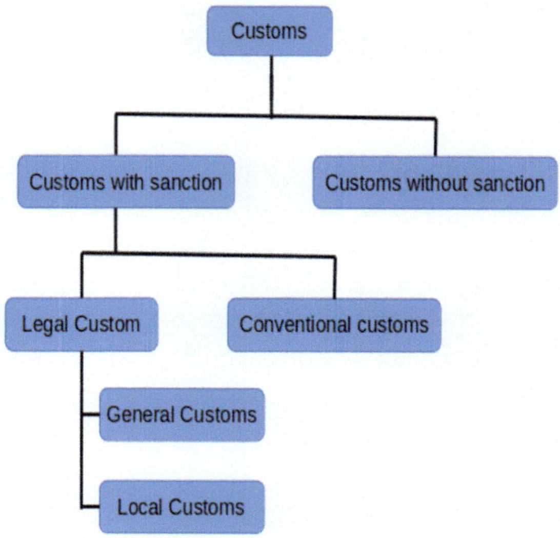

Figure 1.3. Various types of legal customs.

Source: Dr. Ganesh Visavale.

Legal customs have existed since ancient times and continue to play an important role in many societies today (Kelly & Windia, 2019; Kilian, 2019; Kim, 2009, 2020; Kingwill, 2016; Koskenniemi, 1990; Kreso, 2010; Krieger, 2006). In some cases, these customs are codified into statutes or regulations. However, most remain unenforced unless challenged in court. For example, it is generally accepted that people should not steal from one another. This principle is not explicitly stated in any statute but would likely be upheld if someone were to bring a case before a judge.

Customs vary widely between different cultures and countries (Frulli, 2015; Gadzo, 2018; Gagnon-Bergeron, 2018; Gal-Or, 2015; Galindo & Yip, 2017; Gao, 2013; Gillespie & Tran, 2022; Golo et al., 2022). What may be considered acceptable behavior in one place might be completely unacceptable elsewhere. This means that it is important for individuals who travel abroad to familiarize themselves with local customs. Hence, they will ensure that they do not inadvertently break any laws or offend anyone unintentionally.

In addition to providing guidance on how people should behave towards each other, legal customs also help define relationships between citizens and their government or ruler(s) (McCarthy, 1971; McLachlan, 1988; Menski, 1988; Meron, 1987, 1991; Meron et al., 1987; Merry, 1991; Meyer, 2012).

These rules can include things like paying taxes on time or respecting the authority of elected officials. The implication is that failure to comply with such expectations could result in serious consequences depending on the jurisdiction involved.

Overall, legal customs are an integral part of many societies around the world and serve as an important source of stability within those communities (Gray, 2021; Griffiths, 1998; Hager, 2020; Haggenmacher, 2021; Hammond, 2019; Harmathy, 2016; Henry, 2017; Hernández, 2012). They provide both structure and flexibility when interpreting existing laws while helping ensure everyone follows basic principles of decency towards others. This occurs regardless of location or culture differences.

As such, understanding legal customs is essential for anyone wishing to abide by local laws wherever they go (Holleman, 1969, 1972; Horii, 2019; Howell, 2018; Hu, 2017; Huizenga, 2018, 2022; Hulme, 2010). Legal customs can inform certain ordinary activities and procedures such as the construction of a legal document. The legal document is an essential part of any business transaction. It serves as a written agreement between two or more parties, outlining the terms and conditions of their relationship.

A well-crafted legal document can help protect all involved parties from potential disputes and misunderstandings down the line. However, that legal document should broadly chime with the local customs (de Vries, 2021; De Wet, 2004; Debelva & De Broe, 2022; Dekoster, 2019; Demian, 2014; Anthony C Diala, 2017). When creating a legal document, it is important to consider several key elements. These include accuracy, clarity, completeness, consistency, and enforceability. Accuracy means that all information included in the document must be accurate and up to date. Moreover, clarity ensures that each party understands what they are agreeing to. In creating legal documents based on customs, one must have a clear idea of what is binding and not binding (Figure 1.4).

Figure 1.4. Custom as a source of law.

Source: Law corner.

The legal document addresses practicalities that establish and moderate a contractual relationship. For instance, completeness requires that all relevant details are included in the contract. Additionally, consistency ensures that similar language is used throughout the entire document. Finally, enforceability guarantees that both parties will abide by its terms if necessary. It is never clear whether custom alone can achieve all these goals and objectives (Pratiwi et al., 2020; Qerimi, 2020; Quane, 2013; Rautenbach, 2020; Rose, 1989; Rubin, 1990; Russo, 1988; Sarbah, 1904).

That is why custom is a secondary consideration in contract law when there is an established written law. It is important to ensure your legal documents comply with applicable laws in your jurisdiction and that they are consistent with local customs (Rose, 1989; Rubin, 1990; Russo, 1988; Sarbah, 1904; Seidman, 1983; Sheleff, 1994, 2013; Shingleton, 1983). This includes making sure you include any required notices or disclosures for certain types of contracts. A case in point is the level of detail required for certain contracts such as those involving real estate.

To fully benefit from contract law, it is imperative to have legal support which is also aware of local customs and practices (Pedersen, 2014; Pelizzon, 2015; Perreau-Saussine & Murphy, 2007; Petersen, 2007, 2017). For example, you should always have an attorney review your documents before signing them off on behalf of either party. This helps ensure everything is legally binding and valid under local law. When trying to enforce contractual rights, this can become a critical consideration.

Creating custom legal documents may seem like a daunting task at first, bearing in mind the diversity of customs and practices. However, the experts concur that it does not have to be an impossible task or a barrier to engaging in contractual relationships. With the right tools and resources, one can easily create professional-looking documents that are tailored to their specific needs. Having an awareness of local customs and practices can also be of enormous assistance (Crawford, 2012; Criddle, 2013; Cuskelly, 2011; Dahlitz, 1991; Damato, 1973; Damato et al., 1993; Dancer, 2017; Danilenko, 1988).

The attraction of customary law over conventional law is that it is accessible to lay people (Vanboven, 1991; Vergouwen, 2013; Vines, 2017; Watson, 1984; Webber, 2009; Weinberg, 2016; Williams & Klusener, 2013). This extends to the management of contractual documents. One of the most important things to remember when creating legal documents is that they should always be written in plain language. This helps ensure both parties understand what they are agreeing to without any confusion or ambiguity. Additionally, make sure all relevant information is included in the document so there's no room for misinterpretation down the line.

Legal customs will form part of the background knowledge that is necessary to negotiate the intricacies of contracts as well as any accompanying legal documents (Anthony C Diala, 2017; Diala, 2017, 2019; Diala &

Bagni, 2019; Dubner, 1994; Dubois, 1992; Dupont, 2013; Duxbury, 2017). To maintain professional exclusivity, the legal profession has sometimes acted as a serious barrier to those that wish to engage in business and other activities. Hence, the idea that there are segments of the community that will eschew conventional laws in favor of less formal routes. That is why customary law is often linked to the complexities of human behavior.

1.3. UNDERSTANDING PATTERNS OF HUMAN BEHAVIOR

Human behavior is a complex phenomenon that has been studied by scientists for centuries (Jonas & Gunda, 2015; Kadens, 2012; Kammerhofer, 2012; Kane, 1972; Kassoti, 2017; Kelly & Windia, 2019; Kilian, 2019; Kim, 2009). It involves the study of how individuals interact with each other in social situations as well as how they respond to external stimuli such as environmental factors or cultural norms. Patterns of human behavior emerge from these interactions and can be used to better understand why people act the way they do in certain contexts.

One key factor influencing human behavior is genetics (Kumar, 2020; Lagji, 2019; Lavalle, 2014; Laylin, 1976; Lewis, 1983, 2016; Liakopoulos, 2019; Lijnzaad, 2022; Lingaas, 2022). Our genes play an important role in determining our personality traits and behaviors. Additionally, research suggests that early childhood experiences also shape our later behaviors. This includes things like parenting styles or exposure to different environments during development. Moreover, culture plays a major role in shaping patterns of human behavior.

It is notable that different cultures have their own set of values which influence how people think and behave within those societies (Fleck, 2013; Fletcher, 2007; Frulli, 2015; Gadzo, 2018; Gagnon-Bergeron, 2018; Gal-Or, 2015; Galindo & Yip, 2017; Gao, 2013). This is not something to be frowned upon but rather embraced in our contemporary culture of acceptance. Indeed, the notion of cultural relativity is designed to ensure that we do not rank cultures and practices. This is because such ranking can become the precursor to bigotry and unfair treatment.

Indeed, fairness under the law is a crucial aspect of customary law (Lijnzaad, 2022; Lingaas, 2022; Lita et al., 2017; Liu, 2019; Loja, 2014; Lon & Widyawati, 2021; Magnusson, 2013, 2017; Manaka & Corrin, 2021). Human behavior, from which customary law emerges, is a complex collection of patterns of responses to stimuli. To gain a better understanding of human behavior it is important to consider all these factors together rather than looking at them individually. Only then can we begin to uncover the underlying patterns behind why people act the way they do in various contexts.

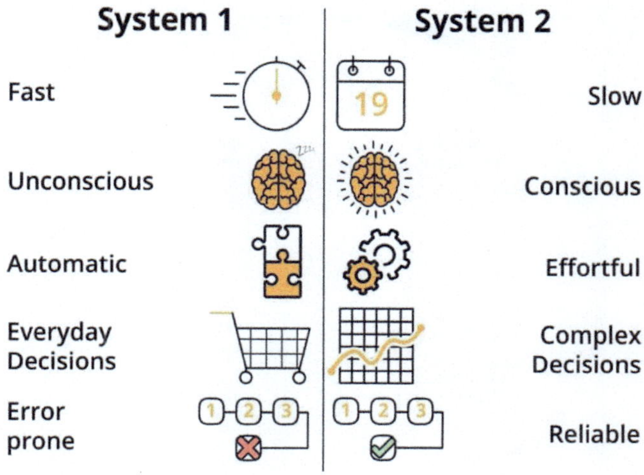

Figure 1.5. Two patterns of human behavior research.

Source: iMotions.

As Figure 1.5 shows, there are two emerging patterns of research into human behavior which might be relevant to our understanding of customary law (Meron et al., 1987; Merry, 1991; Meyer, 2012; Milanovic, 2011; Mnisi & Claassens, 2009; Moore, 1986; Morrison, 2016). The first system considers human behavior to be fast, unconscious, automatic, associated with everyday decisions, and prone to error. The second strand perceives behavior to be slow, conscious, effortful, associated with complex decisions, and reliable. Obvious there is intersection and agreement between these two approaches. The important thing is understanding how and why people respond to stimuli in specific ways.

By doing so we can develop more effective strategies for managing difficult situations or helping individuals reach their full potentials both personally and professionally. It can also be crucial for ensuring better harmonization of differing personalities that exist in communities. Customary law is important in conflict resolution because it moderates human behavior (Bianchi, 2009; Bond, 2009, 2010; Botha & Bekink, 2018; Bourgon, 2020; Budlender et al., 2011; Buss, 2010). If we take the example of human behavior in business, it becomes clear that custom and practice underpins our response in ways that can be interesting (Figure 1.6).

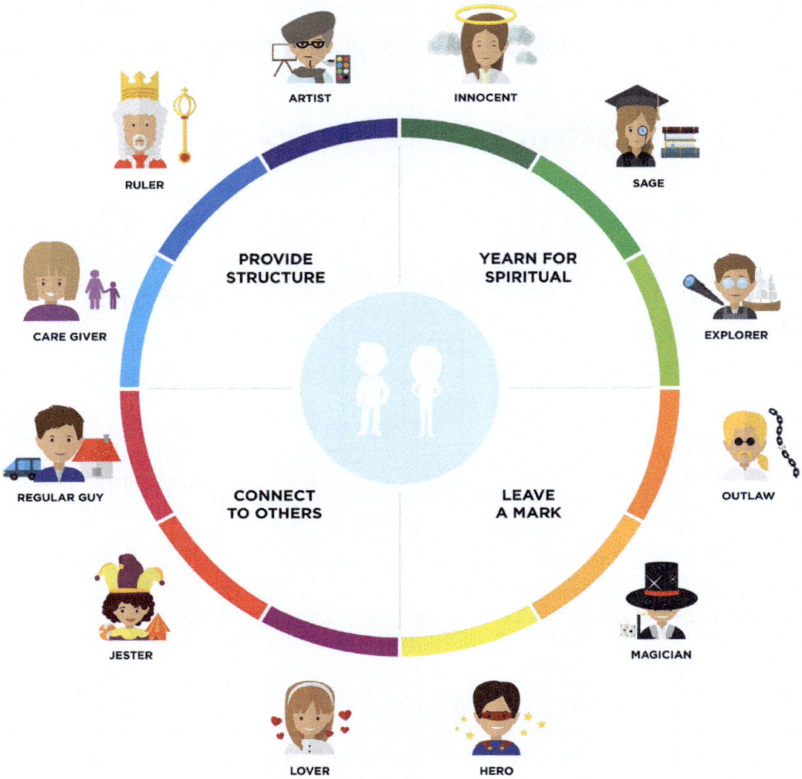

Figure 1.6. Business and human behavior.

Source: Medium.

Business relationships are an integral part of any successful organization. They involve the exchange of goods and services, as well as the sharing of knowledge and resources. As such, it is important to understand how human behavior can impact these relationships to ensure that they remain strong and productive. These relationships are necessarily a function of custom or even the laws that emanate from such customs (Lewis, 2016; Liakopoulos, 2019; Lijnzaad, 2022; Lingaas, 2022; Lita et al., 2017; Liu, 2019; Loja, 2014; Lon & Widyawati, 2021). The impact on business can be enormous.

One way in which human behavior can affect business relationships is through communication. Poor communication between parties can lead to misunderstandings or disagreements, resulting in a breakdown of trust and respect between them. This is an aspect of socialization which is not necessary address by conventional law but has relevance for customary law (Chirayath et al., 2005; Claassens & Mnisi, 2009; Cooter, 1991; Corrin & Mulitalo, 2015; Costa, 1998; Craik, 2020; Crawford, 2012). Business relationships involve mutuality and reciprocity. It is therefore essential for all parties involved to be clear about their expectations from each other, as well as being open and honest when communicating with one another. This will help foster a positive working environment where everyone feels comfortable expressing their opinions without fear of judgment or criticism.

Another factor that affects business relationships is attitude towards change. Indeed, these attitudes may also have implications for the broad acceptance of customary law (Ngira, 2021; Nhlapo, 2017; Nnona, 2018; Norr, 1973; Nwapi, 2016; Nyane, 2019; O'Neill, 2002; Oba, 2002). People often resist change due to fear or uncertainty, but this can have a negative effect on the relationship if not managed properly. It is important for both parties involved to be willing to adapt and embrace new ideas for progress to be made within the relationship itself. If either party refuses to accept changes then this could lead to stagnation or even conflict between them which would ultimately damage the relationship beyond repair.

Overall, it is also important for people involved in business relationships to always show respect towards one another. This holds true regardless of differences in opinion or background experience levels. Respectful behavior helps build trust between individuals which allows them work together more effectively while also creating an atmosphere where everyone feels valued and appreciated by their peers. This is something that should never be taken lightly when dealing with sensitive matters such as those found within business partnerships. Customary law demands the same understanding, respect, and mutuality in community relationships (Bennett, 2009; Benson & Siddiqui, 2014; Bianchi, 2009; Bond, 2009, 2010; Botha & Bekink, 2018; Bourgon, 2020; Budlender et al., 2011).

Understanding how human behavior impacts on business relationships is key for any organization looking achieve success over time. This is an important consideration regardless of whether it is through improved communication practices, embracing change positively or simply showing mutual respect amongst colleagues. All these are all factors that need consideration if you want your partnership flourish. Customary law seeks to regulate human behavior so that there are ground rules on how people behave in specific contexts (Duxbury, 2017; Edmundson, 2015; Elias, 1956;

Enabulele & Bazuaye, 2019; Engel & Kurschilgen, 2013; Farran, 2019; Fenrich et al., 2011). However, the contextual variances and the nature of humanity raises issues of subjectivity and objectivity. The latter is the main topic for the next section.

1.4. OBJECTIVITY IN THE LAW

Judges are tasked with making difficult decisions in the courtroom, and their rulings can have a significant impact on people's lives (Skomerska-Muchowska, 2017; Snyder, 1984; Sprankling, 2014; Sun, 2010; Syaufi & Zahra, 2021; Tan, 1993, 2018). As such, it is important to consider how objective judges are when making these decisions. The concept of judicial objectivity has been debated for centuries. Some argue that judges should be completely impartial and make decisions based solely on the facts presented before them without any personal bias or opinion influencing their decision-making process.

Others believe that judges should take into account their own experiences and opinions when ruling on cases as this could lead to more equitable outcomes for all parties involved (Fenrich et al., 2011; Fleck, 2009, 2013; Fletcher, 2007; Frulli, 2015; Gadzo, 2018; Gagnon-Bergeron, 2018). It is impossible for a judge to be completely unbiased in every case they preside over since they are human beings who bring their own life experiences into the courtroom with them. However, there are steps that can be taken by both lawyers and judges alike to ensure fairness in court proceedings.

To ensure judicial objectivity, certain reforms may be triggered (Benson & Siddiqui, 2014; Bianchi, 2009; Bond, 2009, 2010; Botha & Bekink, 2018; Bourgon, 2020; Budlender et al., 2011; Buss, 2010). For example, attorneys must present evidence objectively so as not to sway the judge's opinion one way or another while also ensuring that all relevant information is included for an informed decision to be made. Judges must also strive towards neutrality by avoiding any preconceived notions about either party involved in a case prior to hearing arguments from both sides of counsel.

Ultimately, complete objectivity may not always be achievable within legal proceedings due to human nature (Horii, 2019; Howell, 2018; Hu, 2017; Huizenga, 2018, 2022; Hulme, 2010; Hutchison, 2020; Hutchison & Sibanda, 2017). Nevertheless, it is still possible for justice systems around the world to strive towards greater levels of fairness through proper training and education of those working within them. The training should be for all including judges themselves. Such interventions are designed to ensure best service and practice for those seeking justice within our courts today. Where subjectivity is the order of the day in judicial process, then judicial bias emerges (Barnabas, 2022; Barrie, 2016; Baxi, 2020; Beavers, 2019; Beer, 2022; Bennett, 2008, 2009, 2015; Benson & Siddiqui, 2014). Judicial bias is a term used to describe the tendency of judges to favor one side over another in legal proceedings. This can be seen in decisions made by judges, as well as their behavior during court hearings and other interactions with parties involved in a case. Judicial bias can have serious implications for the outcome of a trial or hearing. Therefore, it is important that all parties are aware of this potential issue when entering into any kind of legal dispute.

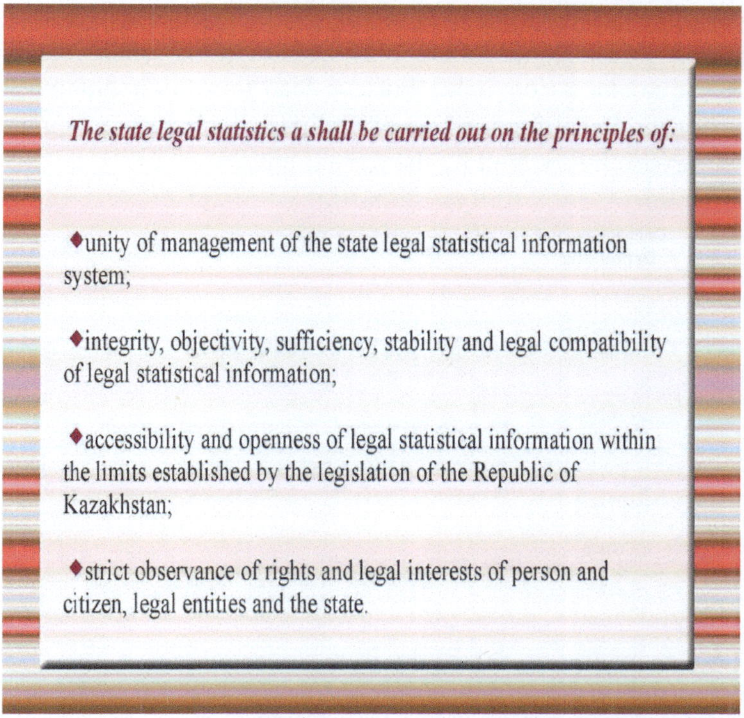

Figure 1.7. Modern collection, processing, and analysis of legal information in Kazakhstan.

Source: BA Amanzholova via ppt-online.

Reporting and recording judicial decisions is very much an integral aspect of ensuring objectivity and fairness in proceedings (Dupont, 2013; Duxbury, 2017; Edmundson, 2015; Elias, 1956; Enabulele & Bazuaye, 2019; Engel & Kurschilgen, 2013; Farran, 2019). Figure 1.7 demonstrates the reporting protocols for judicial decisions in Kazakhstan as a case in point.

Once again, there is an emphasis on objectivity so that the data tells the story rather than focusing too much on personalized experiences and narratives. Of course, those that support judicial discretion may argue that excessive reporting requirements could become perfunctory rather than achieving the expected reforms.

In any case, most aspects of human life including customary law will have some element of objectivity and subjectivity (Masengu, 2016; Mastura, 1994; Maunatlala & Maimela, 2020; Maxim & Titu Maiorescu, 2015; McAuslan, 2015; McCarthy, 1971). Figure 1.8 highlights the key differences between objectivity and subjectivity. The differences between the two approaches does not mean that one is exclusively advantages in all situations. For instance, there may be situations where the biases of the judge are not only inevitable but can lead to a fairer outcome. This is particularly true when the doctrine of equity is deployed to support parties that are otherwise left behind by the formal law.

Categories of Definitions	Subjectivity	Objectivity
Common Use Definitions	Biased, not impartial, based upon opinion, exists only in one's mind, no physical existence, interior experience	Free of bias, impartial, based upon facts, something having physical existence, exterior reality
Grammatical Definition	Pertains to the subject of a verb	Pertains to the object of a verb
Syntactical Definition	At the cause of an action, i.e., "I"	At the effect of an action, i.e., "me"
Current Consciousness Studies Definition	Interior experience, immeasurable, nonphysical (or metaphysical) content	Exterior reality, measured physical bodies

Figure 1.8. Distinguishing objectivity from subjectivity.

Source: Quadernity.

Even where subjectivity is acknowledged, biases in the judicial system must be challenged lest they lead to injustice (Griffiths, 1998; Hager, 2020; Haggenmacher, 2021; Hammond, 2019; Harmathy, 2016; Henry, 2017; Hernández, 2012). The most common form of judicial bias occurs when a judge has an opinion about one party or another before they even hear the evidence presented at trial. This type of prejudice can lead to unfair rulings and verdicts. Such outcomes, which may not reflect the facts presented during litigation, are deemed socially unacceptable. Judges must remain impartial throughout proceedings so that justice is served fairly and without prejudice.

Another form of judicial bias involves personal relationships between judges and attorneys or litigants involved in cases before them. If there is any kind of relationship between these individuals outside the courtroom, it could influence how they view each other's arguments or testimony during trials or hearings. It is important for both sides to disclose any such relationships prior to beginning proceedings so that everyone knows what biases might exist beforehand. The weaknesses of customary law have been partially associated with a failure to account for some of these implicit forms of judicial bias (Murphy, 2014; Mwalimu, 1988; Mwambene, 2012; Mwangi, 2022; Ndulo, 2011; Ngira, 2018, 2021; Nhlapo, 2017).

Some forms of judicial bias involve cultural differences between those appearing before courts around the world. For example, certain cultures may place more emphasis on certain types of evidence than others do. this could lead to different interpretations from different judges depending on their own backgrounds and experiences with similar cases previously heard by them personally or within their jurisdiction overall (Loja, 2014; Lon & Widyawati, 2021; Magnusson, 2013, 2017; Manaka & Corrin, 2021; Manullang, 2021). This has been the case when foreign nationals tend to receive worse judicial outcomes that people who have been socialized into a society. This can have serious implications in areas such as asylum and immigration law.

It is essential for all parties involved in legal disputes to understand how judicial bias works so that they can take steps towards ensuring fairness throughout proceedings. This holds true regardless of whether they are plaintiffs or defendants themselves. Having an awareness of the risks of judicial bias ultimately leads towards better outcomes for everyone involved no matter who wins or loses at trial (Huizenga, 2022; Hulme, 2010; Hutchison, 2020; Hutchison & Sibanda, 2017; Iyi, 2016; Jentoft & Bavinck, 2019). By understanding what constitutes judicial bias ahead-of-time, we can help ensure our justice system remains fair and equitable for all citizens alike going forward into future generations.

Such an approach can contribute towards societal harmony in the same way that customary law has been credited (Meron, 1987, 1991; Meron et al., 1987; Merry, 1991; Meyer, 2012; Milanovic, 2011; Mnisi & Claassens, 2009). It is also important to understand that laws and practices are always contextualized. Hence, the difficulty in transposing laws from foreign lands into communities that have well-established customary laws. This is a process that was last attempted and partially completed during the colonial era. However, there remains a hegemony of laws in which Western and Eurocentric approaches are considered more progressive than the rest of the world. The final section of this chapter considers how societal settings determines the law.

1.5. SOCIETAL SETTINGS AND THEIR LAWS

The creation and implementation of laws is a complex process that involves many different stakeholders (Lon & Widyawati, 2021; Magnusson, 2013, 2017; Manaka & Corrin, 2021; Manullang, 2021; Marasinghe, 1978). It is also heavily influenced by the societal context in which it takes place, as well as the socialization of those involved. This section will explore how these two factors can shape the development and enforcement of laws. In doing so, the section emphasizes the importance of contextualization when conceiving and operationalizing any legal framework.Societal context refers to the cultural, economic, political, and legal environment in which a law is created or implemented (McAuslan, 2015; McCarthy, 1971; McLachlan, 1988; Menski, 1988; Meron, 1987, 1991; Meron et al., 1987). For example, certain countries may have more restrictive laws than others due to their history or culture. A case in point is how the age of consent can vary from 16–21 years depending on the parties and context. Similarly, some societies may be more open to change than others when it comes to introducing new legislation or altering existing ones. The values held by members of society can also play an important role in determining what types of laws are accepted and enforced within a given jurisdiction.

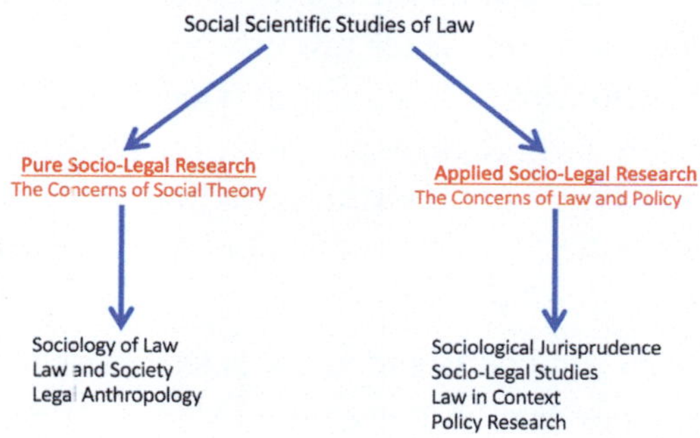

Figure 1.9. Social-scientific studies of law.

Source: Law explorer.

The social-scientific studies of law (Figure 1.9) help us understand how and why legal issues are contextualized. Socialization is another factor that has an impact on law-making processes. Socialization occurs when individuals learn about norms and values from their family members, peers, teachers, and religious leaders. These lessons from society then influences human behavior and attitudes towards certain issues such as crime prevention or public safety measures.

In addition to a direct influence on individual behavior patterns, socialization can also affect how people perceive certain topics related to law-making such as justice systems or criminal punishment methods (Criddle, 2013; Cuskelly, 2011; Dahlitz, 1991; Damato, 1973; Damato et al., 1993; Dancer, 2017; Danilenko, 1988; Davis & Klare, 2010). A case in point is if someone was raised with strong beliefs about capital punishment. The expectation is that they might be less likely to support its use even if other citizens disagree with them on this issue.

Overall, both societal context and socialization have significant impacts on the creation and implementation of laws around the world today (Woodman, 1969, 2001; Worugji et al., 2019; Wu, 2018; Young, 2019; Zamir, 2015; Zarea, 2022; Zenker & Höhne, 2018). Such impact ranges from influencing what types of legislation are passed through parliament to shaping individual opinions regarding specific legal matters like sentencing guidelines for criminals convicted in courtrooms across nations.

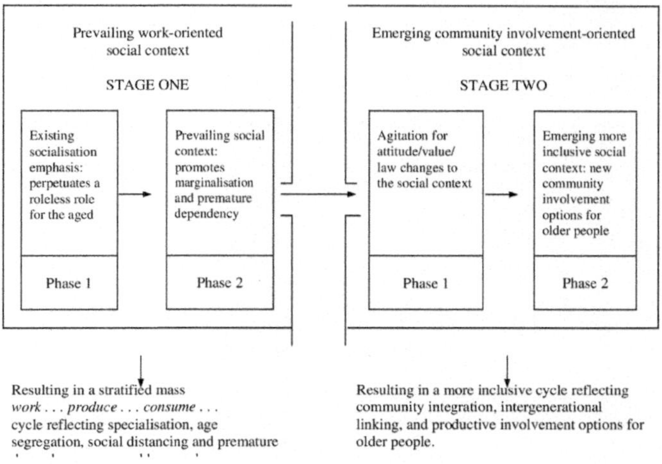

Figure 1.10. Elements of the social context theory.

Source: Earle and Earle (1999).

The social context theory (Figure 1.10) provides a foundation for contextualizing the legislative and judicial process. Understanding these two stages improves our insight into why certain policies exist (or do not exist) at any given time (Demian, 2014; Anthony C Diala, 2017; Diala, 2017, 2019; Diala & Bagni, 2019; Dubner, 1994; Dubois, 1992; Dupont, 2013). In that way, we can work together towards creating fairer systems that benefit all citizens equally regardless of background or personal beliefs and values held by each person. Indeed, this is the foundation for reforming the judicial system.

The issue of specificity is important in all these processes (Gradoni, 2019; Graves, 2017; Gray, 2021; Griffiths, 1998; Hager, 2020; Haggenmacher, 2021; Hammond, 2019; Harmathy, 2016). Currently, it is becoming increasingly important to have laws that are tailored to the specific needs of society. This is because the legal system must adapt and respond quickly to changing social conditions for justice to be served. As such, bespoke laws are necessary for a society's legal framework to remain relevant and effective. The struggle for relevancy is a perpetual judicial practice problem.

Bespoke laws provide an opportunity for lawmakers and legislators to craft legislation that meets the unique needs of their constituents (Meron et al., 1987; Merry, 1991; Meyer, 2012; Milanovic, 2011; Mnisi & Claassens, 2009; Moore, 1986). For example, if a particular region has experienced an influx of immigrants or refugees, then lawmakers can create new immigration policies that address these issues specifically. Similarly, if there is a need for more stringent environmental regulations due to climate change or other factors, then bespoke laws can be crafted accordingly.

Furthermore, bespoke laws allow governments and legislatures greater flexibility when it comes to addressing complex social issues such as poverty or inequality (Poespasari, 2020; Polanski, 2017; Pratiwi et al., 2020; Qerimi, 2020; Quane, 2013; Rautenbach, 2020; Rose, 1989; Rubin, 1990). By crafting legislation that takes into account local circumstances and cultural norms, governments can ensure that their citizens receive fair treatment under the law regardless of their background or economic status. These are precisely some of the advantages that have been associated with customary law.

Generally, having access to bespoke laws allows societies around the world greater autonomy when it comes making decisions about how they want their communities governed (Dubner, 1994; Dubois, 1992; Dupont, 2013; Duxbury, 2017; Edmundson, 2015; Elias, 1956; Enabulele & Bazuaye,

2019; Engel & Kurschilgen, 2013). Rather than relying on outdated statutes from previous eras which may no longer reflect current values or beliefs within a given population group; modern societies now have access tools which enable them craft legislation based on what works best for them at any given time. This is an approach which was not possible before the era of specificity.

Specificity and bespoke legislation cannot be achieved without significant effort being put into researching existing legal frameworks from other countries first (Sibisi, 2020; Siegel, 2015; Sierra, 1995; Singer, 1972; Skomerska-Muchowska, 2017; Snyder, 1984; Sprankling, 2014). Contextualization does not imply insularity or working in silos. Nevertheless, it is clear why having access too tailor-made legislation is so important. First, it increases relevance by allowing governments and legislatures greater freedom when creating new policies. Second, it achieves social justice by providing citizens with fairer treatment under the law. Thirdly, this approach has the effect of giving societies more control over how they wish themselves governed. All these benefits make bespoke laws essential components of any functioning democracy.

CHAPTER 1 SUMMARY

This chapter has introduced customary law to the reader as a preamble to understanding how it is recognized and embedded within modern legal systems. In conceptualization legal customs, this chapter has shown that the law is always contextualized in societies and communities. Moreover, the chapter argues that the law reflects patterns of human behavior. This then raises questions about the extent to which objectivity can be achieved in the law. Such a debate is pertinent when we consider that societal settings have an important role to play in determining what the law is. The next chapter extends this inquiry into how claims are made under customary law.

CHAPTER 2

Claims under Customary Law

Contents

This second chapter considers how and why claims are made under customary law. Hence, the exploration of consuetudinary or unofficial law as well as opinions. In doing so, this chapter interrogates how community standards of behavior are embedded using customary law as an implementing mechanism. The case study of international law shows that this can be a powerful source of legislative influence, if not direct laws. Similar experiences can be attested to during the emergence of the law on piracy. When starting this exploration, it is important to identify situations in which unofficial law holds sway.

2.1. WHAT IS CONSUETUDINARY OR UNOFFICIAL LAW?

Consuetudinary and unofficial law are two terms that are often used interchangeably, but they have distinct meanings (Tomuschat, 2021; Treasure et al., 2016; Tripp, 2004; Tsai, 2015; Robert W Tucker, 1972; Tunkin, 1993). Consuetudinary is a type of customary law that has been developed over time through the practice of people in a particular society or culture. It is based on tradition and custom rather than written laws or statutes. Unofficial law, in contrast, refers to any legal system not recognized by an official government body or court system. This includes both consuetudinary and non-consuetudinary systems such as religious laws, tribal customs, and even private contracts between individuals.

The link between consuetudinary and unofficial law lies in their shared reliance on custom rather than formal legislation for their authority (Rautenbach, 2020; Rose, 1989; Rubin, 1990; Russo, 1988; Sarbah, 1904; Seidman, 1983; Sheleff, 1994, 2013). Both types of legal systems rely heavily on precedent set by past decisions made within the same community or culture to determine how current disputes should be resolved. This means that while there may be no written rules governing these matters, there is still an expectation among members of the community that certain behaviors will be followed when it comes to resolving conflicts or making decisions about important issues affecting them all.

Customary law also plays an important role in both consuetudinary and unofficial legal systems because it provides a framework for understanding how different cultures view certain concepts like justice, fairness, rights, and obligations (Armstrong, 1989; Arowolo, 2019; Asieduakrofi, 1989; Barnabas, 2022; Barrie, 2016; Baxi, 2020; Beavers, 2019). These can then inform decision-making processes within those societies. For example, many indigenous communities around the world use traditional forms of dispute resolution such as mediation instead of relying solely on Western-style courts due to their belief in collective responsibility for maintaining harmony within their communities rather than individual accountability for wrongdoings committed against others outside one's own group.

It is generally recognized that consuetudinary and unofficial law differ from each other in some ways (Sprankling, 2014; Sun, 2010; Syaufi & Zahra, 2021; Tan, 1993, 2018; Tegnan, 2015; Thipe & Buthelezi, 2014). For example, one is noted for being based more heavily upon tradition while the other relies more upon personal agreements. However, they share several commonalities including reliance upon custom rather than formal legislation for authority. Another point of intersection is the recognition of collective responsibility. Furthermore, these two approaches share the utilization of customary laws as guides when making decisions about important matters affecting entire societies or cultures alike.

Figure 2.1. Synonyms of consuetudinary.

Source: Thesaurus plus.

As such these two types of legal systems should not be viewed as mutually exclusive (Figure 2.1). Rather, they should be seen as complementary components necessary for creating effective social structures capable of providing justice to all members (Carrillo-Santarelli, 2017; Castillo & Bian, 2014; Cataldi & Titu Maiorescu, 2015; Chang, 2022; Chanock, 1989; Cheng, 2012). This access must be provided regardless of whether the citizenry lives under officially sanctioned governments or not. Indeed, it could be argued that the principles of fairness in justice hold true even when these two approaches are being utilized. Consuetudinary or unofficial law is a form of legal system that has been in existence since ancient times (Bennett, 2015; Bennett, 2009; Benson & Siddiqui, 2014; Bianchi, 2009; Bond, 2009, 2010; Botha & Bekink, 2018; Bourgon, 2020). It is based on the customs and traditions of a particular society, rather than on written laws. This type of law has been used to regulate social behavior and resolve disputes for centuries. However, its relevance in modern times remains unclear. This is primarily because society has changed, and its needs have followed suit.

The risk associated with relying solely on consuetudinary or customary law is that it can be difficult to enforce due to its lack of codification (Willms, 2009; Wilson, 1961; Wolff, 2016; Woodman, 1988, 1969, 2001; Worugji et al., 2019; Wu, 2018). Without clear rules and regulations, there may be no way to ensure compliance with the law or punish those who violate it. Additionally, this type of legal system often fails to protect vulnerable members of society from exploitation by powerful individuals or groups. That means that it can lead to social injustice and outright oppression if not properly regulated.

	City-states system (Northern-Central Italy)	Feudal system (Southern Italy)
Governance structure	City-level organisations	National organisations, feudal administrations, municipal organs
Actors involved	City administrators, communities	Royal institutions, feudal barons, communities
Legislation	Local laws, consuetudinary norms	National laws, local laws, consuetudinary norms
Resources involved	Territories neighbouring the city belonging to the community	Territories belonging to the kingdom, territories belonging to the feudal barons, territories belonging to the community.

Figure 2.2. Understanding the Southern Italian commons.

Source: Cambridge University Press & Assessment.

The role of traditional or unofficial law remains relevant even in advanced societies such as Italy (Figure 2.2). The key to incorporating these traditional or unofficial forms of justice is to understand their genesis and find ways of harmonizing the intersections they have with contemporary life (Wolff, 2016; Woodman, 1988, 1969, 2001; Worugji et al., 2019; Wu, 2018; Young, 2019; Zamir, 2015). Customary law is often one of the important avenues for bringing unofficial law into the prevailing system. In that way, the advantages of this type of law are acknowledged whilst minimizing the worst negative effects that they could bring.

For consuetudinary and customary law to remain relevant in today's world, certain interventions must be made (Pelizzon, 2015; Perreau-Saussine & Murphy, 2007; Petersen, 2007, 2017; Pocar, 2016; Poespasari, 2020). For example, governments should work towards codifying these laws. This is done so that they are more easily enforced and understood by all parties involved. Furthermore, efforts should also be taken to ensure that these laws are updated regularly so they reflect current societal values and norms as well as protecting vulnerable populations from exploitation. Finally, education initiatives should be implemented so people understand their rights under consuetudinary or customary law as well as how best to use them when necessary.

It could be argued that consuetudinary or unofficial law has served an important role throughout history in regulating social behavior and resolving disputes between individuals within a community (Thipe & Buthelezi, 2014; Thirlway, 1972, 2015, 2017; Tobin, 2014; Tomuschat, 2021; Treasure et al., 2016). Nevertheless, its relevance in modern times depends largely upon the willingness of governments around the world take steps towards ensuring that these laws are properly codified and updated regularly according to changing societal values. By doing so we can ensure that this form of legal system continues providing protection for all citizens regardless their background or status within society. One of the protective mechanisms in contemporary law is the notion of "opinio juris"

2.2. OPINION OF LAW OR NECESSITY OR "OPINIO JURIS"

Opinio juris is a concept that has been used in the legal system for centuries (Kingwill, 2016; Koskenniemi, 1990; Kreso, 2010; Krieger, 2006; Kumar, 2020; Lagji, 2019; Lavalle, 2014; Laylin, 1976; Lewis, 1983). It refers to an opinion or belief held by a person or group of people regarding the lawfulness of their actions. This concept is often used in common law systems, where it serves as an important factor when determining whether certain acts are legally permissible.

The main advantage of opinio juris is that it allows judges to consider more than just the letter of the law when making decisions (Ubink & Weeks, 2017; Ubink, 2008; Utama, 2021; van Caenegem, 2014; van Engelenhoven, 2021).

By taking into account how individuals and groups view their own behavior, judges can make rulings based on what they believe to be right and wrong rather than simply relying on existing laws. This helps ensure that justice is served even if there is not a specific statute addressing a particular issue.

Nevertheless, there are some disadvantages associated with using opinio juris as well (Hutchison, 2020; Hutchison & Sibanda, 2017; Iyi, 2016; Jentoft & Bavinck, 2019; John-Hopkins, 2010; Johnson, 1986; Joireman, 2008). For one thing, it can lead to inconsistent rulings since different judges may have different opinions about what constitutes lawful behavior. Additionally, this approach can also be seen as subjective since it relies heavily on individual beliefs rather than objective facts or evidence.

Despite these drawbacks, opinio juris remains an important part of common law systems today (Claassens & Mnisi, 2009; Cooter, 1991; Corrin & Mulitalo, 2015; Costa, 1998; Craik, 2020; Crawford, 2012; Criddle, 2013). This widespread adoption of the approach is due to its ability to provide flexibility and fairness in decision-making processes. In addition, this concept has become increasingly relevant in recent years due to changes in society such as increased globalization and technological advances which have made traditional laws less applicable across all contexts and jurisdictions around the world.

Overall, while opinio juris does come with some potential risks and challenges associated with its use, its advantages far outweigh any potential negatives when considering its relevance within modern legal systems today (Mwalimu, 1988; Mwambene, 2012; Mwangi, 2022; Ndulo, 2011; Ngira, 2018, 2021; Nhlapo, 2017; Nnona, 2018). As such, understanding this concept should remain an essential part of any lawyer's education so they can better serve their clients no matter what jurisdiction they practice in or situation they find themselves facing. Figure 2.3 highlights the basic tenets of "*opinio juris*."

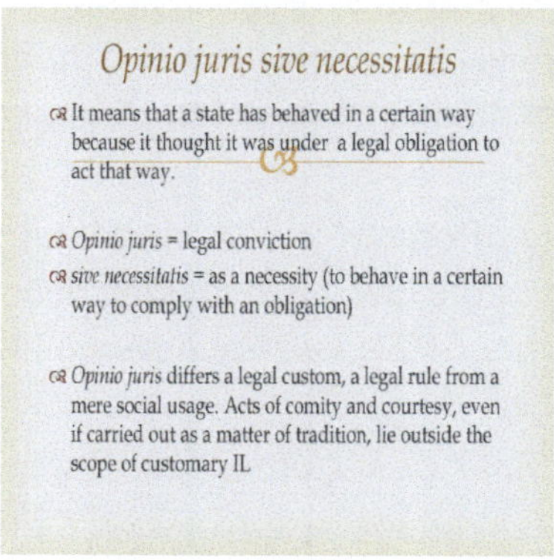

Figure 2.3. Basic conceptualization of "opinio juris".

Source: Prof. Avv. Roberto Baratta, University of Macerata.

Legal opinions are an important tool in the modern legal system (Olaf & Markus, 2018; Omidire, 1990; Orebech et al., 2005; Osman, 2019; Osman & Baase, 2022; Osman & Himonga, 2017). They provide a way for judges to make and reform the law, as well as interpret existing laws. Legal opinions can be used to resolve disputes between parties or clarify ambiguities in statutes or regulations. In addition, they can also be used to create new rules of law that may not have been previously established by statute or common law.

The use of legal opinions has become increasingly popular over time due to their ability to settle disputes quickly and efficiently without having to go through lengthy court proceedings (Olaf & Markus, 2018; Omidire, 1990; Orebech et al., 2005; Osman, 2019; Osman & Baase, 2022; Osman & Himonga, 2017). This is especially beneficial when dealing with complex cases involving multiple parties and issues that require extensive research and analysis before a decision can be made. Additionally, legal opinions often provide more detailed explanations than what would typically be found in a court ruling, allowing for greater clarity on the issue at hand.

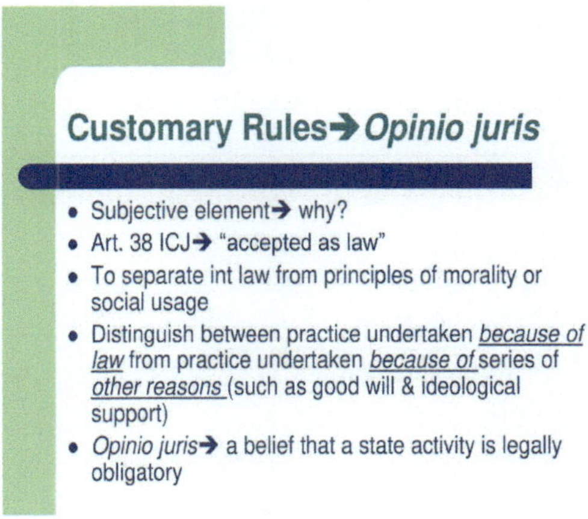

Figure 2.4. Sources of international law.

Source: Amber Mason.

As Figure 2.4 shows, judicial opinions have a role to play in international law (John-Hopkins, 2010; Johnson, 1986; Joireman, 2008; Jonas & Gunda, 2015; Kadens, 2012; Kammerhofer, 2012; Kane, 1972). In many countries around the world, including the United States, courts rely heavily on precedent set by previous decisions when making rulings on similar cases. This means that if there is no clear answer from either statutory or common law sources then judges will look towards prior case decisions for guidance on how best to proceed with their own ruling. By using this method of reasoning, it allows them to ensure consistency across different jurisdictions while still being able to take into account any unique circumstances present in each individual case they hear.

Legal opinions are also useful when attempting to reconcile conflicting interpretations of existing laws (Menski, 1988; Meron, 1987, 1991; Meron et al., 1987; Merry, 1991; Meyer, 2012; Milanovic, 2011; Mnisi & Claassens, 2009). They can also help harmonize regulations between two different jurisdictions within one country or even between two separate countries. By providing an authoritative opinion from an experienced lawyer who specializes in such matters it helps reduce confusion and provides both sides with a better understanding of how best move forward with their dispute resolution process. This is achieved without having resorting costly litigation procedures which could potentially drag out indefinitely depending upon the complexity of the matter at hand.

Overall, legal opinions play an important role today by helping ensure fairness and consistency throughout our judicial systems (Maunatlala & Maimela, 2020; Maxim & Titu Maiorescu, 2015; McAuslan, 2015; McCarthy, 1971; McLachlan, 1988; Menski, 1988). They are responsible for simultaneously providing much needed clarification on difficult topics where traditional methods may fail us short-term solutions the public needs most urgently. As technology continues evolve so too must our approach towards resolving conflicts will evolve thus making these types of documents all but essential going forward into future generations. The next section focuses on the development of standards of community behavior which is an underlying aspect of customary law.

2.3. DEVELOPING COMMUNITY STANDARDS OF BEHAVIOR

Customary law is an important part of the legal system in many countries (Bond, 2009, 2010; Botha & Bekink, 2018; Bourgon, 2020; Budlender et al., 2011; Buss, 2010; Buxbaum, 1968). It is a set of rules and regulations that are based on long-standing traditions, customs, and practices within a particular community or society. Customary law has been used for centuries to develop standards of behavior in communities around the world. Customary law can be divided into two main categories: unwritten customary laws and written customary laws (Osman, 2019; Osman & Baase, 2022; Osman & Himonga,

2017; Ottley, 2016; Parisi, 2001; Pedersen, 2014). Unwritten customary laws are those that have been passed down orally from generation to generation without being formally documented or codified by any government body. These types of laws often reflect traditional values and beliefs held by members of a particular community or society, such as prohibitions against certain activities like stealing or killing another person. Written customary laws, on the other hand, are those that have been officially recognized by governments through legislation or court decisions.

The development of standards of behavior through customary law is an important process for maintaining order within a community or society (Siegel, 2015; Sierra, 1995; Singer, 1972; Skomerska-Muchowska, 2017; Snyder, 1984; Sprankling, 2014; Sun, 2010). By establishing clear expectations about how people should behave towards one another (Figure 2.5 for a summary of pertinent principles), it helps to ensure that everyone's rights are respected and protected while also promoting harmony among individuals living together in proximity with each other. Additionally, these standards help to create an environment where people feel safe enough to express their opinions freely without fear of retribution from others who may disagree with them.

Figure 2.5. 5 Core Principles for open standards development.

Source: The Section of Estratic.

In addition to providing guidance on acceptable behaviors within a given community or society, customary law can also serve as an effective tool for resolving disputes between individuals when they arise due to conflicting interests or interpretations about what constitutes appropriate conduct under certain circumstances (Nyane, 2019; O'Neill, 2002; Oba, 2002, 2008, 2011; Obatusin, 2018; Olaf & Markus, 2018; Omidire, 1990). This type of dispute resolution typically involves mediation rather than litigation. This approach allows parties involved in the dispute to come up with mutually agreeable solutions without having to resorting costly legal proceedings which could take months if not years before reaching its conclusion.

Overall, customary law plays an essential role in developing standards of behavior within communities around the world today as well as helping resolve conflicts between individuals peacefully when necessary so everyone can live harmoniously together despite their differences (Cannizzaro & Bonafe, 2005; Carrillo-Santarelli, 2017; Castillo & Bian, 2014; Cataldi & Titu Maiorescu, 2015; Chang, 2022; Chanock, 1989). As such, it will continue remain relevant even as societies evolve over time.

The standards of behavior in different societies can vary greatly (Mwambene, 2012; Mwangi, 2022; Ndulo, 2011; Ngira, 2018, 2021; Nhlapo, 2017; Nnona, 2018; Norr, 1973). This is due to a variety of factors, including cultural norms, religious beliefs, and even geographical location. It is important to understand the differences between communities when it comes to acceptable behaviors so that we can better interact with one another and foster understanding across cultures.

In some societies, there are strict rules about how people should behave in public spaces (Hu, 2017; Huizenga, 2018, 2022; Hulme, 2010; Hutchison, 2020; Hutchison & Sibanda, 2017; Iyi, 2016; Jentoft & Bavinck, 2019). For example, many Middle Eastern countries have laws that dictate what type of clothing must be worn by both men and women while out in public. In other places such as India or Japan, certain forms of physical contact may be considered inappropriate depending on the context or situation.

Religious beliefs also play an important role in determining social norms within a society (Milanovic, 2011; Mnisi & Claassens, 2009; Moore, 1986; Morrison, 2016; Morudu & Maimela, 2021; Murphy, 2014). Many religions have specific guidelines for how their followers should act and dress which often differ from those found in secular societies. Additionally, these rules may change over time as new interpretations arise or old ones become outdated due to changing societal values or technological advances.

Geographical location can also influence standards of behavior within a community since different regions tend to have distinct customs and traditions that shape local culture over time (Kane, 1972; Kassoti, 2017; Kelly & Windia, 2019; Kilian, 2019; Kim, 2009, 2020; Kingwill, 2016; Koskenniemi, 1990; Kreso, 2010). For instance, rural areas typically adhere more closely to traditional values than urban centers where modern influences are more prevalent. This could lead to variations in accepted behaviors between two neighboring towns located just miles apart from each other. Such disparities have been associated with social injustice.

Nevertheless, it is essential for us all to recognize the variance in standards of behavior among different communities (Fleck, 2009, 2013; Fletcher, 2007; Frulli, 2015; Gadzo, 2018; Gagnon-Bergeron, 2018; Gal-Or, 2015; Galindo & Yip, 2017). This so that we can learn how best to interact with one another without causing offense or misunderstanding our peers' intentions based on our own preconceived notions about what constitutes "proper" conduct within any given society. By doing so, we will create stronger connections between individuals regardless of their backgrounds – ultimately leading towards greater harmony amongst all peoples around the world.

Figure 2.6. Five pillars of the UN socio-economic recovery plan.

Source: United Nations Development Program.

In fact, the social development agenda (Figure 2.6 for an example), is based on this notion of cohesion and mutual respect. Moreover, customary law follows the same values and principles (Chanock, 1989; Cheng, 2012; Chirayath et al., 2005; Claassens & Mnisi, 2009; Cooter, 1991; Corrin &

Mulitalo, 2015; Costa, 1998). Customary law is a set of rules and regulations that are based on the customs, traditions, and practices of a particular society. It has been used for centuries to regulate social behavior in many cultures around the world. In recent years, however, there has been an increasing recognition of the cultural relativity of customary law in contemporary societies.

The concept of cultural relativism recognizes that different cultures have their own unique values and beliefs which should be respected when making decisions about legal matters (Allott, 1984; Anderson, 2003; Angelini, 2012; Armstrong, 1989; Arowolo, 2019; Asieduakrofi, 1989; Barnabas, 2022; Barrie, 2016). This means that laws must take into account local customs and traditions when determining what is acceptable or unacceptable behavior within a given society. For example, certain religious practices may be considered illegal in one country but perfectly acceptable in another due to differences in culture and belief systems.

In addition to recognizing cultural diversity, customary law also provides an important source of stability for communities by providing them with clear guidelines as to how they should behave towards each other (Lewis, 1983, 2016; Liakopoulos, 2019; Lijnzaad, 2022; Lingaas, 2022; Lita et al., 2017; Liu, 2019). By establishing norms for interpersonal relationships within a community, it helps ensure that disputes can be resolved without resorting to violence or other forms of coercion. Furthermore, customary law often serves as an effective deterrent against crime since individuals know what kind of punishment awaits them if they break the rules established by their community's traditional laws.

Despite its advantages however, some critics argue that customary law can lead to discrimination against minority groups who do not conform to majority standards or beliefs regarding certain issues such as gender roles or sexual orientation (Woodman, 2001; Worugji et al., 2019; Wu, 2018; Young, 2019; Zamir, 2015; Zarea, 2022; Zenker & Höhne, 2018). This is certainly true in some cases where traditional laws are used as tools for oppression rather than protection from harm. However, it is important to remember that these same laws can also provide much needed security and stability for those living under them if applied fairly and equitably across all members of society regardless of race or religion and other socially constructed or pre-existing differences.

It could be argued that there are both positive aspects associated with customary law (Parisi, 2001; Pedersen, 2014; Pelizzon, 2015; Perreau-

Saussine & Murphy, 2007; Petersen, 2007, 2017; Pocar, 2016). Examples of such merits include providing stability within communities. Nevertheless, it is essential that we recognize its potential drawbacks too so we can ensure any discriminatory practices are avoided whenever possible going forward into the future. The next section considers the influences of customary on international law.

2.4. INTERNATIONAL LAW AS A FORM OF CUSTOMARY LAW

International law is a set of rules and regulations that govern the conduct of nations in their relations with one another (Dekoster, 2019; Demian, 2014; Anthony C Diala, 2017; Diala, 2017, 2019; Diala & Bagni, 2019; Dubner, 1994). It is also known as public international law, or the law of nations. International law has been around since ancient times, but it was not until after World War II that it became an organized body of laws. The law is responsible for regulating the conduct of nations as well as regional bodies that may encompass more than one country in their reach. Many people seeking justice and failing to gain it in their local courts have considered the option of international law. Figure 2.7 summarizes the notion of international law.

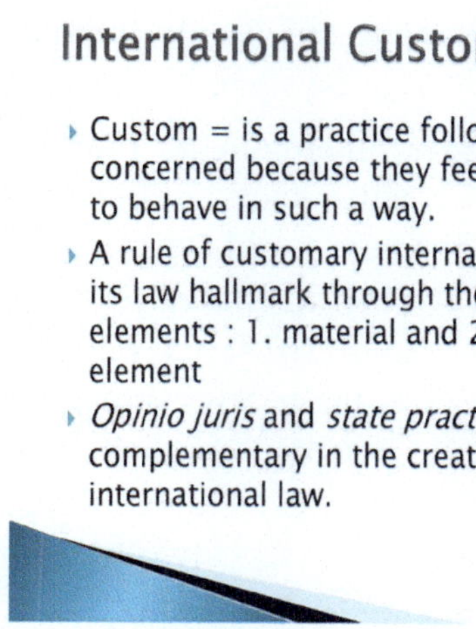

Figure 2.7. The notion of international customary law.

Source: Susanti Hardja.

The main sources of international law are treaties, custom, general principles, and judicial decisions (Krieger, 2006; Kumar, 2020; Lagji, 2019; Lavalle, 2014; Laylin, 1976; Lewis, 1983, 2016; Liakopoulos, 2019; Lijnzaad, 2022; Lingaas, 2022). Treaties are agreements between two or more countries which have been ratified by each country's legislature or executive branch. Customary international law refers to practices that have become accepted as binding on all states through long-term usage and acceptance by other states. General principles refer to those legal concepts which are widely recognized among different legal systems throughout the world such as good faith and "*pacta sunt servanda*" (agreements must be kept). Judicial decisions refer to rulings made by courts in cases involving disputes between two or more countries over matters related to international law.

International organizations such as the United Nations play an important role in developing and enforcing international laws (Thirlway, 1972, 2017; Tobin, 2014; Tomuschat, 2021; Treasure et al., 2016; Tripp, 2004; Tsai, 2015). This is implemented through resolutions passed at its annual meetings, conventions adopted by member states, declarations issued by its various organs such as the Security Council and International Court of Justice (ICJ) as well as other international institutions. The ICJ is responsible for settling disputes between countries based on existing treaties or customary international laws while other UN bodies can issue recommendations regarding certain issues without having any legally binding force unless they are adopted into a treaty or convention signed by member states.

Understanding what constitutes international law is essential for anyone involved in global affairs whether they be diplomats representing their nation's interests abroad or business people engaging in cross-border transactions with foreign entities (Corrin & Mulitalo, 2015; Costa, 1998; Craik, 2020; Crawford, 2012; Criddle, 2013; Cuskelly, 2011; Dahlitz, 1991; Damato, 1973). Knowing how these laws apply can help ensure compliance with them thus avoiding potential conflicts down the line due to misunderstandings about what exactly constitutes acceptable behavior under this body of rules governing interactions between nations worldwide.

Customary law is an important factor in the development of international law (Manullang, 2021; Marasinghe, 1978; Masengu, 2016; Mastura, 1994; Maunatlala & Maimela, 2020; Maxim & Titu Maiorescu, 2015). It has been used to shape and influence the way that countries interact with each other, as well as how they resolve disputes between them. Customary law is based on long-standing practices and beliefs that have been accepted by a particular society or culture over time. This type of law can be seen in many different areas, including trade agreements, human rights conventions, environmental regulations, and more.

When it comes to international relations, customary law plays an important role in setting standards for behavior among nations (Magnusson, 2013, 2017; Manaka & Corrin, 2021; Manullang, 2021; Marasinghe, 1978; Masengu, 2016; Mastura, 1994). For example, when two countries enter into a treaty agreement or sign a contract with one another, they are often guided by principles of customary international law which dictate what is expected from both parties involved. These principles may include things like respecting each other's sovereignty and territorial integrity; refraining from using force against one another; not interfering in each other's internal affairs; providing mutual assistance if needed; and so on.

In addition to helping set standards for behavior between nations, customary international law also helps provide guidance when it comes to resolving disputes between states (Shingleton, 1983; Sibisi, 2020; Siegel, 2015; Sierra, 1995; Singer, 1972; Skomerska-Muchowska, 2017; Snyder, 1984). When two countries disagree about something related to their relationship (such as trade issues), they will often look at existing customs within their respective societies for guidance on how best to proceed with negotiations or arbitration proceedings. This allows them to come up with solutions that are acceptable under both sets of laws without having to resorting to violence or coercion tactics which could further escalate tensions between them instead of resolving them peacefully.

Overall, customary international law serves an important purpose in helping maintain peace and stability among nations around the world by providing guidelines for proper conduct during times of conflict or disagreement (Tripp, 2004; Tsai, 2015; Robert W Tucker, 1972; Tunkin, 1993; Tupper, 1881; Ubink, 2016). At the same time, international law is noted for allowing states some flexibility when it comes time for dispute resolution procedures such as negotiation or arbitration proceedings. By understanding this concept better, we can gain insight into why certain actions taken by governments may seem strange but ultimately make sense given the context within which those decisions were made. This is due to the influence exerted by customary laws throughout history.

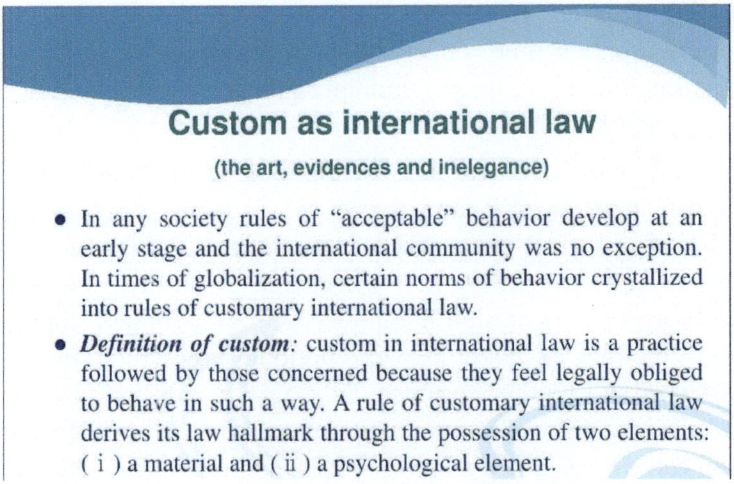

Figure 2.8. Considering international law as a form of customary law.

Source: Eilis Murrily (2014).

Figure 2.8 shows that international law can be considered a form of customary law despite the differences that exist between the two forms of legal frameworks (McLachlan, 1988; Menski, 1988; Meron, 1987, 1991; Meron et al., 1987; Merry, 1991; Meyer, 2012; Milanovic, 2011). The legal systems of the world are complex and varied, with different countries having their own unique laws. Two distinct types of law that exist in many countries are customary law and international law. While both have similarities, there are also some key differences between them. In this section, we will compare these two types of law to better understand how they differ from one another.

Customary law is a type of unwritten legal system based on long-standing traditions and customs within a particular society or culture (Lagji, 2019; Lavalle, 2014; Laylin, 1976; Lewis, 1983, 2016; Liakopoulos, 2019; Lijnzaad, 2022; Lingaas, 2022; Lita et al., 2017). It is often seen as an informal form of justice that relies heavily on community consensus rather than formal legislation or court rulings. Customary laws can vary greatly from region to region depending on local beliefs and values, but generally involve punishments for breaking certain rules such as fines or public shaming.

International law, in contrast, is a set of legally binding rules governing relations between states at an international level (Diala, 2017, 2019; Diala & Bagni, 2019; Dubner, 1994; Dubois, 1992; Dupont, 2013; Duxbury, 2017; Edmundson, 2015). This type of law is created through treaties signed by multiple nations which then become part of each country's domestic legal system once ratified by its governments. International laws cover topics such as human rights protection, trade agreements, environmental regulations and more – all with the aim to promote peace among nations while protecting citizens' rights worldwide.

One major difference between customary and international law lies in their enforcement mechanisms (Sheleff, 2013; Shingleton, 1983; Sibisi, 2020; Siegel, 2015; Sierra, 1995; Singer, 1972; Skomerska-Muchowska, 2017). While customary laws rely mainly on social pressure for compliance (such as ostracism), international laws must be enforced through diplomatic means (e.g., economic sanctions) if violated by any nation state party to the treaty agreements. Additionally, whereas customary laws tend to be localized in nature due to varying cultural norms across regions; international laws apply universally regardless of geographical boundaries since they are agreed upon by multiple countries at once before being implemented domestically within each signatory nation's jurisdictions.

Although both customary and international law share some commonalities (e.g., providing guidance for behavior within societies), there are several key distinctions between them including enforcement methods used when violations occur as well as scope or applicability across different regions or countries respectively (Anderson, 2003; Angelini, 2012; Armstrong, 1989; Arowolo, 2019; Asieduakrofi, 1989; Barnabas, 2022; Barrie, 2016; Baxi, 2020). Understanding these differences can help us better appreciate why it is important for governments around the world to adhere not only their own national legislations but also abide by internationally accepted standards when dealing with matters concerning global affairs in our contemporary world. The final section in this chapter looks at a case study of customary law when dealing with the scourge of piracy.

2.5. CASE STUDY OF CUSTOMARY LAW IN PIRACY

Piracy is a term used to describe the illegal copying, distribution, and use of copyrighted material without permission from the copyright holder (Budlender et al., 2011; Buss, 2010; Buxbaum, 1968; Cannizzaro & Bonafe, 2005; Carrillo-Santarelli, 2017; Castillo & Bian, 2014). It can take many forms, including downloading music or movies illegally from the internet, making copies of software programs for friends or family members without paying for them, and even streaming content online that has not been authorized by the copyright owner. There is a range of responses to piracy with some countries taking it more seriously than others. The consequences of piracy are serious (Kilian, 2019; Kim, 2009, 2020; Kingwill, 2016; Koskenniemi, 1990; Kreso, 2010; Krieger, 2006; Kumar, 2020; Lagji, 2019). Copyright holders have legal rights to their work and when those rights are violated it can result in civil lawsuits as well as criminal prosecution. In addition to potential fines and jail time associated with these cases, victims may also be entitled to damages such as lost profits or other compensation related to their losses due to piracy. It is important for everyone who uses digital media (regardless of whether they are consumers or businesses) to understand what constitutes piracy so they do not inadvertently break any laws.

The best way to avoid being accused of piracy is simply not engaging in activities that could be considered illegal under copyright law (Oba, 2011; Obatusin, 2018; Olaf & Markus, 2018; Omidire, 1990; Orebech et al., 2005; Osman, 2019; Osman & Baase, 2022). This includes downloading unauthorized copies of music or movies from peer-to-peer networks like BitTorrent. It also includes using "cracked" versions of software programs. Others are involved in streaming content online without permission. Then there are those that are more generally sharing copyrighted material with others without authorization from the copyright holders.

Ultimately, understanding what constitutes piracy is key if you want to stay on the right side of the law when it comes to digital media consumption and usage (Ubink & Weeks, 2017; Ubink, 2008; Utama, 2021; van Caenegem, 2014; van Engelenhoven, 2021; Vanboven, 1991). Taking steps like only purchasing legitimate copies of software programs (and avoiding cracked versions) will help ensure you are acting in ways that are consistent with the laws related to intellectual property rights violations. Additionally, educating yourself about your local laws regarding digital media usage can help protect you against potential legal action should someone accuse you of engaging in unlawful activities involving copyrighted works.

Piracy is a major issue that affects the global economy and has been an ongoing problem for centuries (Qerimi, 2020; Quane, 2013; Rautenbach, 2020; Rose, 1989; Rubin, 1990; Russo, 1988; Sarbah, 1904; Seidman, 1983). In recent years, there have been numerous attempts to combat piracy through international law. However, these efforts have not always been successful. As such, it is important to consider other approaches to dealing with this issue. One potential solution is the use of customary law to address piracy-related issues.

Customary law refers to laws that are based on long-standing traditions and customs rather than formal legislation or written codes of conduct (Rautenbach, 2020; Rose, 1989; Rubin, 1990; Russo, 1988; Sarbah, 1904; Seidman, 1983; Sheleff, 1994). This type of legal system can be particularly effective when dealing with complex issues like piracy because it allows for more flexibility in terms of how disputes are resolved. It also has a sophisticated approach when considering how punishments are meted out.

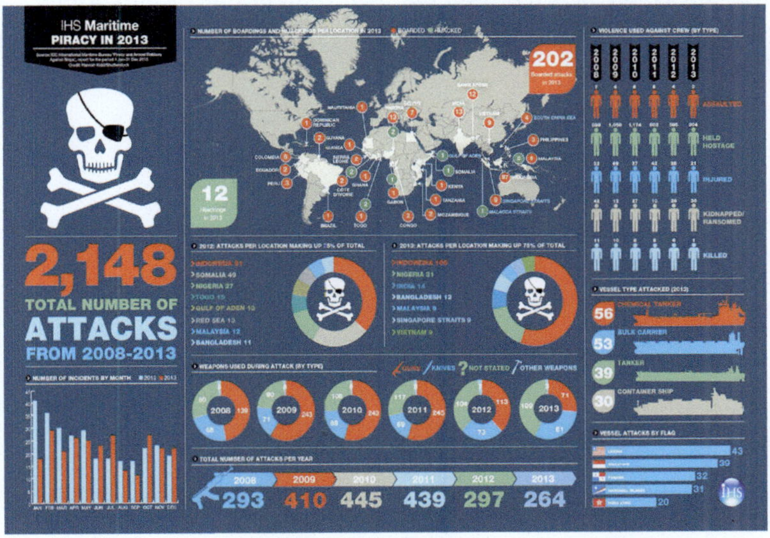

Figure 2.9. The legal challenges in responding to piracy.

Source: Henderson International.

Additionally, customary law often takes into account local cultural norms which can help ensure that any solutions reached will be accepted by those affected by them (Jentoft & Bavinck, 2019; John-Hopkins, 2010; Johnson, 1986; Joireman, 2008; Jonas & Gunda, 2015; Kadens, 2012; Kammerhofer, 2012). If this approach was adopted, it would relieve some of the pressure that has been created by multiple copyright claims across the globe (Figure 2.9 for an idea of the scale and breadth of these challenges). The main argument therefore is that customary law can potentially mitigate the burden that falls under the conventional forms of law. Moreover, the use of customary law will ensure that the management of anti-piracy efforts is not overly onerous.

When using customary law as a means of addressing piracy-related issues, it is important to ensure that all parties involved understand the implications of their actions and agree upon a fair resolution before any action is taken against them (Utama, 2021; van Caenegem, 2014; van Engelenhoven, 2021; Vanboven, 1991; Vergouwen, 2013; Vines, 2017). This could involve engaging local leaders or representatives from affected communities to discuss possible solutions and reach an agreement on how best to proceed with resolving the dispute at hand. Young people are engaged in piracy and remain one of the target populations for intervention (Figure 2.10). It may also be necessary for governments or international organizations such as NATO or INTERPOL to provide assistance in enforcing any agreements made between parties if needed.

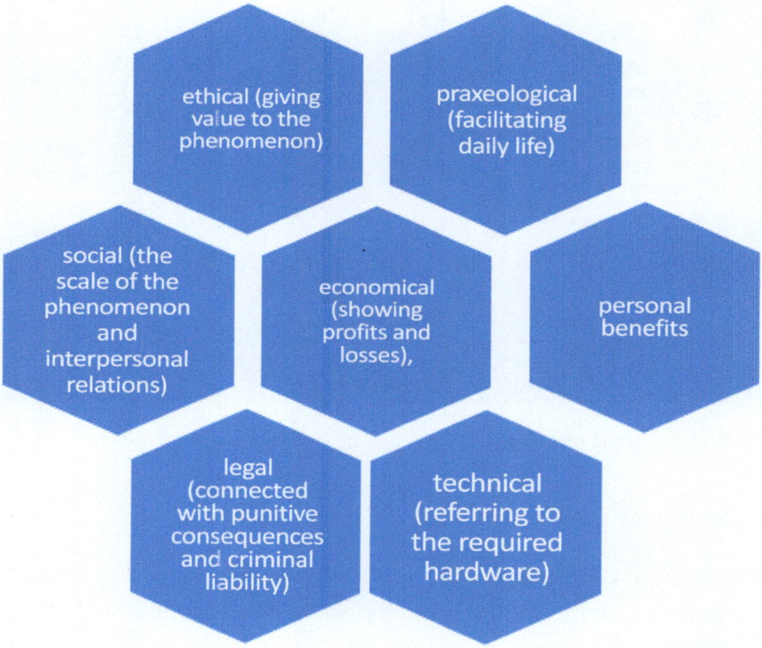

Figure 2.10. Youth evaluations of digital piracy.

Source: Tomczyk (2021) via MDPI.

Traditional methods such as international treaties may still play an important role when tackling piracy-related problems (Williams, 2022; Willms, 2009; Wilson, 1961; Wolff, 2016; Woodman, 1988, 1969, 2001; Worugji et al., 2019). However, incorporating customary law into our approach could prove beneficial. This is due its ability to take into account local customs and cultures when seeking resolutions for disputes involving pirates operating within certain regions around the world. By doing so we can ensure that justice is served fairly while also helping protect innocent victims who may otherwise become caught up in conflicts related to maritime crime activities taking place near their homes or businesses.

Another form of piracy takes place on the sea but is no less harmful. Piracy has been a problem for centuries, and yet it continues to plague the world's oceans. Despite numerous attempts to eradicate piracy through customary law, these efforts have largely failed (Hernández, 2012; Holleman, 1969, 1972; Horii, 2019; Howell, 2018; Hu, 2017; Huizenga, 2018, 2022). It is pertinent to explore why customary law has not been successful in eliminating piracy across the globe. Customary law comprises "the body of unwritten rules that are generally accepted and followed by members of a particular society or culture" (Oxford Languages). It is based on tradition rather than written laws, which makes it difficult to enforce. Customary law relies heavily on social norms and values. If those norms change over time, then so does the effectiveness of the laws themselves.

One reason why customary law has failed to eliminate piracy is because there are no universal standards when it comes to punishing offenders (Harmathy, 2016; Henry, 2017; Hernández, 2012; Holleman, 1969, 1972; Horii, 2019; Howell, 2018; Hu, 2017). Different countries have different approaches when dealing with pirates. For example, some may choose harsher punishments while others may be more lenient. Without consistent enforcement from all nations involved in combating piracy, criminals can easily move between jurisdictions without fear of repercussions for their actions.

Another issue with relying solely on customary law is that many countries lack sufficient resources or personnel needed to effectively combat pirate activity in their waters (Snyder, 1984; Sprankling, 2014; Sun, 2010; Syaufi & Zahra, 2021; Tan, 1993, 2018; Tegnan, 2015). Many governments simply do not have enough money or manpower available to adequately patrol their coasts and apprehend pirates before they commit crimes against ships passing through international waters near them. As such, even if certain countries were able to successfully prosecute pirates under their own laws, other nations would still be vulnerable due to inadequate protection from criminal activity at sea. Finally, another factor contributing towards the failure of customary law in eradicating piracy is its inability to keep up with modern technology (Wu, 2018; Young, 2019; Zamir, 2015; Zarea, 2022; Zenker & Höhne, 2018; Zerner, 1994; Zilberman, 1996). Such technologies are used by criminals today such as GPS tracking systems and satellite communication devices which allow them greater freedom when operating outside territorial boundaries where traditional policing methods cannot reach them quickly enough. Additionally, new tactics employed by organized crime syndicates make it increasingly difficult for authorities around the world who rely only on conventional means like naval patrols, and aerial surveillance to detect illegal activities taking place far away from shorelines.

Although customarily-based legal systems have attempted –and continue–to address this global issue, they remain ineffective due largely due insufficient resources allocated towards enforcing anti-piracy measures (Cooter, 1991; Corrin & Mulitalo, 2015; Costa, 1998; Craik, 2020; Crawford, 2012; Criddle, 2013; Cuskelly, 2011; Dahlitz, 1991). There are varying levels of punishment among different countries. Another problem are the technological advancements made available exclusively for use by criminals. Until these issues are addressed properly, we can expect little progress being made towards ending this age-old problem of piracy.

CHAPTER 2 SUMMARY

This chapter has explored some of the different forms of claims made under customary law. In doing so, the chapter has shown that consuetudinary or unofficial law can sometimes be as powerful as conventional law. Similarly, the chapter has shown how "opinio juris" can be a cardinal form of law-making. To understand how these concepts and principles intersect, the chapter has used the examples of international law and piracy which are classic cases of community standards being codified into law. The third chapter will pick up from this theme to interrogate the ways in which customary law is practiced.

CHAPTER 3

The Practices of Customary Law

Contents

The third chapter in this book focuses on the practices of customary law. We will use a range of cases including the use of customary law to justify the otherwise abhorrent practice of human enslavement. The chapter will also highlight the principles underpinning "*hostis humani generis*." We will consider how case law differs from and intersects with customary law. In doing so, this chapter will summarize some key aspects of the evolution of modern law including its various sources. Perhaps a good starting point for this chapter is a critique and description of the customary law justifications provided for slavery.

3.1. CUSTOMARY LAW AS A JUSTIFICATION FOR SLAVERY

Slavery is a form of exploitation in which one person or group of people are owned by another and forced to work without pay (Hulme, 2010; Hutchison, 2020; Hutchison & Sibanda, 2017; Iyi, 2016; Jentoft & Bavinck, 2019; John-Hopkins, 2010; Johnson, 1986). It has been practiced throughout history, with some estimates suggesting that as many as 40 million people were enslaved worldwide during the transatlantic slave trade alone. Slavery can take many forms, including debt bondage, where individuals are forced to work off debts they cannot afford. Another form is sexual slavery where individuals are exploited for their bodies. Child labor falls within this group and occurs where children are made to do dangerous or exploitative work.

The practice of slavery is illegal in most countries today (Fletcher, 2007; Frulli, 2015; Gadzo, 2018; Gagnon-Bergeron, 2018; Gal-Or, 2015; Galindo & Yip, 2017; Gao, 2013; Gillespie & Tran, 2022). However, it still exists in various forms around the world. Forced labor is often used in industries such as agriculture and mining. Moreover, human trafficking continues to be an issue globally. In addition, there have been reports of modern-day slavery occurring within domestic households and other informal settings.

It is important to understand what constitutes slavery so we can recognize it when we see it and take action against it. The International Labor Organization (ILO) defines forced labor as "all work or service which is exacted from any person under the menace of any penalty and for which the said person has not offered himself voluntarily." This includes both physical coercion and psychological pressure such as threats or intimidation tactics used by employers or traffickers (Davis & Klare, 2010; De ruysscher, 2008; de Vries, 2021; De Wet, 2004; Debelva & De Broe, 2022; Dekoster, 2019; Demian, 2014).

To combat modern-day slavery effectively, governments must ensure that laws protecting workers' rights are enforced properly. This means ensuring that businesses comply with minimum wage requirements and providing access to legal recourse if these rights have been violated (Loja, 2014; Lon & Widyawati, 2021; Magnusson, 2013, 2017; Manaka & Corrin, 2021; Manullang, 2021). Additionally, organizations like Anti-Slavery International provide support services for victims of exploitation so they can rebuild their lives after escaping enslavement.

Ultimately, ending all forms of slavery requires collective action from us all. This can occur through raising awareness about its prevalence today or taking direct action against those who perpetrate it (Orebech et al., 2005; Osman, 2019; Osman & Baase, 2022; Osman & Himonga, 2017; Ottley, 2016; Parisi, 2001). If we want a future free from exploitation then everyone needs to play their part in making sure no one remains enslaved ever again. Nevertheless, it is imperative to recognize the possibility that the economic incentives for slavery (Figure 3.1 for an illustration the original business model for Transatlantic slave trade) create significant barriers to its complete eradication.

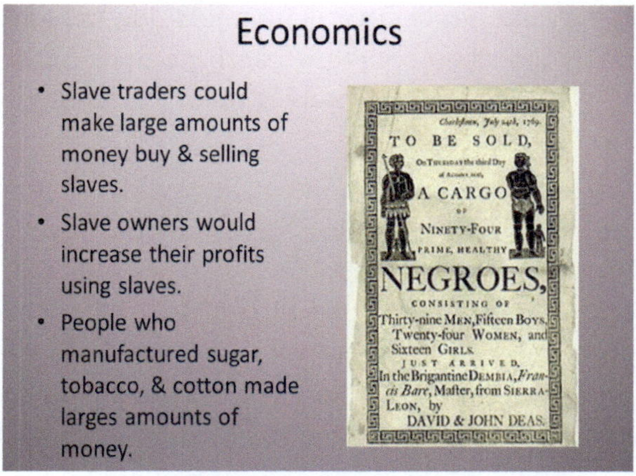

Figure 3.1. Economic incentives for slavery.

Source: Rafe Lewis.

The concept of modern slavery is a complex and multifaceted issue that has been gaining increasing attention in recent years (Castillo & Bian, 2014; Cataldi & Titu Maiorescu, 2015; Chang, 2022; Chanock, 1989; Cheng, 2012; Chirayath et al., 2005). It encompasses a wide range of practices, including human trafficking, forced labor, debt bondage, child labor, and other forms of exploitation. Even though it affects millions of people around the world every year, many are still unaware of its existence or how to identify it.

Modern slavery is often characterized by extreme power imbalances between those who are exploited and their exploiters (Oba, 2008; Oba, 2011; Obatusin, 2018; Olaf & Markus, 2018; Omidire, 1990; Orebech et al., 2005; Osman, 2019). This can manifest itself in various ways such as physical abuse or threats. Other tools include psychological manipulation; economic coercion; or even false promises made by traffickers to lure victims into exploitative situations. In addition to this imbalance of power, modern slavery also involves an element of deception. For instance, victims may be tricked into believing they will receive certain benefits from their situation when they are being taken advantage of for someone else's gain.

It is important to recognize that modern slavery does not only occur in developing countries but can take place anywhere there is poverty and inequality. This type of exploitation can occur in any part of the world including developed nations like the United States and European industrialized nations (Tan, 2018; Tegnan, 2015; Thipe & Buthelezi, 2014; Thirlway, 1972, 2015, 2017; Tobin, 2014). Furthermore, while some individuals may be more vulnerable than others due to factors such as age or gender identity/expression – anyone can become a victim regardless of race or nationality if they find themselves in an exploitative situation with no way out.

In order to effectively combat modern slavery, we must first understand what it looks like on both individual and systemic levels (Edmundson, 2015; Elias, 1956; Enabulele & Bazuaye, 2019; Engel & Kurschilgen, 2013; Farran, 2019; Fenrich et al., 2011; Fleck, 2009). This allows us to better identify potential cases before they escalate further. We must also work together across sectors (government agencies and NGOs for instance) to ensure survivors have access to necessary resources such as legal aid services so they can reclaim their freedom safely without fear of retribution from their exploiters. Finally, we need increased public awareness about this issue so more people know how to spot signs of exploitation when they see them and report any suspicious activity accordingly.

Only then will we truly begin making progress towards ending this global injustice. The concept of modern slavery is a complex and multifaceted issue that has been gaining increasing attention in recent years (van Caenegem, 2014; van Engelenhoven, 2021; Vanboven, 1991; Vergouwen, 2013; Vines, 2017; Watson, 1984).

Modern slavery is often characterized by extreme power imbalances between those who are exploited and their exploiters (Ngira, 2018, 2021; Nhlapo, 2017; Nnona, 2018; Norr, 1973; Nwapi, 2016; Nyane, 2019; O'Neill, 2002). This can manifest itself in various ways such as physical violence or threats; psychological manipulation; economic coercion; or even cultural norms which limit an individual's freedom to make choices about their own life. In addition to this imbalance of power, victims may also experience social isolation due to language barriers or lack of access to resources like education and healthcare. Yet, there is no shortage of political arguments against slavery (Figure 3.2).

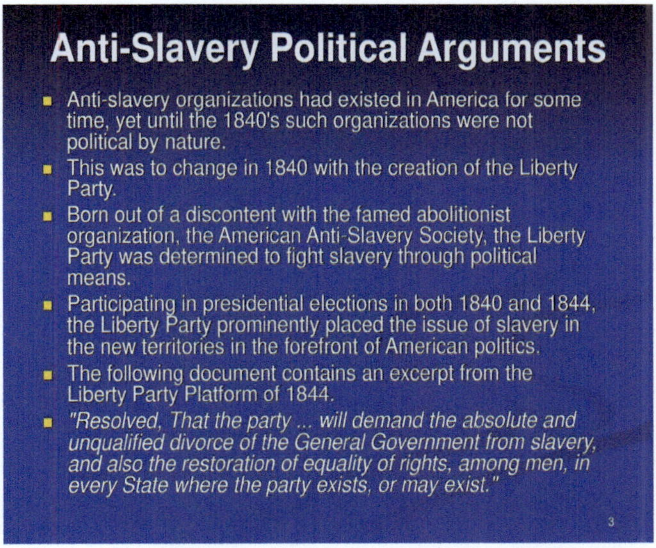

Figure 3.2. Making political arguments against slavery.

Source: William Sherman.

It is important for us all to be aware of the signs associated with modern slavery so we can help protect vulnerable individuals from exploitation. These signs include: working long hours for little pay; being unable to leave one's job without permission; having limited access to medical care or legal representation; living in overcrowded conditions with no privacy (Farran, 2019; Fenrich et al., 2011; Fleck, 2009, 2013; Fletcher, 2007; Frulli, 2015; Gadzo, 2018; Gagnon-Bergeron, 2018). Another indicator is being denied basic rights such as freedom from abuse or harassment. Additionally, this involves not having control over one's passport or identification documents as well as other forms of essential documentation.

In order for us all to effectively combat modern slavery we must first understand what it looks like on a global scale and then work together towards solutions that will ensure everyone's safety and well-being regardless of where they live or what kind of work they do (Perreau-Saussine & Murphy, 2007; Petersen, 2007, 2017; Pocar, 2016; Poespasari, 2020; Polanski, 2017). We must also recognize our collective responsibility when it comes to protecting vulnerable populations from exploitation. This holds true whether through advocacy efforts at local levels or international initiatives aimed at tackling root causes such as poverty and inequality. Sensitization and education are tools for reformers that want justice for those affected by this heinous crime against humanity.

Ultimately, conceptualizing the notion of modern slavery requires us all take actionable steps towards creating a more just society (Kreso, 2010; Krieger, 2006; Kumar, 2020; Lagji, 2019; Lavalle, 2014; Laylin, 1976; Lewis, 1983, 2016; Liakopoulos, 2019). This is where everyone has equal opportunities regardless of race, gender identity, and expression. All this occurs while simultaneously holding perpetrators accountable for their actions wherever possible so that future generations do not have to suffer under similar circumstances again in the future. Only then can we hope to create lasting change within our communities.

Slavery is a heinous crime that has been practiced for centuries, and yet it continues to be an issue in many parts of the world today (Seidman, 1983; Sheleff, 1994, 2013; Shingleton, 1983; Sibisi, 2020; Siegel, 2015; Sierra, 1995; Singer, 1972). Notably, there are numerous laws and regulations in place to combat slavery. For example, there are prohibitive aspects of customary law (or traditional legal systems based on customs and practices) which can also play an important role in tackling this global problem. However, it is important to understand the limitations of customary law when it comes to addressing slavery.

Customary law is often seen as a more effective way of dealing with issues such as slavery because it takes into account local cultural norms and values (Damato, 1973; Damato et al., 1993; Dancer, 2017; Danilenko, 1988; Davis & Klare, 2010; De ruysscher, 2008). This means that solutions can be tailored specifically to each community's needs, rather than relying on one-size-fits-all approaches from international organizations or governments. Additionally, since customary law relies heavily on social pressure from within communities, it can help ensure compliance with anti-slavery measures by creating a sense of collective responsibility among members of those communities. Whereas these advantages make customary law attractive for combating slavery, there are some significant drawbacks that must be taken into consideration before relying solely on this approach (Angelini, 2012; Armstrong, 1989; Arowolo, 2019; Asieduakrofi, 1989; Barnabas, 2022; Barrie, 2016; Baxi, 2020; Beavers, 2019). For example, since customary laws vary widely between different cultures and regions they may not always provide adequate protection against exploitation or abuse. Additionally, they may even condone certain forms of servitude which would otherwise be considered illegal under international standards. Furthermore, due to its reliance on social pressure rather than formal enforcement mechanisms (like courts or police forces), violations may go unpunished if individuals do not feel obligated to report them out of fear or shame.

In conclusion, while customary law does have potential benefits when used alongside other methods for tackling slavery such as legislation and education campaigns; its limitations should also be kept in mind when considering how best to address this global issue effectively and sustainably over time (Golo et al., 2022; Gradoni, 2019; Graves, 2017; Gray, 2021; Griffiths, 1998; Hager, 2020; Haggenmacher, 2021; Hammond, 2019). Ultimately any successful strategy will need to take into account both the strengths and weaknesses associated with using traditional legal systems so that all stakeholders involved can work together towards eliminating modern day slavery once. Another challenging problem for modern legal systems is the existence of crimes against humanity.

3.2. THE PRINCIPLES OF "HOSTIS HUMANI GENERIS"

The Latin phrase "hostis humani generis" is a legal term that has been used in various contexts throughout history (Chang, 2022; Chanock, 1989; Cheng, 2012; Chirayath et al., 2005; Claassens & Mnisi, 2009; Cooter, 1991; Corrin & Mulitalo, 2015). It translates to "enemy of all mankind." This phrase is typically used to refer to someone who commits an act so heinous that they are considered beyond the pale of humanity. This type of infringement of international and human law calls for exceptional punishment as a deterrent and retribution for the suffering of victims.

In international law, this phrase was first used by the English jurist Sir Edward Coke in 1608 when he wrote about piracy as being hostis humani generis. This meant that pirates were enemies of all nations and could be prosecuted by any nation whose ships or citizens had been attacked or robbed by them. The concept was later adopted into international law with the Declaration of Paris in 1856 which declared piracy a crime against all nations and allowed for universal jurisdiction over those accused of such crimes (Osman & Baase, 2022; Osman & Himonga, 2017; Ottley, 2016; Parisi, 2001; Pedersen, 2014; Pelizzon, 2015).

Today, this phrase is still commonly used in legal documents to describe individuals who have committed acts so egregious that they are deemed outside the bounds of acceptable behavior for members of society. For example, terrorists may be referred to as hostes humani generis because their actions threaten not only individual countries but also global peace and security (Koskenniemi, 1990; Kreso, 2010; Krieger, 2006; Kumar, 2020; Lagji, 2019; Lavalle, 2014; Laylin, 1976; Lewis, 1983, 2016). Similarly, war criminals can also be labeled as such due to their disregard for basic principles like respect for life and property during times of conflict.

NATIONALISM - SOME IMPLICATIONS

Crimes Against Humanity - the ultimate ultranationalist nightmare.

Estimated Victims of Genocide and Mass Murders in the 20th Century

National Group	Number Killed
Armenians	1.5 million
Bengalis	1.5 million
Burundians	250 000
Cambodians	1.7 million
Chinese	25 million
East Timorese	200 000
Guatemalans	200 000
Ibos	1 million
Indonesians	500 000
Jews	6 million

National Group	Number Killed
Kosovars	10 000
North Koreans	2 million
Roma and Sinti	250 000
Russians	25 million
Rwandans	800 000
Slavs	6 million
Sudanese	2 million
Ugandans	500 000
Ukrainians	3 million

Crimes Against Humanity

1. Using the map as a resource, which part of the world is most represented by the statistics?

2. Why do we know of some more than others?

3. Under the heading "Naming the Crimes", page 155, write the three categories and their definitions.

Figure 3.3. Estimated victims of genocide and mass murders in the 20th century crimes against humanity.

Source: Walter Martin.

Overall, "hostes humani generis" is an important legal term with a long history behind it (Marasinghe, 1978; Masengu, 2016; Mastura, 1994; Maunatlala & Maimela, 2020; Maxim & Titu, 2015). The legal concept serves as a reminder that certain acts cannot go unpunished regardless of where they occur or who commits them. The implication is these perpetrators must face justice no matter what country they come from or how powerful they may seem on paper. In short, this phrase stands for justice without borders. This is something we should strive towards if we want our world to become a more peaceful and secure place for everyone. Figure 3.3 shows that crimes against humanity continue throughout the 20th century.

The phrase "hostis humani generis" is Latin for "enemy of all mankind." It has been used to describe pirates and other criminals who commit acts that are considered so heinous, they are seen as a threat to the entire world (Lita et al., 2017; Liu, 2019; Loja, 2014; Lon & Widyawati, 2021; Magnusson, 2013, 2017; Manaka & Corrin, 2021). This concept has been around since ancient times, but it was popularized in 17th century England when Sir Edward Coke wrote about it in his Institutes of the Lawes of England.

In modern times, this phrase is often associated with customary law (Allott, 1957, 1984; Anderson, 2003; Angelini, 2012; Armstrong, 1989; Arowolo, 2019; Asieduakrofi, 1989; Barnabas, 2022). This is a set of rules and regulations that have developed over time through custom or tradition rather than formal legislation. Customary law can be found in many different societies across the globe and is based on local customs and beliefs rather than written laws. In some cases, these laws may even contradict those established by governments or international organizations such as the United Nations (UN).

Customary law plays an important role in protecting people from harm caused by individuals who could be considered enemies of all mankind (De Wet, 2004; Debelva & De Broe, 2022; Dekoster, 2019; Demian, 2014; Diala, 2017, 2019). For example, if someone commits a crime against another person or group that violates their rights under customary law, then they can be held accountable for their actions regardless of whether there is any formal legislation governing them at the time. This helps ensure justice is served even when no official laws exist to protect victims from certain types of crimes.

At its core, customary law serves as a way to protect people from those who would do them harm without regard for morality or ethics (Weinberg, 2016; Williams & Klusener, 2013; Williams, 2022; Willms, 2009; Wilson,

1961; Wolff, 2016; Woodman, 1988). Hence, essentially acting like hostis humani generis themselves. By providing clear guidelines on how people should behave towards one another within a given society, it helps create an environment where everyone feels safe and respected regardless of their background or beliefs. This is the essence and foundation of cohesive societies.

Ultimately, while "hostis humani generis" may seem like an outdated concept today (Cheng, 2012; Chirayath et al., 2005; Claassens & Mnisi, 2009; Cooter, 1991; Corrin & Mulitalo, 2015; Costa, 1998; Craik, 2020). However, its underlying principles remain relevant thanks to customary law which continues to provide protection against those who would seek to cause harm without consequence. As long as we continue upholding these values through our legal systems worldwide then we can ensure that justice will prevail no matter what form it takes.

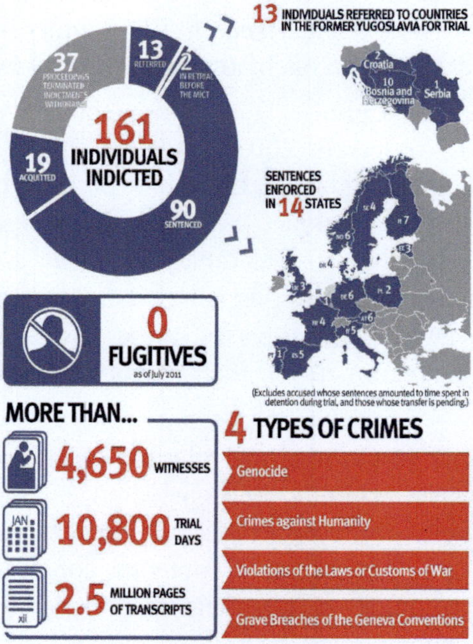

Figure 3.4. The work of the international criminal tribunal for the former Yugoslavia.

Source: World without Genocide.

As Figure 3.4 poignantly shows, industrialized societies such as the ones existing in Europe today still face the threat of crimes against humanity.

Researchers continue to explore the motivations and modalities of these crimes (Magnusson, 2017; Manaka & Corrin, 2021; Manullang, 2021; Marasinghe, 1978; Masengu, 2016; Mastura, 1994; Maunatlala & Maimela, 2020). These investigations are meant to ensure an early warning system so that ordinary members of the public are not caught up in misdeeds over which they have very limited control. Even with all these efforts, crimes against humanity are still polluting the earth.

Crimes against humanity are some of the most heinous acts that can be committed, and they must be addressed with the utmost seriousness (Tupper, 1881; Ubink, 2016; Ubink & Weeks, 2017; Ubink, 2008; Utama, 2021; van Caenegem, 2014; van Engelenhoven, 2021). Unfortunately, customary law is often not enough to adequately address these crimes. Customary law is a set of rules and regulations that have been established by a particular community or society over time. It has traditionally been used as an alternative form of justice in many parts of the world, but it does have its limitations when it comes to fighting crimes against humanity.

One limitation of customary law is that it tends to focus on punishing individuals rather than addressing systemic issues or preventing future atrocities from occurring (Adebola, 2021; Akande, 2004; Albakjaji, 2022; Allott, 1957, 1984; Anderson, 2003; Angelini, 2012). This means that while perpetrators may face punishment for their actions, there is no guarantee that similar crimes will not occur again in the future due to underlying social conditions or other factors. Additionally, customary laws tend to lack clear definitions for what constitutes a crime against humanity. This makes it difficult for prosecutors and judges to determine whether certain acts should be considered criminal under international standards.

Another limitation of customary law is its reliance on traditional methods such as mediation and arbitration instead of more modern approaches like trials before independent courts or tribunals (Watson, 1984; Webber, 2009; Weinberg, 2016; Williams & Klusener, 2013; Williams, 2022; Willms, 2009; Wilson, 1961). These traditional methods do not always provide victims with adequate access to justice since they rely heavily on negotiation between parties rather than impartial adjudication based on evidence presented in court proceedings. Furthermore, these methods can also lead to lenient punishments which fail to reflect the severity of the crime committed and do little towards deterring future offenders from committing similar acts in the future. Finally, customary laws are often limited by cultural norms (Sarbah, 1904; Seidman, 1983; Sheleff, 1994, 2013; Shingleton, 1983; Sibisi, 2020;

Siegel, 2015; Sierra, 1995). These may prevent victims from speaking out about their experiences or seeking redress through legal channels due to fear of retribution or stigma associated with certain types of violence (such as sexual assault). This further limits access to justice for those who have suffered at the hands of criminals perpetrating crimes against humanity since they may feel unable or unwilling to seek help through formal legal systems due cultural taboos surrounding their experiences.

It could be concluded that customary law can play an important role in providing communities with alternative forms of justice outside formal legal systems (Wilson, 1961; Wolff, 2016; Woodman, 1988, 1969, 2001; Worugji et al., 2019; Wu, 2018; Young, 2019). Nevertheless, it is not without its limitations that make it inadequate when dealing with serious offenses such as crimes against humanity which require more robust measures. Such measures are necessary if crimes against humanity are going to be effectively addressed and prevented from happening again in the future.

Therefore, governments must take steps to ensure that all citizens have access to proper judicial processes so perpetrators can be held accountable according to international standards regardless where they live (Thipe & Buthelezi, 2014; Thirlway, 2015, 2017; Thirlway, 1972; Tobin, 2014; Tomuschat, 2021; Treasure et al., 2016). Only then will we truly begin combating these terrible violations of human rights.

When it comes to fighting crimes against humanity such as genocide or war crimes, customary law falls short in several ways (Elias, 1956; Enabulele & Bazuaye, 2019; Engel & Kurschilgen, 2013; Farran, 2019; Fenrich et al., 2011; Fleck, 2009, 2013). First of all, customary law does not provide any legal protection for victims who may have suffered from these types of atrocities. This means that perpetrators can go unpunished if there are no other forms of justice available to them. Additionally, since customary law relies heavily on tradition and culture-specific norms, it may not always reflect current international standards regarding human rights violations or criminal activity more generally.

Furthermore, customary law is largely unwritten and unenforced by any central authority (such as a government) (Engel & Kurschilgen, 2013; Farran, 2019; Fenrich et al., 2011; Fleck, 2009, 2013; Fletcher, 2007; Frulli, 2015; Gadzo, 2018). Therefore, its enforcement can vary greatly depending on where you are located geographically or culturally speaking. This makes it difficult for victims to seek justice through this system if their case involves multiple countries or cultures with different sets of customs governing how certain offenses should be handled legally speaking. Finally, even when cases involving crimes against humanity do make their way into courtrooms under traditional systems like common law or civil code systems (which rely heavily on written statutes), judges may still struggle with determining appropriate punishments due to lack of precedent in such cases (Graves, 2017; Gray, 2021; Griffiths, 1998; Hager, 2020; Haggenmacher, 2021; Hammond, 2019; Harmathy, 2016). This is something which would likely be less problematic under a more comprehensive system like international criminal courts (ICCs) which specialize in prosecuting individuals accused of committing serious human rights abuses around the world. While customarily laws remain important tools for regulating behavior within societies they cannot alone provide adequate protection from those who commit grave injustices such as genocide and war crimes. Hence, making alternative measures necessary if we hope to bring perpetrators truly accountable for their actions. The next section will consider the differences and links between case law and customary law.

3.3. CASE LAW VERSUS CUSTOMARY LAW

The legal systems of many countries are based on either case law or customary law (Ubink, 2016; Ubink & Weeks, 2017; Ubink, 2008; Utama, 2021; van Caenegem, 2014; van Engelenhoven, 2021). While both provide a framework for resolving disputes, there are some key differences between the two that should be considered when deciding which system is best suited to a particular situation. Case law is derived from judicial decisions made by courts and other tribunals in response to specific cases brought before them. This type of law is based on precedent, meaning that similar cases will be decided in the same way as previous ones. It also allows for flexibility since judges can interpret laws differently depending on the circumstances of each case.

Customary law, by way of contrast, is based on long-standing traditions and practices within a community or society rather than court rulings (Edmundson, 2015; Elias, 1956; Enabulele & Bazuaye, 2019; Engel & Kurschilgen, 2013; Farran, 2019). This type of law tends to be more rigid since it relies heavily on tradition and does not allow much room for interpretation or change over time. Additionally, customary laws may vary significantly from one region to another due to cultural differences between communities. When considering which system would work best in any given situation, it is important to consider how much flexibility you need and whether you want your decision-making process to rely heavily upon established precedents or traditional customs instead.

The legal system of any country is composed of two main components: case law and customary law (Vergouwen, 2013; Vines, 2017; Watson, 1984; Webber, 2009; Weinberg, 2016; Williams & Klusener, 2013; Williams, 2022). Both have their own advantages and disadvantages, which must be taken into account when considering the relative merits and demerits of each. Case law, also known as common law or judge-made law, is based on judicial decisions made in court cases. This type of legal system has several advantages over customary laws. Firstly, it allows for greater flexibility in interpreting the laws since judges are able to make rulings based on their interpretation of existing statutes or precedents set by previous cases. Secondly, it provides a more consistent approach to decision making since all courts must follow the same rules when deciding similar cases. Finally, case law can be used to create new laws that reflect changing social values or technological advances without having to go through lengthy legislative processes.

There are some drawbacks associated with relying solely on case law for legal guidance (Tegnan, 2015; Thipe & Buthelezi, 2014; Thirlway, 1972, 2015, 2017; Tobin, 2014; Tomuschat, 2021). For one thing, this type of system can lead to an excessive amount of litigation since parties may disagree about how a particular ruling should be interpreted or applied in different circumstances. Additionally, because judges are not elected officials they may lack public accountability if they make unpopular decisions that do not reflect public opinion or sentiment at large. Furthermore, due to its reliance on precedent setting judgments from higher courts it can take longer for lower courts' rulings to become binding than would otherwise be necessary under a statutory framework where legislation is passed directly by lawmakers rather than through judicial interpretation alone.

Case law provides greater flexibility but may require more research into past decisions (Fenrich et al., 2011; Fleck, 2009, 2013; Fletcher, 2007; Frulli, 2015; Gadzo, 2018; Gagnon-Bergeron, 2018; Gal-Or, 2015). Meanwhile customary laws tend to offer less leeway but can often provide quicker resolution times due their reliance upon well-established norms within a community or society at large. Ultimately, understanding these distinctions can help ensure that whatever legal system you choose works best for your needs and those affected by its application. Figure 3.5 contrasts common law with civil law with some areas of intersection.

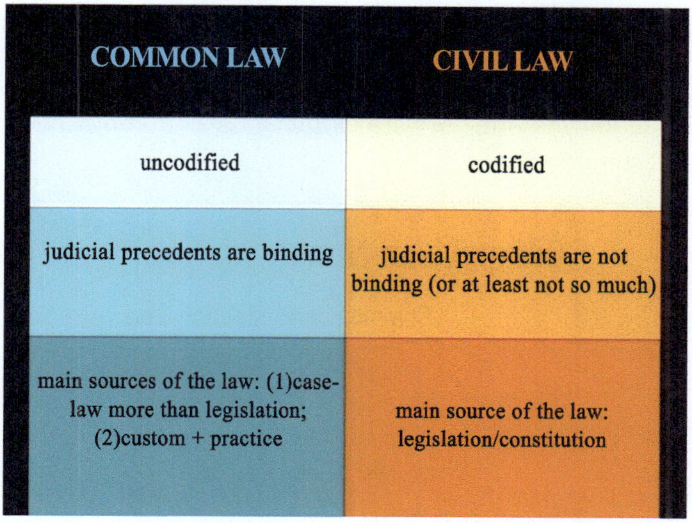

Figure 3.5. Comparing common law with civil law.

Source: Law Help via YouTube.

Customary laws refer primarily to those practices which have been accepted as legally binding within certain communities over time due largely to tradition rather than formal codification into written statutes like those found in most modern societies today (Pocar, 2016; Poespasari, 2020; Polanski, 2017; Pratiwi et al., 2020; Qerimi, 2020; Quane, 2013). One advantage associated with this type of legal system is that it tends to provide greater stability since customs tend not change quickly unlike statutory frameworks which can often undergo rapid revisions depending upon political winds at any given moment. Additionally, customary laws tend promote social cohesion among members within a community who share similar beliefs and values regarding what constitutes acceptable behavior.

Nevertheless, there are some potential drawbacks associated with relying too heavily upon traditional customs as well (Craik, 2020; Crawford, 2012; Criddle, 2013; Cuskelly, 2011; Dahlitz, 1991; Damato, 1973; Damato et al., 1993; Dancer, 2017). For instance, such systems may fail to adequately address issues related to gender equality racial discrimination and other forms of oppression. This is particularly true if these matters were never addressed during earlier times when such customs first developed. Moreover, because customarily accepted behaviors vary widely across different cultures even within countries themselves disputes between individuals belonging distinct groups could arise leading potentially costly conflict resolution efforts down the road. Both case law and customary offer unique benefits and disadvantages depending upon the context of the situation being considered thus important consider relative merits demerits each before determining best course action moving forward. Figure 3.6 is a comparative chart of common and statutory law.

Comparison chart

	Common Law	Statutory Law
Creation of new laws	The law evolves with new decisions made by judges in courts.	New laws are issued by various government agencies.
Operational Level	Procedural	Substantive
Also known as	Case law	Written law
Nature	Instructive	Prescriptive
Origin	Precedent or judiciary	Government or legislature

Figure 3.6. Comparing common law with statutory law.

Source: nselmi.com via Twitter.

The legal system of any country is a complex and ever-evolving entity (Koskenniemi, 1990; Kreso, 2010; Krieger, 2006; Kumar, 2020; Lagji, 2019; Lavalle, 2014; Laylin, 1976). It is composed of both case law, which is based on judicial decisions, and customary law, which relies on the customs and traditions of a particular society. Both forms of law are essential for ensuring justice in a nation. However, they must be regularly updated to keep up with changing times.

Reforming and modernizing both case law and customary law can help ensure that laws remain relevant to current social conditions (Thirlway, 1972, 2015, 2017; Tobin, 2014; Tomuschat, 2021; Treasure et al., 2016; Tripp, 2004). This process involves reviewing existing laws to identify areas where changes may be necessary or beneficial. For example, outdated statutes may need to be amended or repealed altogether if they no longer reflect the values held by society today. Similarly, traditional practices that have become obsolete should also be reevaluated so as not to impede progress towards greater equality or other important goals.

In addition to updating existing laws, new legislation should also be introduced when appropriate to address emerging issues such as climate change or technological advances like artificial intelligence (AI). Such measures can help ensure that our legal systems remain responsive to the needs of citizens while still protecting their rights under the rule of law (Costa, 1998; Craik, 2020; Crawford, 2012; Criddle, 2013; Cuskelly, 2011; Dahlitz, 1991; Damato, 1973; Damato et al., 1993). Finally, it is important for governments around the world to recognize that reforming and modernizing both case law and customary law requires collaboration between different stakeholders including lawmakers, judges, lawyers, academics, and civil society organizations among others.

By working together these groups can develop effective solutions for addressing contemporary challenges while preserving fundamental principles such as human dignity and respect for diversity within societies worldwide (De Ruysscher, 2008; de Vries, 2021; De Wet, 2004; Debelva & De Broe, 2022; Dekoster, 2019; Demian, 2014; Anthony C Diala, 2017). Hence the idea that reforming and modernizing both case law and customary law are essential steps towards creating an equitable legal system capable of responding effectively to changing circumstances over time without sacrificing its core values along the way. Doing so will enable us all – regardless of background –to benefit from fair treatment under the rule of just law. The next section will consider the evolution of modern law.

3.4. THE EVOLUTION OF MODERN LAW

Modern law is a term used to describe the legal system that has evolved over time (Barrie, 2016; Baxi, 2020; Beavers, 2019; Beer, 2022; Bennett, 2008, 2009, 2015; Benson & Siddiqui, 2014). It encompasses all the laws and regulations that govern our society today, from criminal justice to civil rights. The modern legal system is based on principles such as fairness, equality, and justice for all. The development of modern law began in the late 18th century with the emergence of nation-states and their need for a unified set of laws to govern them. This led to an increase in codified legislation which was designed to ensure consistency across different jurisdictions. Over time, this body of legislation has grown significantly and now covers almost every aspect of life including business transactions, family matters, property ownership, taxation and more.

In addition to codified legislation there are also common law systems which rely on precedent rather than written statutes or regulations (Mastura, 1994; Maunatlala & Maimela, 2020; Maxim & Titu Maiorescu, 2015; McAuslan, 2015; McCarthy, 1971; McLachlan, 1988). Common law systems have been around since ancient times, but they continue to be used today in many countries around the world including England & Wales and Australia & New Zealand. In these countries judges make decisions based on previous cases rather than relying solely on written statutes or regulations when making rulings about disputes between parties involved in litigation proceedings.

Modern law also includes international agreements between nations such as treaties or conventions which can be enforced by domestic courts if necessary (Enabulele & Bazuaye, 2019; Engel & Kurschilgen, 2013; Farran, 2019; Fenrich et al., 2011; Fleck, 2009, 2013; Fletcher, 2007). These agreements often cover areas like human rights protection or environmental protection where it is important for governments around the world to work together towards achieving shared goals without infringing upon each other's sovereignty too much. Overall modern law is an ever-evolving field that seeks to provide fair outcomes while protecting individuals' rights within society at large. Figure 3.7 highlights some key events in the development of common law.

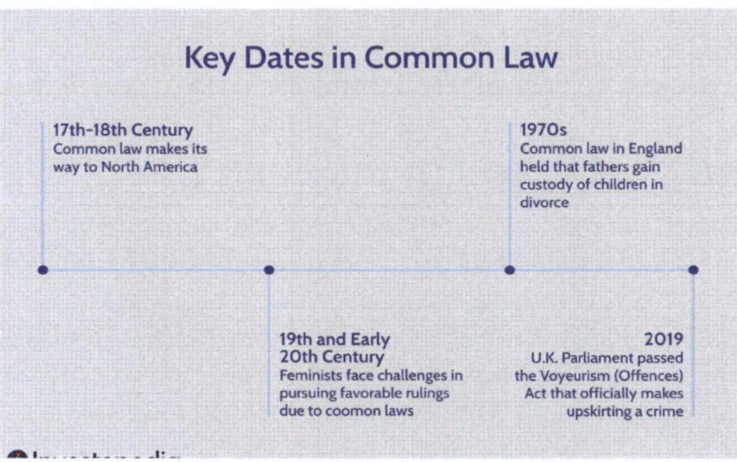

Figure 3.7. Key developments in common law.

Source: Investopedia.

The modern legal system is a complex and ever-evolving entity (Morrison, 2016; Morudu & Maimela, 2021; Murphy, 2014; Mwalimu, 1988; Mwambene, 2012; Mwangi, 2022). It has been shaped by centuries of development, with laws being amended and updated to reflect the changing needs of society. As such, it can be difficult to assess its strengths and weaknesses in an objective manner. However, there are some key points that can be identified which provide insight into how effective the current legal framework is at protecting citizens' rights and ensuring justice is served.

One of the major strengths of modern law is its ability to adapt quickly to new situations or changes in public opinion (Ubink, 2008; Utama, 2021; van Caenegem, 2014; van Engelenhoven, 2021; Vanboven, 1991; Vergouwen, 2013);. This allows for laws to remain relevant even as social norms evolve over time. Additionally, many countries have adopted international standards when it comes to human rights protection, meaning that individuals around the world are afforded certain basic protections regardless of their location or nationality.

Contrastingly, one potential weakness of modern law lies in its complexity (Armstrong, 1989; Arowolo, 2019; Asieduakrofi, 1989; Barnabas, 2022; Barrie, 2016; Baxi, 2020; Beavers, 2019; Beer, 2022; Bennett, 2008). This is due to its long history and numerous amendments over time, understanding all aspects of a particular legal system can be challenging even for experienced lawyers or judges. Furthermore, while international standards exist regarding human rights protection they may not always be enforced effectively on a local level due to lack of resources or political will from governments in power at any given moment.

It could therefore be argued that modern law does offer many advantages compared with earlier systems. These include greater flexibility and more comprehensive coverage (Woodman, 1988, 1969, 2001; Worugji et al., 2019; Wu, 2018; Young, 2019; Zamir, 2015; Zarea, 2022). However, there are still areas where improvements could be made if we want our legal frameworks to truly serve justice for all citizens across the globe. By continuing efforts towards simplifying existing legislation while also strengthening enforcement mechanisms for international standards we can ensure that everyone enjoys equal access to justice no matter where they live or what their background may be.

In one way or another, it appears that while modern law does offer some advantages compared with previous systems (such as greater flexibility), there are also significant drawbacks which need addressing if we want our legal frameworks to truly serve everyone equally and fairly no matter where they live or what their background might be (Tucker, 1972 Tunkin, 1993; Tupper, 1881; Ubink, 2016; Ubink & Weeks, 2017; Ubink, 2008). The legal system is constantly evolving, and modern law must take into account the lessons learned from common law. Common law has been around for centuries, and it provides a valuable source of insight into how laws should be structured to best serve society. We explore some of the ways that modern law can be reformed using lessons learned from common law.

One way that modern law can benefit from common law is by recognizing the importance of precedent (Robert W Tucker, 1972; Tunkin, 1993; Tupper, 1881; Ubink, 2016; Ubink & Weeks, 2017; Ubink, 2008; Utama, 2021). Precedent is an important part of common law because it allows judges to make decisions based on past cases rather than relying solely on their own opinions or interpretations of statutes. This helps ensure consistency in court rulings and prevents arbitrary decisions being made without any basis in existing case history. By incorporating precedent into modern legislation, lawmakers can help ensure that justice is served fairly and consistently across all jurisdictions. As Figure 3.8 shows, both common and statute law work as complements to each other.

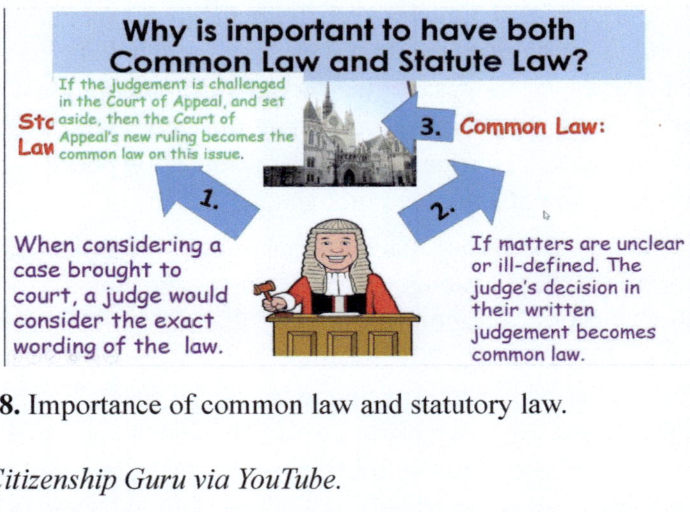

Figure 3.8. Importance of common law and statutory law.

Source: Citizenship Guru via YouTube.

Another lesson that can be taken from common law is the concept of stare decisis (Hager, 2020; Haggenmacher, 2021; Hammond, 2019; Harmathy, 2016; Henry, 2017; Hernández, 2012; Holleman, 1969, 1972). This is Latin for "to stand by things decided." It means that courts are bound by previous judicial decisions when making new ones. This principle ensures stability within the legal system as well as providing guidance for future cases with similar facts or issues at hand. Modern legislatures should consider implementing this principle when drafting new laws to provide greater certainty about how those laws will be interpreted and applied in practice.

Finally, another key lesson learned from common law relates to equity (Oba, 2002, 2008, 2011; Obatusin, 2018; Olaf & Markus, 2018; Omidire, 1990; Orebech et al., 2005; Osman, 2019). This relates to fairness between parties involved in a dispute or transaction regardless of what may have been agreed upon beforehand or written down legally speaking (e.g., contracts). Equity serves as an important check against unjust outcomes resulting from overly rigid application of rules; thus, allowing judges more flexibility when deciding cases where one party may have suffered due to unforeseen circumstances beyond their control (e.g., natural disasters). Incorporating equitable principles into modern legislation would help ensure fairer outcomes for all parties involved while still maintaining respect for contractual agreements between them whenever possible.

There are many lessons that can be taken away from studying common law which could prove invaluable when reforming our current legal systems today; such as recognizing the importance of precedent, implementing stare decisis principles and taking equity considerations into account during decision-making processes (Botha & Bekink, 2018; Bourgon, 2020; Budlender et al., 2011; Buss, 2010; Buxbaum, 1968; Cannizzaro & Bonafe, 2005; Carrillo-Santarelli, 2017). Doing so would not only improve access to justice but also promote greater fairness throughout society overall. This is something all nations strive towards achieving.

Another lesson that modern lawmakers can learn from common law is the value of flexibility when creating new laws or amending existing ones (Worugji et al., 2019; Wu, 2018; Young, 2019; Zamir, 2015; Zarea, 2022; Zenker & Höhne, 2018; Zerner, 1994). Common Law was designed with flexibility in mind. For instance, its rules were meant to evolve over time according to changing social norms and values rather than remain static forevermore. This means that legislators today should not be afraid to amend existing laws if necessary, nor create new ones if needed – provided they do so within reasonable limits set by constitutional principles such as due process rights and equal protection under the law for all citizens alike.

Finally, another key lesson which modern lawmakers can learn from common Law relates to judicial discretion (Cannizzaro & Bonafe, 2005; Carrillo-Santarelli, 2017; Castillo & Bian, 2014; Cataldi & Titu Maiorescu, 2015). This relates to the leeway judges have when interpreting statutes or deciding cases based on facts presented before them. Common Law recognizes the need for judicial discretion but also sets certain boundaries within which judges must operate. These include respecting established precedents (as discussed above) but also taking into account relevant public policy considerations such as fairness and justice for all parties involved in a dispute resolution process etcetera). By following these guidelines closely while still allowing room for individual interpretation where appropriate, contemporary courts will be able to better serve their communities while ensuring justice prevails.

There are many lessons which contemporary lawmakers can learn from studying Common Law (Baxi, 2020; Beavers, 2019; Beer, 2022; Bennett, 2008, 2009, 2015; Benson & Siddiqui, 2014; Bianchi, 2009). These include recognizing the importance of precedent setting. Another reform involves embracing flexibility when creating or amending legislation. This also calls for understanding judicial discretion's role within our legal system. These reforms are all with an aim towards reforming our current legal framework, so it better serves society's needs. It is important to bear in mind that the law is sourced from different institutions and elements of society. This fact can have a significant impact on how the law is conceived, operationalized, and interpreted. Therefore, the next section pays attention to the various sources of the law.

3.5. VARIOUS SOURCES OF THE LAW

Court decisions serve an important role in interpreting existing laws when there is ambiguity about their meaning or application in particular cases (Gillespie & Tran, 2022; Golo et al., 2022; Gradoni, 2019; Graves, 2017; Gray, 2021; Griffiths, 1998; Hager, 2020; Haggenmacher, 2021). These interpretations become binding precedent for future cases involving similar issues unless overturned by higher courts with jurisdiction over them. Executive orders are issued directly from the president (or governor) without legislative approval. While not legally binding themselves, they often direct government agencies to take certain actions within their scope of authority that must then be followed until revoked or modified through subsequent legislation passed by Congress (or state legislature).

Finally, legal commentaries provide insight into how different aspects of law interact with one another through analysis conducted by scholars who specialize in a range of niches such as constitutional law or contract law (Thirlway, 1972; Tobin, 2014; Tomuschat, 2021; Treasure et al., 2016;

Tripp, 2004; Tsai, 2015; Tucker, 1972). This type of research can help inform decision-making processes when dealing with complex matters where multiple factors need consideration before reaching a conclusion about what action should be taken next. All these various sources work together to ensure justice is served fairly throughout society according to established principles laid down long ago but still relevant today despite the changing times we live in now. Figure 3.9 shows how laws are derived from the courts and parliament.

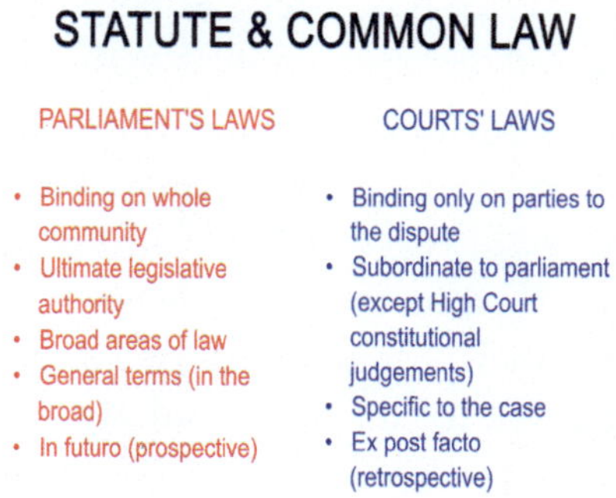

Figure 3.9. Laws derived from parliament and the courts.

Source: Doddy Santoso.

Making laws is an important part of the democratic process (Marasinghe, 1978; Masengu, 2016; Mastura, 1994; Maunatlala & Maimela, 2020; Maxim & Titu Maiorescu, 2015; McAuslan, 2015). In a parliamentary system, it is the responsibility of parliament to create and pass legislation that governs how people live their lives. But how does this process work? We can take the example of the legislative process in the United Kingdom. This is a particularly compelling example given the fact that Britain colonized many nations which adopted or mimicked its parliamentary processes. Indeed, there is literature that speaks of the British parliament as the mother of parliaments.

Although lacking a written constitution, there are specific protocols for making laws in the United Kingdom. Many other parts of the world follow a similar process (Albakjaji, 2022; Allott, 1957, 1984; Anderson, 2003; Angelini, 2012; Armstrong, 1989; Arowolo, 2019; Asieduakrofi, 1989). The first step in making a law is for a Member of Parliament (MP) to introduce a bill into the House of Commons or Senate. This bill outlines what changes are proposed and why they should be made. The MP then presents their case for why the bill should become law, which can include speeches from other MPs who support or oppose it.

Once debate has taken place, members vote on whether to accept or reject the proposed legislation. If accepted by majority vote, it will move onto its second reading where further discussion takes place before being voted on again at third reading stage. At this point amendments may be added if necessary before finally passing through both Houses with Royal Assent from His Majesty's Government – meaning that it has been approved by all parties involved and can now become law in England and Wales (or Scotland/Northern Ireland depending on jurisdiction).

It is worth noting that not all bills make it through these stages successfully (Danilenko, 1988; Davis & Klare, 2010; De ruysscher, 2008; de Vries, 2021; De Wet, 2004; Debelva & De Broe, 2022; Dekoster, 2019). Some may fail due to lack of support or because they have been deemed too controversial by certain groups within society. There will be a myriad of interest groups and campaigners such as religious organizations or pressure groups and lobbyists. Inevitably, many proposals and bills fail to materialize. However, those which do succeed will go on to shape our lives in one way or another!

The processes adopted by the United Kingdom can seem archaic, but they have served the nation for centuries and inspired many legislative regimes across the Commonwealth and the old empire (Lingaas, 2022; Lita et al., 2017; Liu, 2019; Loja, 2014; Lon & Widyawati, 2021; Magnusson, 2013, 2017; Manaka & Corrin, 2021). Having an overview of how parliament makes laws in Britain today is instructive for students of the law. It is certainly an interesting process but one which ensures that any new regulations are thoroughly discussed before becoming official policy.

That then raises questions about the role of the courts? How do they make laws? Should they be making laws at all? In fact, courts can and do make laws through judicial precedent (Kim, 2009, 2020; Kingwill, 2016; Koskenniemi, 1990; Kreso, 2010; Krieger, 2006; Kumar, 2020; Lagji, 2019; Lavalle, 2014). This is when judges use previous cases to decide how current ones should be judged – meaning that if two similar cases have been heard before then the same ruling will likely apply again. This helps to ensure consistency and fairness within our legal system as well as providing an effective way of making sure that all parties involved are treated equally under the law. In addition to this, judges can also create new laws by interpreting existing legislation in different ways or by introducing new concepts into their rulings which may not have been considered previously (Nhlapo,

2017; Nnona, 2018; Norr, 1973; Nwapi, 2016; Nyane, 2019; O'Neill, 2002; Oba, 2002, 2008, 2011). For example, a judge might interpret a particular piece of legislation differently than it was originally intended – thus creating a 'new' law. For critics, this is a problematic approach since parliament is meant to have primacy in the legislative process. Indeed, debates about the role of judges in making laws have dominated many Supreme Court rulings in the USA between activist judges on the liberal side and judicial restraint.

The US judicial system is a complex and ever-evolving entity. It has been shaped by centuries of legal precedent, as well as the changing political landscape of the country. One area that has seen significant change over time is judicial activism, which refers to judges making decisions based on their own personal beliefs or values rather than strictly adhering to established law (Tunkin, 1993; Tupper, 1881; Ubink, 2016; Ubink & Weeks, 2017; Ubink, 2008; Utama, 2021; van Caenegem, 2014). Various theories and practices of judicial activism in the US judicial system have shaped its procedures and outcomes.

Judicial activism can be divided into two main categories: liberal and conservative (Gal-Or, 2015; Galindo & Yip, 2017; Gao, 2013; Gillespie & Tran, 2022; Golo et al., 2022; Gradoni, 2019; Graves, 2017; Gray, 2021; Griffiths, 1998). Liberal activists believe that judges should interpret laws broadly to protect individual rights from government interference; they are more likely to strike down laws they deem unconstitutional or otherwise unjustified. Conservative activists take a more restrained approach, believing that judges should defer to legislative bodies when it comes to interpreting laws; they are less likely to overturn existing statutes unless there is clear evidence of unconstitutionality or injustice.

In practice, both types of judicial activism have had an impact on the US judiciary system over time. For example, liberal activists have pushed for greater protection for civil liberties such as freedom of speech and religion; while conservative activists have sought stricter enforcement of criminal laws and tougher sentences for offenders. Both sides also tend to favor certain interpretations when it comes to constitutional issues like abortion rights or same-sex marriage – though these views may differ depending on who holds office at any given time (Singer, 1972; Skomerska-Muchowska, 2017; Snyder, 1984; Sprankling, 2014; Sun, 2010; Syaufi & Zahra, 2021).

Ultimately, both theories and practices of judicial activism play an important role in shaping our nation's legal framework (Debelva & De Broe, 2022; Dekoster, 2019; Demian, 2014; Anthony C Diala, 2017, 2019; Diala

& Bagni, 2019). However, it is important not to forget that each case must still be decided according to its merits within the context of existing law before any activist decision can be made either way. By understanding how different ideologies shape our courts today, we can better appreciate why certain rulings come out one way versus another – even if we do not always agree with them personally.

The justice system is a cornerstone of democracy, designed to ensure that all citizens are treated fairly and equitably (Nhlapo, 1997; Nhlapo, 2017; Nnona, 2018; Norr, 1973; Nwapi, 2016; Nyane, 2019; O'Neill, 2002; Oba, 2002, 2008). However, in recent years it has become increasingly politicized and co-opted into the culture wars. This has had serious implications for how justice is administered and perceived by the public. It also threatens public confidence in the judges who are now seen as part of the political debates that ought to ideally take place in elected parliaments.

In many countries around the world, politicians have sought to use the justice system as a tool for advancing their own political agendas (Orebech et al., 2005; Osman, 2019; Osman & Baase, 2022; Osman & Himonga, 2017; Ottley, 2016; Parisi, 2001). This can be seen in attempts to pass laws that disproportionately target certain groups or individuals based on their race, religion, or other characteristics. It can also be seen in efforts to manipulate judicial appointments so that judges with ideological leanings are appointed to key positions within the court system.

This politicization of the justice system has led to an erosion of trust between citizens and those responsible for administering justice (Huizenga, 2018, 2022; Hulme, 2010; Hutchison, 2020; Hutchison & Sibanda, 2017; Iyi, 2016; Jentoft & Bavinck, 2019). When people perceive that decisions are being made based on politics rather than facts or evidence, they lose faith in the fairness of proceedings and may even begin to question whether they will receive impartial treatment from authorities if they ever find themselves involved in legal proceedings.

Furthermore, this politicization has resulted in a situation where some cases take precedence over others due to their political significance rather than any inherent merit or importance within society at large (Pedersen, 2014; Pelizzon, 2015; Perreau-Saussine & Murphy, 2007; Petersen, 2007, 2017; Pocar, 2016). This means that important issues such as domestic violence or child abuse may not get adequate attention because they do not fit neatly into one side's narrative about what constitutes "justice" – leading victims of these crimes feeling ignored by those who should be protecting them most closely: our courts and law enforcement agencies. It is essential that we recognize this problem before it becomes too entrenched within our societies (Holleman, 1972; Horii, 2019; Howell, 2018; Hu, 2017; Huizenga, 2018, 2022; Hulme, 2010; Hutchison, 2020; Hutchison & Sibanda, 2017). Otherwise, we risk undermining one of our most fundamental democratic principles: equal access to justice regardless of background or beliefs. We must strive towards creating an environment where everyone feels safe enough coming forward with complaints without fear of retribution from powerful interests seeking only further entrenchment through manipulation of legal systems worldwide. Only then can we truly say we have achieved true equality under law – something which every citizen deserves but few currently enjoy today due its increasing politicization.

It is important to remember that the law is constantly evolving and changing as society progresses (Laylin, 1976; Lewis, 1983, 2016; Liakopoulos, 2019; Lijnzaad, 2022; Lingaas, 2022; Lita et al., 2017; Liu, 2019; Loja, 2014). This means that both parliament and courts must be prepared to adapt their approach to keep up with the times – something which can only benefit us all. It is therefore not surprising that some voices have been calling for a reform of the legislative process as well as the administration of justice. This is something that happens in a range of jurisdictions across the globe.

The legislative process and justice systems of the world are in need of reform (de Vries, 2021; De Wet, 2004; Debelva & De Broe, 2022; Dekoster, 2019; Demian, 2014; Anthony C Diala, 2017). In recent years, several ideas have been proposed to improve these systems and make them more equitable for all citizens. Here we will explore some of the most popular proposals for reforming the legislative process and justice systems around the world.

One idea that has gained traction is to increase public participation in decision-making processes (Joireman, 2008; Jonas & Gunda, 2015; Kadens, 2012; Kammerhofer, 2012; Kane, 1972; Kassoti, 2017; Kelly & Windia, 2019; Kilian, 2019). This could be done by allowing citizens to vote on legislation or even participate directly in policy debates through online forums or other means. By giving people a greater say in how their government operates, it would help ensure that laws reflect the wishes of those they affect most directly.

Another proposal is to reduce barriers to access within legal proceedings, such as reducing court fees or providing free legal aid services for those who cannot afford representation (Akande, 2004; Albakjaji, 2022; Allott,

1957, 1984; Anderson, 2003; Angelini, 2012; Armstrong, 1989; Arowolo, 2019). This would help ensure that everyone has an equal opportunity when it comes time to defend themselves against charges brought against them by authorities or seek redress from wrongs committed against them by others.

A third suggestion is to create independent oversight bodies with authority over both legislators and law enforcement officials alike (Vanboven, 1991; Vergouwen, 2013; Vines, 2017; Watson, 1984; Webber, 2009; Weinberg, 2016; Williams & Klusener, 2013). This is proposed to prevent abuse of power and corruption within these institutions. Such bodies could investigate complaints made about either group's actions while also ensuring compliance with existing laws and regulations governing their activities.

Finally, there have been calls for increased transparency throughout all levels of government operations (including making information regarding budgets, contracts awarded, etc.,) available publicly so that citizens can hold their representatives accountable if necessary (Young, 2019; Zamir, 2015; Zarea, 2022; Zenker & Höhne, 2018; Zerner, 1994; Zilberman, 1996; Zitzke, 2022; Zwalve, 2012). Additionally, this could help reduce instances where powerful individuals use their influence behind closed doors without any accountability whatsoever from those affected by their decisions or actions taken on behalf of society at large.

All these ideas represent potential solutions towards improving our current legislative process and justice system worldwide (Ndulo, 2011; Ngira, 2018, 2021; Nhlapo, 2017; Nnona, 2018; Norr, 1973; Nwapi, 2016; Nyane, 2019). However, further research must be conducted before any changes can be implemented effectively across different countries' contexts. It is clear though that something needs to change if we want our governments to truly serve its citizens fairly and justly going forward into the future.

But what about legal commentaries? How do they contribute to the process of making laws? Legal commentaries are written by experts in the field and provide an analysis of existing legislation (Quane, 2013; Rautenbach, 2020; Rose, 1989; Rubin, 1990; Russo, 1988; Sarbah, 1904; Seidman, 1983; Sheleff, 1994). They can be used as a reference point for both parliamentarians and judges when considering how to interpret or apply a particular law. This is especially useful when it comes to complex areas such as tax, employment, or human rights – where there may be multiple interpretations of the same piece of legislation. By providing an impartial view on these matters, legal commentaries help ensure that everyone is treated equally under the law. In addition to this, legal commentaries can also act as a source of inspiration for new laws or amendments to existing ones (Hutchison & Sibanda, 2017; Iyi, 2016; Jentoft & Bavinck, 2019; John-Hopkins, 2010; Johnson, 1986; Joireman, 2008; Jonas & Gunda, 2015). For example, if a commentator identifies an area which could benefit from additional regulation then this could prompt parliamentarians into action. Similarly, if commentators identify any potential loopholes in current regulations then these too can be addressed through legislative changes.

Overall, legal commentaries play an important role in helping shape our laws today (Gal-Or, 2015; Galindo & Yip, 2017; Gao, 2013; Gillespie & Tran, 2022; Golo et al., 2022; Gradoni, 2019). While legal commentaries can be incredibly useful in helping to shape our laws, they also bring with them several problems. One of the most significant issues is that having so many different entities making laws can lead to confusion and inconsistency. This is because each commentator may have their own interpretation or opinion on how a particular law should be applied – which could result in conflicting advice being given out.

Furthermore, it is not always easy for people to keep up to date with all the latest developments in legislation (Cuskelly, 2011; Dahlitz, 1991; Damato, 1973; Damato et al., 1993; Dancer, 2017; Danilenko, 1988; Davis & Klare, 2010; De ruysscher, 2008). This is especially true if they are not familiar with the area or do not have access to reliable sources of information. As such, this could mean that individuals end up relying on outdated advice when trying to interpret or apply a particular law – something which could potentially lead to costly mistakes.

Finally, there is also the risk that commentators may become too influential when it comes to shaping our laws (Nnona, 2018; Norr, 1973; Nwapi, 2016; Nyane, 2019; O'Neill, 2002; Oba, 2002, 2008, 2011; Obatusin, 2018). While their opinions should certainly be taken into account by legislators, ultimately it should still be parliamentarians who make the final decisions about what goes into new legislation and amendments. If commentators start taking over then this could undermine democracy. We cannot speak of addressing the democratic deficit if important decisions are dominated by so-called experts who may not have the best experiences of real life. In conclusion then, while legal commentaries can provide invaluable insights into how our laws are made today there are some potential drawbacks associated with having so many different entities involved in this process (Graves, 2017; Gray, 2021; Griffiths, 1998; Hager, 2020; Haggenmacher, 2021; Hammond,

2019; Harmathy, 2016; Henry, 2017). It is therefore important for us all to remain aware of these issues and ensure that any changes made through legislative processes reflect public opinion rather than just those of individual commentators. The question of how countries harmonize and rationalize the various sources of law is an important one. In many countries, laws are derived from a variety of sources including statutes, common law, case law, international treaties, and legal commentaries. This can make it difficult for individuals to understand what their rights and obligations are under the law as there may be conflicting interpretations or advice available on any given issue.

One way in which this problem could be addressed is through greater collaboration between different branches of government when it comes to creating new legislation or amending existing laws (John-Hopkins, 2010; Johnson, 1986; Joireman, 2008; Jonas & Gunda, 2015; Kadens, 2012; Kammerhofer, 2012). By having all relevant stakeholders involved in the process then we can ensure that everyone's views are taken into account before any decisions are made – something which should help to reduce confusion amongst citizens about their rights and responsibilities.

Another potential solution would be for governments to create more comprehensive databases containing information about all applicable laws so that people have access to up-to-date advice whenever they need it (Galindo & Yip, 2017; Gao, 2013; Gillespie & Tran, 2022; Golo et al., 2022; Gradoni, 2019; Graves, 2017; Gray, 2021; Griffiths, 1998; Hager, 2020). This could also help prevent outdated opinions from influencing current debates as commentators would no longer have such a monopoly over legal knowledge. In addition, governments should also consider introducing measures which encourage public participation in legislative processes by providing citizens with opportunities to voice their opinions on proposed changes or amendments before they become official policy. Doing so will not only give people a say in how our laws evolve but also provide legislators with valuable insights into what matters most to those affected by them – something which could ultimately lead to better decision making.

The legal system of any country is based on a set of laws that govern the behavior and actions of its citizens (O'Neill, 2002; Oba, 2002, 2008, 2011; Obatusin, 2018; Olaf & Markus, 2018; Omidire, 1990). These laws are derived from various sources, which can be divided into two main categories: primary sources and secondary sources. Primary sources include constitutions, statutes, regulations, treaties, court decisions and executive orders. Secondary sources include legal commentaries such as books or articles written by lawyers or judges about the law.

Constitutions are the highest form of law in most countries and provide a framework for all other laws to follow (Tan, 1993, 2018; Tegnan, 2015; Thipe & Buthelezi, 2014; Thirlway, 1972, 2015, 2017). They outline fundamental rights and freedoms as well as establish governmental structures and powers. Statutes are enacted by legislatures at both federal and state levels to create specific rules governing certain areas such as criminal offenses or taxation policies. Regulations are issued by administrative agencies to implement statutes in more detail; they often contain detailed instructions on how to comply with particular requirements under the law. Treaties involve agreements between two or more nations that have been ratified by their respective governments; these may cover topics such as trade relations or military alliances between countries.

There are many different types of primary and secondary sources available for understanding what constitutes lawful behavior within any given society today – each playing an important role in helping ensure justice is served fairly across all individuals regardless of background or circumstance (Moore, 1986; Morrison, 2016; Morudu & Maimela, 2021; Murphy, 2014; Mwalimu, 1988; Mwambene, 2012). Understanding where our laws come from will help us better understand why we must abide by them. This is something essential if we wish to maintain order throughout our communities.

The sources of law are the foundations upon which legal systems are built (Asieduakrofi, 1989; Barnabas, 2022; Barrie, 2016; Baxi, 2020; Beavers, 2019; Beer, 2022; Bennett, 2008, 2009, 2015). It is important to critically evaluate these sources in order to understand how they interact and shape our laws. In section, we explore the various sources of law and their implications for society.

First, let us consider common law. Common law is based on precedent set by judges in previous cases that have been decided by courts of higher authority (Norr, 1973; Nwapi, 2016; Nyane, 2019; O'Neill, 2002; Oba, 2002, 2008, 2011; Obatusin, 2018). This means that when a court makes a decision about a case, it sets an example for future cases with similar facts or circumstances. This type of law can be seen as beneficial because it allows for consistency in decisions made by different courts across jurisdictions; however, it also has its drawbacks since there may be no clear guidance from higher authorities on certain issues or if the precedents set do not reflect current societal values or norms.

Second, statutory laws are those created by legislatures such as Congress or state legislatures through statutes and regulations passed into effect after being voted on and approved by elected officials (Obatusin, 2018; Olaf & Markus, 2018; Omidire, 1990; Orebech et al., 2005; Osman, 2019; Osman & Baase, 2022). These types of laws provide more specific guidance than common law but can also be subject to change depending on who is in power at any given time and what their political agenda may be. Additionally, some statutes may conflict with existing common-law principles making them difficult to enforce without further clarification from higher authorities such as appellate courts or even the Supreme Court itself. Complexity remains a key feature of these processes. For instance, Figure 3.10 shows that there is a difference in the law-making processes for common law and civil law as a case in point of the complexities of the legal system.

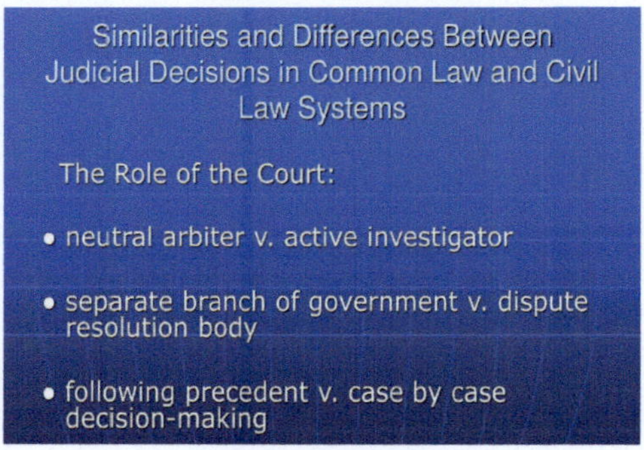

Figure 3.10. Differences in the decision-making process for common law and civil law.

Source: Ebony Hermans (2012).

Thirdly, constitutional laws are those established within a nation's constitution which serve as the highest form of legal authority within that country's jurisdiction (Chang, 2022; Chanock, 1989; Cheng, 2012; Chirayath et al., 2005; Claassens & Mnisi, 2009; Cooter, 1991). They cannot be changed except through amendments ratified according to procedures outlined within each nation's respective constitution documents. Constitutional laws often protect citizens' rights against government interference while providing limits on governmental powers so that individuals remain free from oppressive rule. However, due to their rigid nature they can sometimes become outdated over time if not amended accordingly when necessary changes arise in society's values or needs.

Finally international treaties between nations create another source of binding legal obligations among countries involved in said treaty agreements (Osman & Himonga, 2017; Ottley, 2016; Parisi, 2001; Pedersen, 2014; Pelizzon, 2015; Perreau-Saussine & Murphy, 2007). These treaties usually involve trade agreements between two countries but could also include human rights conventions amongst many other topics related to international relations between states. International treaties must adhere strictly to all parties involved otherwise one party could take advantage over another leading potentially disastrous consequences both economically and politically speaking.

Understanding how each source interacts with one another helps us better comprehend our own legal system while allowing us to make informed decisions regarding potential changes needed either legislatively, judicially, constitutionally, or internationally (Haggenmacher, 2021; Hammond, 2019; Harmathy, 2016; Henry, 2017; Hernández, 2012; Holleman, 1969, 1972; Horii, 2019). By critically evaluating these various sources we gain insight into how our societies function under different forms of governance thus enabling us to make more educated choices when voting for representatives who will ultimately decide what kind policies should govern our lives going forward.

CHAPTER 3 SUMMARY

The third chapter in this book sought to clarify some of the practices of customary law. For example, the chapter showed how economic and moral justifications were cloaked under the auspices of customary law to justify slavery. We have considered how crimes against humanity emerged as a concept that is deeply rooted in customary law. The chapter then compared customary law with case law and statutory law as part of the evolution of modern law from a range of sources. In the next chapter we explore the processes of establishing customary law.

CHAPTER 4

The Establishment of Customary Law

Contents

The fourth chapter highlights the various ways in which customary law is established in communities and societies. Hence, the chapter will explore the methodologies of law as well as their relationship to Classic Western theories of jurisprudence. This will allow us to engage in conceptual analyzes of customary law. The chapter will introduce the notion of social behavior as opposed to its antisocial counterparts or social deviance. The key issues in this chapter cannot be fully understood without first identifying the methodologies of law.

4.1. THE METHODOLOGIES OF THE LAW

The law is a complex and ever-evolving system that governs our society (Meron, 1991; Meron et al., 1987; Merry, 1991; Meyer, 2012; Milanovic, 2011; Mnisi & Claassens, 2009; Moore, 1986). It is essential to understand the methods of the law in order to ensure justice and fairness for all. This section will discuss some of the most common methods used by legal professionals when dealing with cases. One method commonly used by lawyers is litigation, which involves taking a case to court in order to resolve it through a trial or settlement. Litigation can be expensive and time consuming, but it often provides an effective way for parties involved in disputes to reach an agreement without having to go through lengthy negotiations or mediation processes.

Another popular method employed by legal professionals is arbitration, which allows two parties who are unable to come to an agreement on their own terms (such as those involved in contract disputes, labor issues, or other civil matters) to have their dispute resolved outside of court with the help of a neutral third party known as an arbitrator (Morrison, 2016; Morudu & Maimela, 2021; Murphy, 2014; Mwalimu, 1988; Mwambene, 2012; Mwangi, 2022). Arbitration can be less costly than litigation and may provide more flexibility when it comes time for both sides of the dispute to reach a resolution. It also means that some of the animosity that is associated with these conflicts is moderated by the arbitrator. This gives the parties space to come to a fairly amicable settlement.

Mediation is another option available for resolving conflicts between two parties without going through formal court proceedings (Kammerhofer, 2012; Kane, 1972; Kassoti, 2017; Kelly & Windia, 2019; Kilian, 2019; Kim, 2009, 2020; Kingwill, 2016; Koskenniemi, 1990). In this process, both sides agree upon using a mediator who helps them negotiate towards finding common ground on which they can agree upon while avoiding any further conflict or disagreement between them. Mediation has become increasingly popular due its cost effectiveness and ability for both sides of the dispute to come away feeling satisfied with the outcome reached during negotiations rather than leaving one side feeling like they were taken advantage of during litigation proceedings.

Finally, negotiation is also frequently used by attorneys when attempting to settle disputes out-of-court before resorting to more costly options such as arbitration or litigation (Williams, 2022; Willms, 2009; Wilson, 1961; Wolff, 2016; Woodman, 1988; Woodman, 1969, 2001). Negotiation requires strong communication skills from both parties involved so that each side understands what they are agreeing to while still being able achieve their desired outcomes from any potential agreements made during these discussions. Overall, there are many different methods available within our legal system that allow individuals, businesses, organizations, etc., to resolve conflicts without having to take part in lengthy courtroom battles. Understanding how each approach works best depending on your particular situation can help you make informed decisions about how best handle your case moving forward.

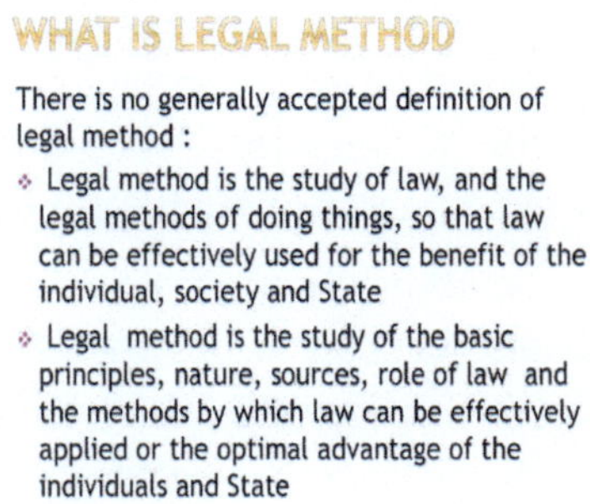

Figure 4.1. Components of the legal method.

Source: Laurence Stone.

The law is a complex system that can be difficult to navigate (Lewis, 1983, 2016; Liakopoulos, 2019; Lijnzaad, 2022; Lingaas, 2022; Lita et al., 2017; Liu, 2019; Loja, 2014; Lon & Widyawati, 2021). A legal method (Figure 4.1) can be a supportive framework for service users. Different methods of the law are available to help individuals and organizations understand their rights and obligations, as well as how to resolve disputes. Each method has its own advantages and disadvantages, so it is important to consider all options before making a decision.

One popular method of the law is litigation, which involves taking legal action against another party in court (Liu, 2019; Loja, 2014; Lon & Widyawati, 2021; Magnusson, 2013, 2017; Manaka & Corrin, 2021; Manullang, 2021). Litigation can be expensive and time-consuming but it offers an opportunity for both parties to present evidence in front of a judge or jury who will make a final ruling on the case. This process also allows for appeals if either side disagrees with the outcome. The downside is that litigation can take years before reaching resolution, during which time both sides may incur significant costs associated with lawyers' fees and other expenses related to preparing for trial.

Another option is arbitration, which involves having an impartial third-party mediator review evidence from both sides and make a binding decision on the dispute without going through formal court proceedings (Merry, 1991; Meyer, 2012; Milanovic, 2011; Mnisi & Claassens, 2009; Moore, 1986; Morrison, 2016; Morudu & Maimela, 2021). Arbitration tends to be faster than litigation since there are no lengthy trials or appeals processes involved; however, this method does not provide any recourse if one side disagrees with the arbitrator's ruling since it cannot be appealed like in court cases. Additionally, arbitration often requires payment of fees upfront by both parties regardless of whether they win or lose their case – something that could potentially put smaller businesses at a disadvantage compared to larger ones who have more resources available for such payments.

Finally, negotiation is another common approach used when resolving disputes outside of courtrooms or arbitration hearings (Nhlapo, 2017; Nnona, 2018; Norr, 1973; Nwapi, 2016; Nyane, 2019; O'Neill, 2002; Oba, 2002, 2008). Negotiation typically involves two parties discussing their differences until they reach an agreement that satisfies them both without involving any third-party mediators or judges – although sometimes attorneys may still need to get involved depending on the complexity of the situation at hand (e., g., contract negotiations). The main advantage here is cost savings since neither party needs to pay lawyer fees unless they choose to; however, this type of settlement also carries some risk because each side must trust that their counterpart will honor whatever deal was reached between them without any legal enforcement behind it should things go wrong down the line.

Ultimately deciding which method best suits your particular situation depends on many factors including budget constraints as well as how quickly you want resolution. Service users are typically advised to research carefully before committing themselves. In some industrialized nations a citizen's advice bureau might take on this important role. The Citizens Advice Bureau (CAB) is an invaluable resource for citizens seeking advice and assistance in navigating the complexities of the justice system. It provides a range of services, from providing legal information to helping people access legal aid and representation. The CAB also offers support to those who are unable to afford or access traditional legal services, such as victims of domestic violence or those with disabilities.

In recent years, there has been an increased focus on bringing the justice system closer to citizenry by making it more accessible and user-friendly (Omidire, 1990; Orebech et al., 2005; Osman, 2019; Osman & Baase, 2022; Osman & Himonga, 2017; Ottley, 2016). This has led to initiatives such as online court hearings, virtual courtrooms and digital case management systems that allow individuals to manage their cases without having to physically attend court proceedings. However, these technological advances can be difficult for some members of society – particularly those who lack basic computer literacy skills – which is where the CAB comes in.

The CAB provides free advice on how best to use technology when engaging with the justice system; this includes guidance on how best to prepare for online hearings or submit documents electronically via email or other digital platforms. Furthermore, they provide practical help with filling out forms correctly and understanding complex legal jargon so that individuals can make informed decisions about their cases without feeling overwhelmed by technical language used in courts or tribunals.

By offering this kind of support, the CAB helps bridge any gaps between citizens and their rights within the law; it ensures that everyone has equal access regardless of financial means or educational background. In addition, its presence allows vulnerable members of society – such as refugees fleeing persecution – a safe space where they can seek help without fear of judgment or discrimination based on race/ethnicity/religion etc. Overall then, it is clear that CAB plays an important role in ensuring fairness within our justice system by providing much needed assistance for all citizens regardless of socio-economic status; thus allowing them greater autonomy over their own lives while simultaneously promoting social cohesion through shared understanding across different communities within our society today.

Some of these developments are a consequence and outcome of rigorous legal research (Liakopoulos, 2019; Lijnzaad, 2022; Lingaas, 2022; Lita et al., 2017; Liu, 2019; Loja, 2014; Lon & Widyawati, 2021; Magnusson,

2013, 2017). Legal academic research is an important tool for advancing our knowledge of the justice system. It can take many forms, from empirical studies to theoretical analyzes, and each type has its own unique role in helping us understand how the law works. It is pertinent to explore some of the different types of legal academic research and their importance in furthering our understanding of the justice system. Empirical studies are one form of legal academic research that involve collecting data on a particular issue or topic related to law and then analyzing it to draw conclusions about how laws work in practice (Pocar, 2016; Poespasari, 2020; Polanski, 2017; Pratiwi et al., 2020; Qerimi, 2020; Quane, 2013; Rautenbach, 2020). This type of research often involves surveys or interviews with people who have experience with a certain area of law, such as criminal defense attorneys or judges. By gathering information from these individuals, researchers can gain insight into how laws are applied in real-world situations and what challenges they face when trying to uphold them. Theoretical analysis is another form of legal academic research that focuses on examining existing theories about law and developing new ones based on those findings (Diala, 2017, 2019; Diala & Bagni, 2019; Dubner, 1994; Dubois, 1992; Dupont, 2013; Duxbury, 2017). This type of study typically involves looking at past court decisions or other sources to identify patterns or trends that could be used to develop new theories about how laws should be interpreted and applied. The goal here is not only to better understand existing laws but also create more effective ones by taking into account various perspectives on a given issue. Figure 4.2 summarizes the classification of legal research in ways that are consistent with the description above.

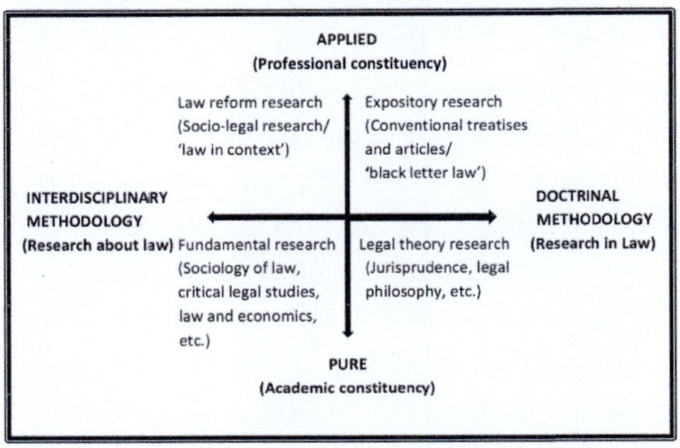

Figure 4.2. Classification of legal research.

Source: Adapted from Chynoweth (2008, 29).

Finally, comparative studies are yet another form of legal academic research that looks at different countries' approaches towards similar issues within their respective justice systems (Howell, 2018; Hu, 2017; Huizenga, 2018, 2022; Hulme, 2010; Hutchison, 2020; Hutchison & Sibanda, 2017; Iyi, 2016). By comparing different countries' approaches towards a particular problem – such as drug policy – researchers can gain valuable insights into which strategies may be most effective for addressing similar problems elsewhere around the world. Comparative studies also provide an opportunity for scholars to learn from each other's experiences so they can apply successful strategies across multiple jurisdictions without having to reinvent the wheel every time something needs fixing within their own country's justice system.

Legal academics play an essential role in advancing our knowledge about the justice system through their various forms of research mentioned above (empirical studies, theoretical analysis & comparative) (Maxim & Titu Maiorescu, 2015; McAuslan, 2015; McCarthy, 1971; McLachlan, 1988; Menski, 1988; Meron, 1987, 1991). Through these efforts we can better understand both current practices as well as potential solutions for improving them going forward – ultimately leading us closer towards achieving true social equity & fairness under the rule-of-law worldwide. The law is an ever-evolving entity, and the methods of its application have changed drastically over time. From ancient times to modern day, the way in which legal matters are handled has been subject to a variety of influences. It is pertinent to explore how these changes have taken place throughout history.

In ancient societies, laws were often based on religious or moral codes that had been passed down through generations (Tobin, 2014; Tomuschat, 2021; Treasure et al., 2016; Tripp, 2004; Tsai, 2015; Tucker, 1972). These laws were enforced by local rulers who acted as both judge and jury when it came to settling disputes between individuals or groups. This system was largely informal and relied heavily on tradition rather than written statutes or regulations. As civilizations grew more complex, so too did their legal systems. During the Middle Ages in Europe, for example, monarchs began codifying laws into written documents known as "statutes" that could be used to settle disputes between citizens and punish those found guilty of breaking them. This marked a shift away from relying solely on tradition towards a more formalized approach to justice that would become increasingly common over time.

During the Enlightenment period in Europe (17th – 18th centuries), there was an increased emphasis placed on individual rights and freedoms within society – something which had not previously been given much consideration before then (Mwangi, 2022; Ndulo, 2011; Ngira, 2018, 2021; Nhlapo, 2017; Nnona, 2018; Norr, 1973; Nwapi, 2016). As such, new forms of legislation were created with the aim of protecting people's liberties while also ensuring fairness in court proceedings; this included introducing concepts such as due process and habeas corpus into lawmaking processes across many countries around the world at this time period.

Today's legal systems are highly sophisticated compared to those seen even just a few hundred years ago; they now incorporate elements from various sources including international treaties and conventions alongside domestic legislation crafted by governments themselves (Damato et al., 1993; Dancer, 2017; Danilenko, 1988; Davis & Klare, 2010; De ruysscher, 2008; de Vries, 2021; De Wet, 2004). The use of technology has also revolutionized how cases are managed, with digital databases allowing lawyers access to vast amounts of information quickly without having to manually search through physical records.

Additionally, advances in communication technologies mean that lawyers can now collaborate remotely with colleagues located anywhere around the globe – something which would have seemed impossible only decades ago. Overall, it is clear that our understanding of what constitutes fair treatment under law has evolved significantly since its inception thousands years ago (Manaka & Corrin, 2021; Manullang, 2021; Marasinghe, 1978; Masengu, 2016; Mastura, 1994; Maunatlala & Maimela, 2020). With each passing generation comes new ideas about justice, leading us closer towards achieving true equality for all citizens regardless of their background or circumstances. It is therefore essential that we continue to strive for progress if we wish to ensure everyone receives equal protection under law going forward into the future. One of the most compelling contributors to these reforms in justice are classic western theories of jurisprudence.

4.2. CLASSIC WESTERN THEORIES OF JURISPRUDENCE

Natural Law Theory is one of the oldest and most well-known theories in Western jurisprudence (Gagnon-Bergeron, 2018; Gal-Or, 2015; Galindo & Yip, 2017; Gao, 2013; Gillespie & Tran, 2022; Golo et al., 2022; Gradoni, 2019; Graves, 2017). This theory holds that there are certain laws which exist independently from any human authority or legislation; they are inherent in nature itself and can be discovered through reason alone. Natural law theorists believe that these laws should form the basis for all other legal systems, as they provide an objective standard against which all other laws can be judged.

One of the contributors to these philosophies was English law (Beer, 2022; Bennett, 2008, 2009, 2015; Benson & Siddiqui, 2014; Bianchi, 2009; Bond, 2009, 2010). It is therefore pertinent to briefly explore the history of English law. English law is one of the oldest legal systems in the world, with its roots stretching back to Anglo-Saxon times.

The development of English law has been shaped by a variety of influences over the centuries, including Roman and European laws as well as local customs and traditions.

The earliest known written laws in England date back to 6th century AD when King Aethelberht I issued his code for Kent. This was followed by other codes from various kings throughout England during this period, such as Alfred's Laws (890) and Edward's Laws (1272).

These early codes were based on Germanic tribal custom rather than any formal system of justice or legislation. In 1066, William the Conqueror invaded England and brought with him Norman French Law which became known as Common Law.

This new system was based on precedent rather than statute; meaning that judges would make decisions based on previous cases rather than relying solely on written rules or regulations. Common Law remained largely unchanged until 1189 when Henry II introduced a more structured approach to justice through his Assize Courts which allowed for appeals against verdicts made at lower courts. Figure 4.3 highlights some of the key events in the history of English law.

During this time, Parliament began to play an increasingly important role in shaping English law through statutes passed by both Houses – Commons and Lords – which had become established by 1295 under Edward I's reign. Statutes continued to be passed throughout subsequent centuries up until modern day where they remain an integral part of the UK legal system alongside common law principles developed over time through judicial decisions made in courtrooms across England and Wales from 1189 onwards.

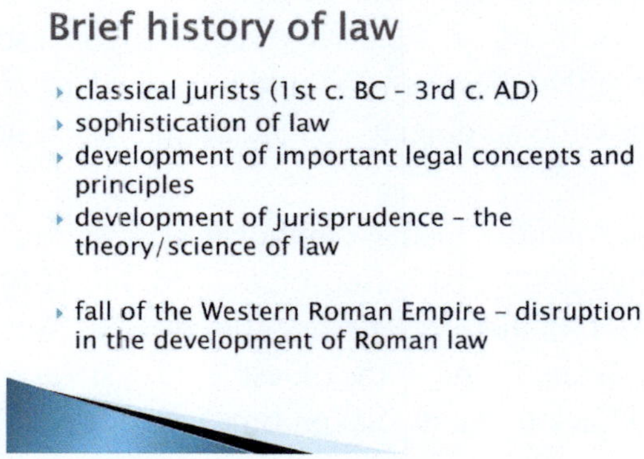

Figure 4.3. Brief history of English law.

Source: Miljen Matijašević.

Today, English law is still heavily influenced by these two sources: statutes created by Parliament and common law principles developed through case precedents set out in court judgments over hundreds of years ago. These two sources have the effect of making it one of the most complex yet fascinating legal systems around (Arowolo, 2019; Asieduakrofi, 1989; Barnabas, 2022; Barrie, 2016; Baxi, 2020; Beavers, 2019; Beer, 2022; Bennett, 2008; Bennett, 2015). It continues to evolve with each passing year thanks to changes made within both Houses but also due to advances in technology that have enabled us to access information faster than ever before.

One of the important theories that have influenced English law is Legal Positivism (Huizenga, 2022; Hulme, 2010; Hutchison, 2020; Hutchison & Sibanda, 2017; Iyi, 2016; Jentoft & Bavinck, 2019; John-Hopkins, 2010). This is a perspective and method which states that law exists only when it has been created by a legitimate source such as a government or court system.

The study of jurisprudence, or the philosophy of law, has been around for centuries (Ndulo, 2011; Ngira, 2018, 2021; Nhlapo, 2017; Nnona, 2018; Norr, 1973; Nwapi, 2016; Nyane, 2019). It is a complex field that encompasses many different theories and approaches to understanding the legal system. One way to categorize these theories is by looking at classic Western jurisprudence. This section will explore some of the most influential and widely accepted theories in this area. Figure 4.4 summarizes the key theories of the law.

	NATURALIST	POSITIVIST	SOCIOLOGIST
THEORY	• a legal theory that recognises law of nature/ moral law • believes that laws must be good and just to govern human relation. • It's the nature of every human being to know from his conscience what is righteous and therefore lawful. • They believe that human laws are defined by morality, and not by an authority figure like a government king. • **NATURALIST: OVERLAP THESIS** • all forms of natural law theory supports the necessary relation between the concepts of law and morality.	• Positivists believe that only positive law is law. Positive laws are laws that have been established by the authority of the state (sovereign). • Positivists are blind to values. • Positive law has nothing to do with ideal or just law, it has no regard to goodness or badness or the law. • Recognize only positive facts and excludes considerations towards concepts of jurisprudence. • **POSITIVIST: SEPARABILITY THESIS** • Positivism is not concerned with whether law is moral, just or unfair.	• Law is wholly concerned with its effect and results on society rather than treating law as will of god or command of the sovereign as law exists for the needs of the society. • Main concern of socialist is Interpreting the law in the social context, to bring good to the society. • Law regulates all kinds of relationships in a society and controls the behavior of its members.Hence, it is considered as a form of social control. • Law is not only about legality and punishment.
JURIST	→ BLACKSTONE ◆ Laws of nature dictated by god himself that are superior to any other	→ JOHN AUSTIN ◆ Law is a command made by a political sovereign. ◆ Rule is only legally valid	→ ROSCOE POUND ◆ Law is an instrument of social engineering. Its

Figure 4.4. Theories of law.

Source: Izzati Syahirah Zainudin.

Another important theory is Legal Positivism, which states that law exists only when it has been created by a legitimate source such as a government or court system (Webber, 2009; Weinberg, 2016; Williams & Klusener, 2013; Williams, 2022; Willms, 2009; Wilson, 1961; Wolff, 2016). According to this view, any law not created by an authorized body does not have any real force or effect on society; instead it must be enforced through social pressure or coercion if necessary. Legal positivists also argue that morality cannot be used as a basis for determining whether something should be considered legally binding since morality varies between cultures and individuals while positive law remains constant across societies regardless of their moral beliefs.

Analytical Jurisprudence is another major school of thought within Western jurisprudence which focuses on analyzing existing legal systems rather than creating new ones from scratch like natural lawyers do with their own set of principles derived from nature itself (Tripp, 2004; Tsai, 2015; Tucker, 1972; Tunkin, 1993; Tupper, 1881; Ubink, 2016; Ubink & Weeks, 2017). Analytical jurists look at how various rules interact with each other within a given jurisdiction's legal framework in order to determine what kind of outcomes would result from applying them together in specific cases. They also examine how changes made to one part may affect others parts, allowing them to make more informed decisions about potential reforms.

Finally, Sociological Jurisprudence looks at how people actually behave when faced with particular situations involving questions about legality (Ottley, 2016; Parisi, 2001; Pedersen, 2014; Pelizzon, 2015; Perreau-Saussine & Murphy, 2007; Petersen, 2007, 2017). Rather than relying solely on abstract concepts like those found in analytical jurisprudence, sociological theorists take into account factors (e.g., culture, religion, economics, and politics) when making judgments about what constitutes lawful behavior. By doing so they attempt to create more realistic models for predicting how people will act under certain circumstances thus providing valuable insight into why certain behaviors occur even though they may technically violate established norms.

In conclusion, there are several classic Western theories of jurisprudence including Natural Law Theory, Legal Positivism, Analytical Jurisprudence and Sociological Jurisprudence each offering unique perspectives on understanding our current legal system better. While none offer absolute answers regarding every situation we face today, collectively these four schools provide us with invaluable insights into both past practices and future possibilities concerning justice administration throughout history up until now. The next issue to tackle is how conceptual analyzes can be applied to different forms of judicial systems including customary law.

4.3. CONCEPTUAL ANALYZES OF CUSTOMARY LAW

Customary law is an important part of the legal system in many countries around the world and therefore subject to analyzes (Corrin & Mulitalo, 2015; Costa, 1998; Craik, 2020; Crawford, 2012; Criddle, 2013; Cuskelly, 2011; Dahlitz, 1991). It comprises a set of rules and regulations that are based on long-standing traditions, customs, and practices within a particular society or community. Customary law has been used for centuries to resolve disputes between individuals and communities, as well as to regulate social behavior. In recent years, there has been increased interest in understanding how customary law works and its implications for modern societies.

In order to gain insight into this complex area of study, researchers have developed various conceptual analyzes of customary law (Lavalle, 2014; Laylin, 1976; Lewis, 1983, 2016; Liakopoulos, 2019; Lijnzaad, 2022; Lingaas, 2022; Lita et al., 2017; Liu, 2019). These analyzes involve examining the underlying principles behind customary laws and their application in different contexts. For example, some studies focus on how certain aspects of traditional culture influence the development of specific types of laws or regulations within a given society. Other research looks at how changes in technology or economic conditions can affect existing customary laws over time. This analysis then raises a range of interrelated concepts (Figure 4.5).

Figure 4.5. Concepts and sources of law.

Source: Zafar & associates.

One key concept that has emerged from these studies is that custom does not necessarily equate with legality (Kadens, 2012; Kammerhofer, 2012; Kane, 1972; Kassoti, 2017; Kelly & Windia, 2019; Kilian, 2019; Kim, 2009, 2020; Kingwill, 2016). Rather, it reflects values held by members of a particular community or society which may be subject to change over time depending on external factors such as technological advances or shifts in public opinion about certain issues.

This means that while custom may provide guidance when making decisions about legal matters, it should not be seen as an absolute source of authority when interpreting legislation or resolving disputes between parties involved in litigation proceedings.

Another important concept related to customary law is its relationship with other forms of regulation such as statutory law (laws passed by legislatures) and common law (judge-made precedents) (Damato, 1973; Damato et al., 1993; Dancer, 2017; Danilenko, 1988; Davis & Klare, 2010; De ruysscher, 2008; de Vries, 2021; De Wet, 2004). While all three systems are designed to ensure justice is served according to established standards, they often operate independently from one another due to differences in scope and interpretation methods employed by each type's respective practitioners/experts/authorities. As such, it is essential for those studying this field to understand both the similarities between them, as well as any potential conflicts which could arise if two sets overlap.

Overall, conceptual analysis provides valuable insights into how customary laws work, and why they remain relevant today despite changing times (Meyer, 2012; Milanovic, 2011; Mnisi & Claassens, 2009; Moore, 1986; Morrison, 2016; Morudu & Maimela, 2021). By better understanding these concepts, we can more effectively use them when dealing with legal matters involving our own communities.

Furthermore, it helps us appreciate just how much impact tradition still plays even amidst rapid modernization across many parts of the globe. In recent years, there has been increased interest in understanding how customary law works and its implications for modern societies. The history of the law of the sea is a case in point that can be subjected to this type of conceptual analysis.

The law of the sea is a body of international law that governs activities related to the oceans and seas. It has been in existence since ancient times, with various civilizations developing their own laws and regulations for maritime activity (Henry, 2017; Hernández, 2012; Holleman, 1969, 1972; Horii, 2019; Howell, 2018; Hu, 2017; Huizenga, 2018). Over time, these laws have evolved into an internationally accepted set of rules governing navigation, fishing rights, territorial waters, environmental protection and other matters related to ocean use.

In 1982, the United Nations Convention on the Law of the Sea (UNCLOS) was adopted by most countries around the world as a way to codify existing customary international law regarding maritime issues. This convention established a framework for allocating resources among nations and provided guidelines for resolving disputes over marine boundaries or exploitation of natural resources in areas beyond national jurisdiction. The UNCLOS also created exclusive economic zones (EEZs), which give coastal states control over certain activities within 200 nautical miles from their shores. Figure 4.6 summarizes the history of the law of the sea.

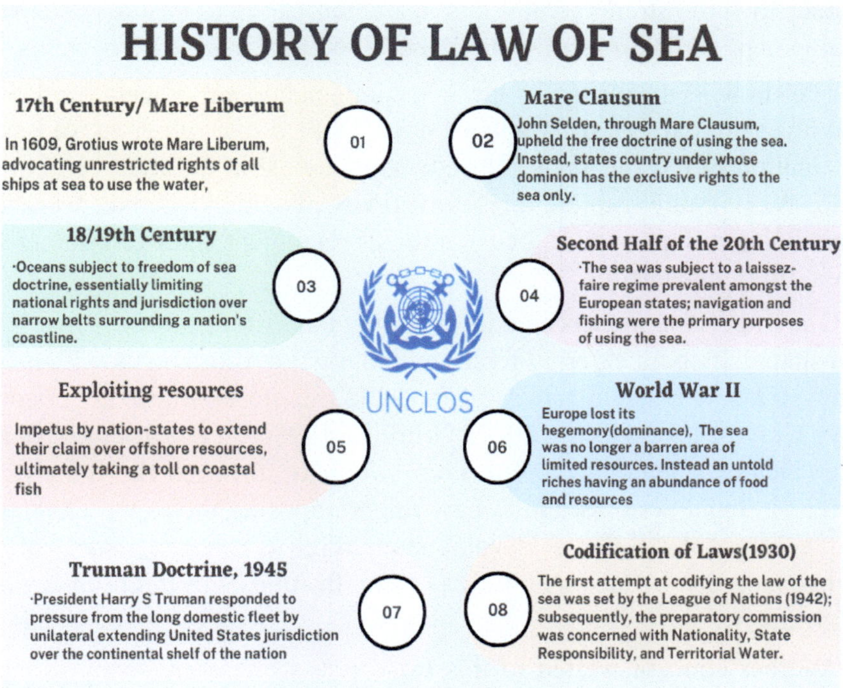

Figure 4.6. Historical incidents in the law of the sea.

Source: theyouthedge.com.

Since its adoption more than three decades ago, UNCLOS has had far-reaching implications for global politics and economics. For example, it has enabled countries to claim large swaths of ocean territory as part of their EEZs – something that would not have been possible without this agreement in place. This has led to increased competition between nations vying for access to valuable fisheries or mineral deposits located beneath the seabed outside traditional territorial waters limits. Additionally, UNCLOS provides legal protections against pollution caused by ships operating in international waters – something that could potentially help reduce damage done by oil spills or other forms of contamination across vast stretches of open waterway.

At present there are still some unresolved issues surrounding implementation and enforcement mechanisms under UNCLOS (Rubin, 1990; Russo, 1988; Sarbah, 1904; Seidman, 1983; Sheleff, 1994, 2013; Shingleton, 1983; Sibisi, 2020). However, overall it remains one of the most important pieces of legislation when it comes to regulating human activity at sea worldwide. As such, it is essential that governments continue working together towards strengthening this agreement so as to ensure sustainable development while protecting our planet's precious marine ecosystems.

The study of the history of law is a complex and multifaceted endeavor. It involves an analysis of how laws have evolved over time, as well as an examination of the various legal systems that exist in different parts of the world. We will now explore a brief overview of some key concepts related to this field, with particular focus on the development and evolution of law across different societies.

One important concept in understanding the history of law is that it has been shaped by both external forces and internal developments within each society (Gao, 2013; Gillespie & Tran, 2022; Golo et al., 2022; Gradoni, 2019; Graves, 2017; Gray, 2021; Griffiths, 1998; Hager, 2020). External forces include things like colonization or conquest, which can bring about changes in legal systems due to new rulers imposing their own laws upon conquered peoples. Internal developments refer to changes made within a given society itself, such as reforms or codifications enacted by its leaders or citizens.

Another concept related to this topic is that there are many different types of legal systems around the world today (Cataldi & Titu Maiorescu, 2015; Chang, 2022; Chanock, 1989; Cheng, 2012; Chirayath et al., 2005; Claassens & Mnisi, 2009). These range from common law systems based on English precedent, civil law systems derived from Roman Law principles, Islamic Sharia Law-based systems found mainly in Muslim countries, customary laws based on traditional practices found among indigenous populations, and more recently developed hybrid models combining elements from multiple sources into one system. Each type has its own unique characteristics and features which must be taken into account when studying any particular country's legal system. Finally, it should also be noted that while certain aspects may remain constant throughout history (such as basic human rights), other aspects are constantly changing due to social progress or technological advances (such as cybercrime legislation) (Diala & Bagni, 2019; Dubner, 1994; Dubois, 1992; Dupont, 2013; Duxbury, 2017; Edmundson, 2015; Elias, 1956; Enabulele & Bazuaye, 2019). Therefore, it is important for those interested in this field to stay up-to-date with current trends so they can better understand how these changes affect existing laws and regulations around the world today. Understanding the history of law requires knowledge not only about past events but also about present realities; examining both external influences and internal developments; recognizing various types of legal systems; and staying abreast with current trends affecting them all together provides us with valuable insight into our ever-evolving global landscape when it comes to matters concerning justice worldwide.

Overall, conceptual analysis provides valuable insights into how customary laws work, and why they remain relevant today despite changing times (Treasure et al., 2016; Tripp, 2004; Tsai, 2015; Tucker, 1972; Tunkin, 1993; Tupper, 1881). By better understanding these concepts, we can more effectively use them when crafting new policies aimed at protecting citizens' rights while also ensuring fairness across all sectors. One of the important dimensions of common law that we will explore in the next section is social behavior.

4.4. THE NOTION OF SOCIAL BEHAVIOR

Social behavior is a complex and fascinating topic that has been studied by sociologists for centuries (Vines, 2017; Watson, 1984; Webber, 2009; Weinberg, 2016; Williams & Klusener, 2013; Williams, 2022; Willms, 2009). It encompasses the way people interact with each other, how they form relationships, and how their actions are influenced by social norms. In this section, we will explore what social behavior is from a sociological perspective.

At its core, social behavior refers to the ways in which individuals interact with one another in society (Gadzo, 2018; Gagnon-Bergeron, 2018; Gal-Or, 2015; Galindo & Yip, 2017; Gao, 2013; Gillespie & Tran, 2022; Golo et al., 2022; Gradoni, 2019). This includes both verbal and nonverbal communication as well as physical contact such as handshakes or hugs. Social behavior also involves understanding the expectations of others within a given context and responding accordingly. For example, when attending a formal event like a wedding or funeral, it would be expected that you dress appropriately and act respectfully towards those around you. Antisocial behavior is culturally defined. Figure 4.7 highlights the constituent elements of culture.

Figure 4.7. Constituent elements of culture.

Source: Dreamstime.

Culture is an integral part of any society, and it has been studied extensively by anthropologists and sociologists (Buss, 2010; Buxbaum, 1968; Cannizzaro & Bonafe, 2005; Carrillo-Santarelli, 2017; Castillo & Bian, 2014; Cataldi & Titu Maiorescu, 2015). It is defined as the shared beliefs, values, customs, behaviors, and artifacts that characterize a particular group or society. As such, culture plays a major role in how people interact with each other and their environment.

In order to understand the different theories of culture across societies around the world, it is important to critically analyze them (Dancer, 2017; Danilenko, 1988; Davis & Klare, 2010; De ruysscher, 2008; de Vries, 2021; De Wet, 2004; Debelva & De Broe, 2022). One theory suggests that cultures are shaped by environmental factors such as geography or climate. This means that certain cultural traits may be more common in certain regions due to their physical characteristics. For example, some cultures may have developed agricultural practices suited for dry climates while others may have adapted fishing techniques suitable for coastal areas.

Another theory proposes that culture is determined by historical events or influences from other societies through contact or migration (Adebola, 2021; Akande, 2004; Albakjaji, 2022; Allott, 1957, 1984; Anderson, 2003; Angelini, 2012; Armstrong, 1989). This could explain why some countries share similar cultural elements despite being geographically distant from one another; they were likely influenced by similar external forces at some point in history. Additionally, this theory can also help us understand why certain aspects of a given culture remain unchanged over time even when its population changes drastically; these elements are deeply rooted within its history and identity as a nation or region.

Finally, there are those who believe that culture evolves organically over time based on internal dynamics rather than external influences like geography or history alone (Sun, 2010; Syaufi & Zahra, 2021; Tan, 1993, 2018; Tegnan, 2015; Thipe & Buthelezi, 2014; Thirlway, 2015). This means that individuals within a given society will shape its cultural norms through their own experiences and interactions with one another without necessarily relying on outside sources for guidance or inspiration. In this way we can see how cultures evolve naturally over generations without having to rely solely on predetermined factors like location or past events for explanation purposes only.

There are many different theories about how cultures develop across different societies in the world (Russo, 1988; Sarbah, 1904; Seidman, 1983; Sheleff, 1994, 2013; Shingleton, 1983; Sibisi, 2020; Siegel, 2015). By critically analyzing these theories, we can gain insight into why certain aspects of our own cultures remain unchanged while others change rapidly. Ultimately, understanding these various perspectives helps us better appreciate our own unique identities as well as those of other nations around the globe.

The concept of prosocial behavior is one that has been studied extensively in the field of psychology. It refers to voluntary actions taken by individuals or groups to benefit others, often without any expectation of reward or recognition (Williams & Klusener, 2013; Williams, 2022; Willms, 2009; Wilson, 1961; Wolff, 2016; Woodman, 1988; Woodman, 1969). While there are many factors that can influence an individual's propensity for prosocial behavior, culture plays a particularly important role in determining how it manifests itself within different communities across the world.

In some cultures, such as those found in East Asia and Latin America, collectivism is highly valued and encouraged (Dubois, 1992; Dupont, 2013; Duxbury, 2017; Edmundson, 2015; Elias, 1956; Enabulele & Bazuaye, 2019; Engel & Kurschilgen, 2013). This means that people tend to prioritize group goals over individual ones and place greater emphasis on cooperation rather than competition. As a result, prosocial behaviors like helping out neighbors or volunteering at community events are more common among these populations than they would be elsewhere.

Western societies tend to emphasize individualism more heavily than their Eastern counterparts do (Dubner, 1994; Dubois, 1992; Dupont, 2013; Duxbury, 2017; Edmundson, 2015; Elias, 1956; Enabulele & Bazuaye, 2019; Engel & Kurschilgen, 2013). This leads to a focus on self-interest and personal achievement which can make it difficult for people from these backgrounds to engage in altruistic activities without feeling guilty about not prioritizing their own needs first. Despite this challenge though, research suggests that even those who come from cultures with strong individualist values still demonstrate significant levels of prosociality when given the opportunity – suggesting that cultural norms may not be as influential as previously thought when it comes to influencing our behavior towards others positively.

While culture does play an important role in shaping our attitudes towards prosocial behavior, its effects should not be overestimated either (Lagji, 2019; Lavalle, 2014; Laylin, 1976; Lewis, 1983, 2016; Liakopoulos, 2019; Lijnzaad, 2022; Lingaas, 2022; Lita et al., 2017). Sociologists have identified several key components of social behavior including conformity, cooperation, competition, aggression, altruism, and reciprocity. Conformity refers to an individual's willingness to adhere to accepted standards of conduct while cooperation involves working together towards common goals without expecting anything in return from others involved in the process. Competition occurs when two or more parties strive for limited resources while aggression is defined as hostile behavior intended to cause harm or distress to another person or group of people. Altruism describes selfless acts done out of kindness whereas reciprocity implies mutual exchange between two parties where each provides something beneficial for the other party involved in order for them both to benefit equally from the interaction.

In addition to these components of social behavior there are also various theories which attempt to explain why humans behave certain ways within different contexts (Edmundson, 2015; Elias, 1956; Enabulele

& Bazuaye, 2019; Engel & Kurschilgen, 2013; Farran, 2019). Examples include evolutionary theory which suggests that our behaviors are shaped by natural selection. This contrasts with symbolic interactionism which focuses on how symbols shape our interactions. The third major framework is the functionalist theory which looks at how societies function based on shared values. Then there is the conflict theory which examines power dynamics between groups. Finally, there is the rational choice theory which states that individuals make decisions based on cost-benefit analysis.

Overall it can be seen that understanding social behavior requires looking at multiple factors including biological influences, cultural norms, personal experiences, economic conditions, political systems etc. (Sarbah, 1904; Seidman, 1983; Sheleff, 1994, 2013; Shingleton, 1983; Sibisi, 2020; Siegel, 2015; Sierra, 1995). By taking all these elements into account we can gain insight into why people behave certain ways within different contexts thus allowing us better understand human nature itself. There are many necessary societal or institutional processes which are impacted by social behavior. A case in point is behavior change communication (Figure 4.8).

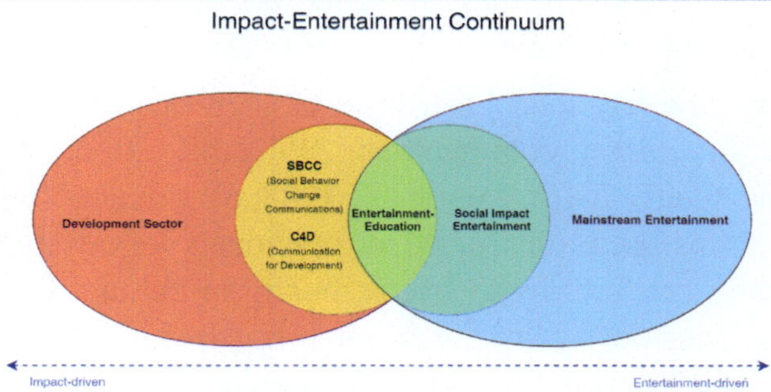

Figure 4.8. Social and behavior change communication.

Source: Wikipedia.

Altruism describes selfless acts done out of kindness whereas reciprocity implies mutual exchange between two parties where each provides something beneficial for the other party involved in order for them both to benefit from it equally over time.

In addition to these components of social behavior there are also various theories which attempt explain why certain behaviors occur such as evolutionary theory which suggests that humans evolved certain behaviors due to natural selection; symbolic interactionism which states that our interactions with others are based on shared meanings; functionalist theory which argues that all parts of society work together harmoniously; conflict theory which posits that power dynamics play an important role in shaping our interactions; and rational choice theory which claims that individuals make decisions based on cost-benefit analysis. Social behavior can be seen as an intricate web composed of many different elements ranging from biological factors through psychological ones right up until cultural influences. By understanding these components better we can gain insight into why people behave the way they do – allowing us not only understand ourselves but also those around us better too.

The relationship between customary law and social behavior has been a topic of interest for many scholars throughout socio-cultural history (Damato, 1973; Damato et al., 1993; Dancer, 2017; Danilenko, 1988; Davis & Klare, 2010; De ruysscher, 2008; de Vries, 2021; De Wet, 2004). Customary law is defined as the body of unwritten rules that are accepted by members of a particular society or culture, while social behavior refers to the way people interact with each other in their respective societies. It is important to understand how these two concepts have interacted over time in order to gain insight into the development of various cultures and societies.

Customary law has long been used as a means of regulating social behavior within certain communities (Williams, 2022; Willms, 2009; Wilson, 1961; Wolff, 2016; Woodman, 1988; Woodman, 1969, 2001). In some cases, it was used to ensure that individuals followed certain norms and expectations set forth by their community or culture. For example, in ancient Greece, customary laws were established which dictated what type of clothing could be worn by men and women, who could marry whom, and even what types of food were acceptable for consumption. These laws served as an effective way to maintain order within society at large.

In addition to providing structure for societal norms, customary law also had an impact on how people interacted with one another on a daily basis (Horii, 2019; Howell, 2018; Hu, 2017; Huizenga, 2018, 2022; Hulme, 2010; Hutchison, 2020; Hutchison & Sibanda, 2017). This was especially true when it came to matters such as marriage contracts or inheritance rights; both areas where custom played an important role in determining outcomes based on family ties or economic status. By understanding how these customs shaped relationships between individuals within different cultures we can gain valuable insight into the evolution of those societies over time.

Finally, it is worth noting that customary law often changed depending upon the context in which it was applied; this allowed for greater flexibility when dealing with issues related to social behavior across different cultures and eras throughout history (Diala, 2019; Diala & Bagni, 2019; Dubner, 1994; Dubois, 1992; Dupont, 2013; Duxbury, 2017; Edmundson, 2015; Elias, 1956). As such, studying the relationship between customary law and social behavior provides us with invaluable information about past civilizations which can help inform our understanding of today's world more effectively than ever before. The diametric opposite of social behavior is antisocial behavior.

4.5. ANTISOCIAL BEHAVIOR AND DEVIANCY

The relationship between antisocial behavior, motives, emotions, and competencies is a complex one that has been studied extensively in the field of psychology. Antisocial behavior can be defined as any action or attitude that violates social norms and disrupts the functioning of society. It can range from minor infractions such as shoplifting to more serious offenses such as assault or murder. Motives are the underlying reasons why people engage in certain behaviors; they may include financial gain, revenge, power, or even boredom. Emotions play an important role in how individuals respond to their environment and interact with others; these feelings can either facilitate or inhibit antisocial behavior depending on their intensity and duration. Finally, competencies refer to an individual's ability to understand and manage their own emotions as well as those of others around them.

Research suggests that there is a strong link between all four factors when it comes to understanding why someone might engage in antisocial behavior. For example, studies have found that people who lack emotional regulation skills are more likely to act out aggressively than those who possess better self-control abilities (Konrad et al., 2020). Similarly, research has shown that individuals with higher levels of impulsivity tend to display more aggressive tendencies than those with lower levels (Lambert & Kootstra-Rambach 2021). Additionally, some studies suggest that certain motives—such as revenge—may lead people down a path towards criminal activity (Gillespie et al., 2019).

It is also important to note that not all forms of antisocial behavior stem from negative intentions; sometimes it may simply be due to ignorance or misunderstanding about what constitutes acceptable social conduct (Hoffman & Miller 2018). Furthermore, while some individuals may have difficulty controlling their impulses due to mental health issues like depression or anxiety disorders (Brunet et al., 2017), this does not necessarily mean they will always behave inappropriately in every situation they encounter.

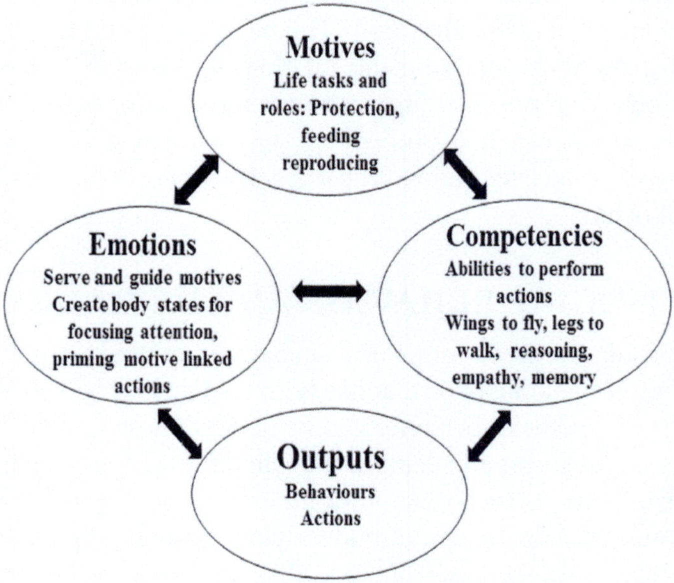

Figure 4.9. Interactions between motives, emotions, competencies, and output.

Source: Gilbert and Basran (2019).

In conclusion, it is clear from existing research evidence that there are multiple links between antisocial behavior and various psychological factors including motives, emotions, and competencies (Figure 4.9). While further investigation into this area would certainly be beneficial for developing effective interventions for reducing crime rates, it should also be noted that not everyone who displays problematic behaviors necessarily intends harm (Osman & Himonga, 2017; Ottley, 2016; Parisi, 2001; Pedersen, 2014; Pelizzon, 2015; Perreau-Saussine & Murphy, 2007). Therefore, it is essential for professionals working within this field to take into account both internal motivations behind actions along with external environmental influences when attempting to assess risk factors associated with criminal activities.

From a sociological standpoint it is important to understand why certain behaviors occur and how they relate to larger societal issues rather than simply labeling them "anti-social" and punishing those who engage in them without understanding the root cause behind their actions (Fenrich et al., 2011; Fleck, 2009, 2013; Fletcher, 2007; Frulli, 2015; Gadzo, 2018;

Gagnon-Bergeron, 2018). For example, if someone vandalizes property it may be because they feel frustrated with their economic situation and do not have access to other outlets for expressing this frustration constructively. In this case addressing the underlying issue would be more effective than simply punishing the individual for engaging in antisocial behavior without providing any sort of support system for them going forward.

It is also important to recognize that while some forms of antisocial behavior are criminalized (such as theft or assault) there are many instances where it is not necessarily illegal but still has an impact on society at large (such as littering) (Wolff, 2016; Woodman, 1988, 1969, 2001; Worugji et al., 2019; Wu, 2018; Young, 2019; Zamir, 2015). In these cases we need to look beyond just punishment and focus on educating individuals about why certain behaviors are not acceptable so that we can create a healthier environment for everyone involved instead of just relying on punitive measures alone which often fail at actually solving the problem long term.

Overall understanding what drives people towards engaging in antisocial behaviors from a sociological perspective is key when trying to address these issues effectively both individually and collectively within our societies today (Elias, 1956; Enabulele & Bazuaye, 2019; Engel & Kurschilgen, 2013; Farran, 2019; Fenrich et al., 2011; Fleck, 2009, 2013). By recognizing how different aspects such as poverty, inequality or lack of opportunity contribute towards creating environments where people feel compelled to act out negatively, we can start working together towards finding solutions that benefit us all instead of focusing solely on punishment which rarely leads anywhere positive in the end. Anti-social behavior is a term used to describe any type of behavior that goes against accepted social norms (Diala, 2017, 2019; Diala & Bagni, 2019; Dubner, 1994; Dubois, 1992; Dupont, 2013; Duxbury, 2017). It can range from minor infractions such as talking too loudly in public, to more serious offenses like vandalism or assault. From a sociological perspective, anti-social behavior is seen as an expression of underlying social issues and power dynamics within society. At its core, anti-social behavior is the result of individuals feeling powerless or marginalized by their environment. This could be due to poverty, discrimination, lack of education or other factors that lead people to feel excluded from mainstream society. When these feelings are not addressed properly they can manifest themselves in negative ways such as aggression towards others or destruction of property. This can lead to complex psychosocial dynamics such as evolved dispositions (Figure 4.10).

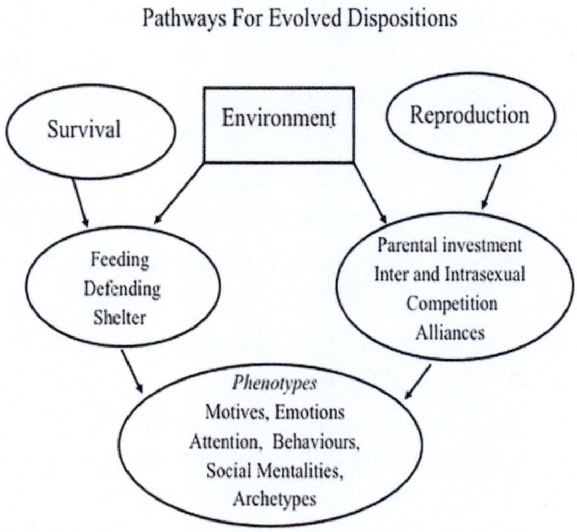

Figure 4.10. Relationship between evolved strategies, phenotypes, motives, and social mentalities.

Source: Gilbert and Basran (2019).

Humans are social creatures, and our behavior is shaped by a variety of factors (Craik, 2020; Crawford, 2012; Criddle, 2013; Cuskelly, 2011; Dahlitz, 1991; Damato, 1973; Damato et al., 1993; Dancer, 2017). From evolutionary strategies to phenotypes, motives, and social mentalities, the way we interact with each other can be complex and fascinating. It is useful to explore how these different elements influence our behavior in society. Evolutionary strategies play an important role in shaping human behavior. Our ancestors developed certain behaviors that helped them survive and reproduce more successfully than their peers; these behaviors have been passed down through generations until they became part of our genetic makeup today. For example, humans tend to cooperate with others because it increases their chances of survival; this trait has been passed down from generation to generation as a result of natural selection.

Phenotypes also shape human behavior in many ways. Phenotypes refer to physical characteristics such as height or eye color that are determined by genetics but can also be influenced by environmental factors like diet or exercise habits. These physical traits can affect how people interact with one another; for instance, taller individuals may be seen as more authoritative figures while shorter individuals may appear less intimidating or approachable.

Motives are another factor that influences human behavior in society. Motives refer to the reasons why people do things – whether it's out of self-interest or altruism – which ultimately determine how they act towards others around them. People who have strong motives for helping others will likely behave differently than those who only care about themselves; understanding someone's motives can help us better understand why they act the way they do in certain situations.

Finally, social mentalities shape our interactions with one another on a daily basis too. Social mentalities refer to the beliefs and attitudes we hold about ourselves and other people based on past experiences or cultural norms; these beliefs often dictate how we think about ourselves and treat those around us accordingly (e.g., being kind versus rude). Understanding someone's social mentality helps us better comprehend why they might behave a certain way when interacting with others – even if it does not always make sense at first.

There are many different elements that contribute to shaping human behavior: evolutionary strategies, phenotypes, motives, and social mentalities all play an important role in determining how we interact with each other on a daily basis. By understanding these various components better – both within ourselves as well as those around us –we can become more aware of our own actions so that we can strive towards creating healthier relationships between everyone involved.

Ultimately, understanding what drives people towards engaging in antisocial behavior from a sociological perspective allows us to create better solutions which address both the immediate problem at hand but also look beyond just punishment towards finding long term solutions which benefit everyone involved – both those committing acts deemed "anti-socials" and wider society alike.

The relationship between customary law and antisocial behavior has been a topic of debate for many years (Mwambene, 2012; Mwangi, 2022; Ndulo, 2011; Ngira, 2018, 2021; Nhlapo, 2017; Nnona, 2018; Norr, 1973). Customary law is defined as the set of rules, norms, and values that are accepted by a particular community or society. It is often based on tradition and culture, rather than written laws. On the other hand, antisocial behavior refers to any type of conduct that violates social norms or causes harm to others. In recent years, there has been an increasing focus on understanding how customary law affects people's attitudes towards antisocial behavior (Pelizzon, 2015; Perreau-Saussine & Murphy, 2007; Petersen, 2007,

2017; Pocar, 2016; Poespasari, 2020). Studies have shown that in some communities where traditional customs are still practiced, individuals may be more likely to engage in criminal activities such as theft or violence due to their belief in these customs. For example, some cultures may view stealing from outsiders as acceptable if it is done for survival purposes or out of necessity. Similarly, certain societies may condone physical aggression against those who violate their traditions or beliefs.

At the same time, research suggests that adherence to customary law can also lead to positive outcomes when it comes to preventing crime and promoting prosocial behaviors among members of a community (Liakopoulos, 2019; Lijnzaad, 2022; Lingaas, 2022; Lita et al., 2017; Liu, 2019; Loja, 2014; Lon & Widyawati, 2021; Magnusson, 2013, 2017). In particular, studies have found that individuals who follow traditional customs tend to be less likely to commit crimes compared with those who do not adhere strictly enough to them.

This could be because they feel more connected with their cultural identity and thus take greater responsibility for upholding its values and principles within their own lives and actions. Additionally, following customary laws can help create stronger bonds between members of a community which can further reduce instances of crime since people will feel more accountable for each other's actions if they share similar beliefs about what constitutes right versus wrong behavior within their group context.

While there appears evidence suggesting both positive and negative relationships between customary law and antisocial behavior, it is important not to make generalizations about this issue without taking into account individual contexts. Further research should therefore explore how different types of customary law interact with various forms of antisocial behavior across diverse settings. Only then will we gain better insight into how best to address this complex issue effectively.

CHAPTER 4 SUMMARY

This chapter has considered the ways in which customary law is established. We started by exploring the methodologies of law. The chapter then considered the role and influence of Classic Western theories of jurisprudence. This then led to a review of the analyzes of customary law. Finally, the chapter considered how social and antisocial behavior evolved in communities. This is a theme that is extended in the next chapter which considers how laws are an expression of societal norms.

CHAPTER 5

Customary Law as an Expression of Norms

Contents

In this chapter, we consider how customary laws can become a conduit for expressing societal norms. This chapter will conceptualize a series of important components of culture. These include norms, values, and folkways. Such concepts are important when trying to understand human and social anthropology. They may also be useful when identifying and confirming the legitimacy of judicial decisions. Often, norms are the starting point for these discussions.

5.1. WHAT ARE NORMS?

Norms are the accepted standards of behavior that exist within a particular society or culture (Koskenniemi, 1990; Kreso, 2010; Krieger, 2006; Kumar, 2020; Lagji, 2019; Lavalle, 2014; Laylin, 1976; Lewis, 1983, 2016). They can be both explicit and implicit, meaning they may be written down in laws or other documents, or they may simply be understood by members of the group without being explicitly stated. Norms provide guidance on how people should act in certain situations and help to maintain order and stability within a society.

Norms vary from one culture to another, as well as between different groups within a single culture (Hager, 2020; Haggenmacher, 2021; Hammond, 2019; Harmathy, 2016; Henry, 2017; Hernández, 2012; Holleman, 1969, 1972). For example, norms regarding appropriate dress codes will differ depending on whether you are attending a formal event or going out for drinks with friends. Similarly, norms around acceptable levels of politeness also vary depending on who you are interacting with; it would not be considered polite to address your boss in the same way you would address your best friend!

It is important to note that while norms are generally seen as positive forces that promote social cohesion and harmony, they can also have negative consequences if taken too far (Crawford, 2012; Criddle, 2013; Cuskelly, 2011; Dahlitz, 1991; Damato, 1973; Damato et al., 1993; Dancer, 2017; Danilenko, 1988). For instance, some cultures place an emphasis on conformity which can lead to individuals feeling unable to express themselves freely or take risks due to fear of judgment from others. Additionally, when norms become rigidly enforced this can lead to discrimination against those who do not conform – such as minority groups – which further reinforces existing power structures and inequalities within society.

Overall then it is clear that understanding cultural norms is essential for navigating any given situation successfully (Ngira, 2018, 2021; Nhlapo,

2017; Nnona, 2018; Norr, 1973; Nwapi, 2016; Nyane, 2019; O'Neill, 2002). However, we must also remember that these rules should never be used as an excuse for excluding those who do not fit into our own definition of 'normal' behavior. There exists a relationship between norms, values, and culture as exemplified by Figure 5.1. Indeed, it is this relationship that has often been referenced when seeking ways of changing norms towards those that are more acceptable to the functioning of society.

Figure 5.1. How to create healthy group norms for team communication.

Source: Doist Section.

Customary law and norms are two closely related concepts that often overlap (Meron et al., 1987; Merry, 1991; Meyer, 2012; Milanovic, 2011; Mnisi & Claassens, 2009; Moore, 1986). Customary law is a set of rules, practices, and customs that have been accepted by a particular community or society over time. These laws can be enforced through social pressure or other means of enforcement such as fines or imprisonment. Norms, on the other hand, refer to the expectations of behavior within a given group or society. They are not necessarily legally binding but they do influence how people behave in certain situations.

The relationship between customary law and norms is complex but it can be broken down into three main components: legal recognition, enforcement mechanisms, and cultural acceptance (Chirayath et al., 2005; Claassens & Mnisi, 2009; Cooter, 1991; Corrin & Mulitalo, 2015; Costa, 1998; Craik, 2020; Crawford, 2012). Legally speaking, customary law has more weight than norms because it is recognized by the state as having authority over its citizens' actions. However, this does not mean that all customary laws are followed without question – many communities may choose to ignore certain aspects of their own traditional laws if they feel those laws no longer serve them well.

Enforcement mechanisms for both customary law and norms vary from one culture to another (Holleman, 1972; Horii, 2019; Howell, 2018; Hu, 2017; Huizenga, 2018, 2022; Hulme, 2010; Hutchison, 2020; Hutchison & Sibanda, 2017). Some societies rely heavily on informal sanctions such as gossiping while others use formal punishments like fines or jail time for violations of either type of rule-set. In addition to these methods of enforcement there is also an element of cultural acceptance at play when it comes to following either type of rule-set – if members within a given community believe strongly enough in the importance of adhering to their traditional values then they will likely follow them even if there is not any legal backing behind them.

Although there are differences between customary law and norms they share many similarities in terms of their purpose (to regulate behavior) and how they are enforced (through various forms) (Mastura, 1994; Maunatlala & Maimela, 2020; Maxim & Titu Maiorescu, 2015; McAuslan, 2015; McCarthy, 1971; McLachlan, 1988). Ultimately though it comes down to each individual community deciding which rules best suit their needs – whether those rules come from established custom or simply shared expectations among its members. Customary law and norms are two closely related concepts that often overlap.

Norms are an integral part of any culture, and they can vary greatly from one society to another (Petersen, 2017; Pocar, 2016; Poespasari, 2020; Polanski, 2017; Pratiwi et al., 2020; Qerimi, 2020; Quane, 2013; Rautenbach, 2020). As such, it is important to understand the various typologies of norms that exist across cultures in order to better comprehend how different societies interact with each other. It is therefore pertinent to use theory to critique various typologies of norms that are referenced across cultures in the world. Figure 5.2 highlights some types of social norms.

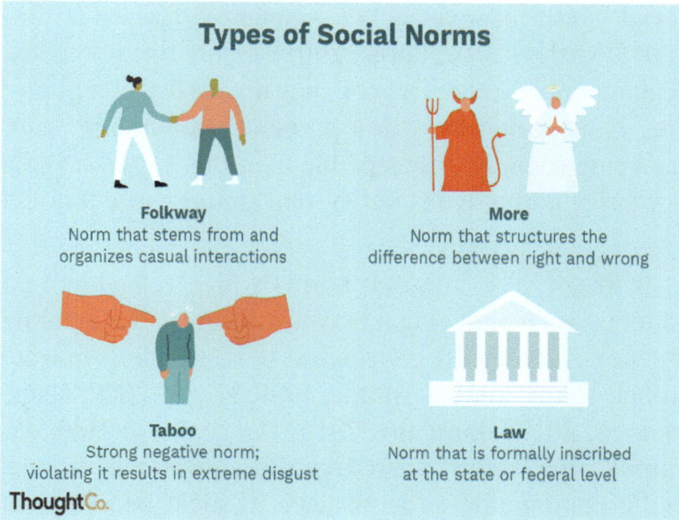

Figure 5.2. Typologies of social norms.

Source: ThoughtCo.

One type of norm is known as a prescriptive norm (Johnson, 1986; Joireman, 2008; Jonas & Gunda, 2015; Kadens, 2012; Kammerhofer, 2012; Kane, 1972; Kassoti, 2017; Kelly & Windia, 2019). This type of norm dictates what people should do or not do within a given context. For example, many cultures have rules about proper etiquette when dining at someone's home or attending certain events. Prescriptive norms also dictate how people should dress for certain occasions and even how they should behave in public spaces like parks or beaches.

Another type of norm is known as a descriptive norm (Skomerska-Muchowska, 2017; Snyder, 1984; Sprankling, 2014; Sun, 2010; Syaufi & Zahra, 2021; Tan, 1993, 2018). This type of norm describes what people actually do within a given context rather than prescribing what they ought to do according to some external standard or rule set by society at large. Descriptive norms often reflect cultural values and beliefs; for instance, if most members of a particular culture tend to greet each other with hugs upon meeting then this would be considered a descriptive norm within that culture's social environment.

A third type of norm is known as an injunctive norm which refers to the perceived approval or disapproval associated with certain behaviors within a given context (i.e., whether something is seen as socially acceptable)

(Orebech et al., 2005; Osman, 2019; Osman & Baase, 2022; Osman & Himonga, 2017; Ottley, 2016; Parisi, 2001). Injunctive norms can be either positive (encouraging behavior) or negative (discouraging behavior). For example, if most members in a particular community view smoking cigarettes as being socially unacceptable then this would be considered an injunctive negative normative belief system among those individuals living there.

Finally, there are also informal norms which refer more generally to accepted patterns and practices that may not necessarily be codified into law but still influence everyday life nonetheless (e.g., standing up when someone enters the room) (Gray, 2021; Griffiths, 1998; Hager, 2020; Haggenmacher, 2021; Hammond, 2019; Harmathy, 2016; Henry, 2017; Hernández, 2012). Informal norms often reflect shared values and beliefs among members within specific communities; for instance, if most people living in rural areas tend towards politeness when interacting with strangers then this could be seen as an informal normative belief system among those individuals living there.

Overall, it is clear that understanding these various types of norms can help us gain insight into different cultures around the world and their respective social environments – both formalized ones based on laws/rules/regulations and informal ones based on shared values/beliefs amongst its citizens alike (Syaufi & Zahra, 2021; Tan, 1993, 2018; Tegnan, 2015; Thipe & Buthelezi, 2014; Thirlway, 2015; Thirlway, 2017). By critically analyzing these typologies through theoretical lenses such as symbolic interactionism, functionalism, etc., we can gain further insight into why certain behaviors might be encouraged while others discouraged depending on where you live – ultimately helping us become more culturally aware global citizens. Underpinning this awareness is the notion of cultural values.

5.2. WHAT ARE VALUES?

Values are the beliefs and principles that guide our behavior (Lijnzaad, 2022; Lingaas, 2022; Lita et al., 2017; Liu, 2019; Loja, 2014; Lon & Widyawati, 2021; Magnusson, 2013, 2017; Manaka & Corrin, 2021). They shape how we think, act, and interact with others. Values can be personal or shared by a group of people. They can also be cultural or religious in nature. At their core, values provide us with direction and purpose in life. They help us make decisions about what is important to us and how we want to live our lives. Values can also influence our relationships with other people as well as our overall outlook on life.

When it comes to making decisions, values play an important role in helping us determine what is right for ourselves and those around us (Tegnan, 2015; Thipe & Buthelezi, 2014; Thirlway, 1972, 2015, 2017; Tobin, 2014; Tomuschat, 2021). For example, if you value honesty then you may choose not to lie even when it would benefit you personally because lying goes against your moral code of conduct. Similarly, if you value family then you may prioritize spending time with them over pursuing career opportunities that could take away from quality time spent together as a family unit. Figure 5.3 demonstrates in vivid terms how values can influence human behavior.

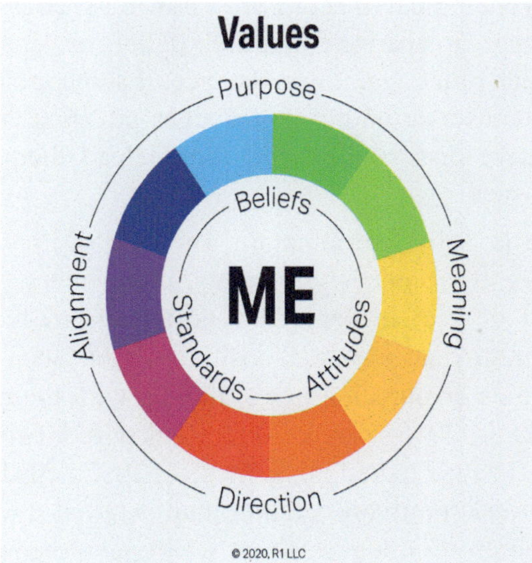

Figure 5.3. The role of value types on influencing human behavior.

Source: R1 LCC (2020).

Values and behavior are two concepts that have been studied extensively by psychologists, sociologists, and other social scientists (Lingaas, 2022; Lita et al., 2017; Liu, 2019; Loja, 2014; Lon & Widyawati, 2021; Magnusson, 2013, 2017; Manaka & Corrin, 2021). Different theories attempt to explain the relationship between values and behavior in different ways. It is therefore pertinent to compare and contrast how various theories approach this topic. One of the most prominent theories is Social Learning Theory (SLT) (Lon & Widyawati, 2021; Magnusson, 2013, 2017; Manaka & Corrin, 2021; Manullang, 2021; Marasinghe, 1978). This theory suggests that people learn behaviors through observation of others' actions as well as reinforcement or punishment for their own actions. SLT also states that values influence behavior because they provide a framework for understanding what is right or wrong in any given situation. For example, if someone has a strong value system based on honesty, then they may be more likely to act honestly even when faced with temptation to do otherwise.

Another popular theory is Cognitive Dissonance Theory (CDT) (Williams & Klusener, 2013; Williams, 2022; Willms, 2009; Wilson, 1961; Wolff, 2016; Woodman, 1988; Woodman, 1969). CDT proposes that individuals strive for consistency between their beliefs and behaviors; thus, if an individual holds certain values but behaves contrary to those values it can cause psychological discomfort known as cognitive dissonance which motivates them to change either their beliefs or behaviors so they are consistent with each other again. For instance, if someone believes strongly in environmental conservation but drives a gas-guzzling car then they may experience cognitive dissonance which could lead them to purchase an electric vehicle instead.

Finally, there is Self-Determination Theory (SDT) which posits that humans have three basic needs: autonomy, competence, and relatedness; these needs must be met in order for individuals to feel satisfied with themselves and motivated towards positive action such as engaging in meaningful activities or pursuing goals aligned with their personal values (Young, 2019; Zamir, 2015; Zarea, 2022; Zenker & Höhne, 2018; Zerner, 1994; Zilberman, 1996; Zitzke, 2022; Zwalve, 2012). SDT emphasizes the importance of intrinsic motivation rather than external rewards like money or recognition; therefore it suggests that when people engage in activities driven by internal motivations such as fulfilling core values then they are more likely to persist despite obstacles along the way since these activities bring greater satisfaction than those done solely out of obligation or reward seeking purposes.

It is notable that different theories offer varying explanations about how our values shape our behavior but all agree on one thing: our beliefs play an important role in determining how we act upon them (Hutchison & Sibanda, 2017; Iyi, 2016; Jentoft & Bavinck, 2019; John-Hopkins, 2010; Johnson, 1986; Joireman, 2008; Jonas & Gunda, 2015). It is important for us all to take time to periodically reflect on our own personal value systems so we can ensure our decisions align with what matters most deeply within ourselves – only then can we truly live authentically according to who we really are.

Values are often shaped by experiences throughout life such as growing up in a certain culture or religion or being exposed to different types of media like books or movies which contain messages about morality and ethics that resonate deeply within us over time (Siegel, 2015; Sierra, 1995; Singer, 1972; Skomerska-Muchowska, 2017; Snyder, 1984; Sprankling, 2014; Sun, 2010). It is important to recognize the power of these influences so that we can consciously decide which values will best serve ourselves and those around us going forward into adulthood and beyond. Ultimately, understanding your own values is key for living an authentic life full of meaning and purpose – one where your actions align with who you truly are at heart. Humans ought to reflect on what matters most to them so that life brings more clarity into why it is worth existing.

We can see that there is indeed an intimate relationship between values and customary law – one which has been established over time as societies have evolved into more complex entities requiring greater regulation than ever before (Chang, 2022; Chanock, 1989; Cheng, 2012; Chirayath et al., 2005; Claassens & Mnisi, 2009; Cooter, 1991; Corrin & Mulitalo, 2015). By understanding this connection we can better appreciate why such laws exist today – not only do they reflect our shared beliefs but they also serve to protect us from harm while allowing us to express ourselves freely within our respective communities. Customary law is a set of rules and regulations that are based on the customs, traditions, and practices of a particular community or society. It is an unwritten form of law that has been passed down through generations and is still in use today. Customary law can be seen as a reflection of the values held by members of the community or society in which it exists.

Values are beliefs about what is important to us as individuals or groups (Marasinghe, 1978; Masengu, 2016; Mastura, 1994; Maunatlala & Maimela, 2020; Maxim & Titu, 2015). They shape our attitudes towards life, guide our behavior, and influence how we interact with others. Values also provide guidance for decision-making processes within communities and societies; they help determine what actions should be taken when faced with certain situations or dilemmas. The relationship between values and customary law can be seen in many ways (Vines, 2017; Watson, 1984; Webber, 2009; Weinberg, 2016; Williams & Klusener, 2013; Williams, 2022; Willms, 2009). For example, if a particular value system holds that honesty is important then this will likely be reflected in the laws governing theft or fraud within that community or society; similarly if respect for elders is valued then there may be laws protecting them from abuse or neglect. In addition to reflecting values directly through its content, customary law also serves to reinforce those same values by providing sanctions against those who violate them – thus helping ensure their continued observance over time.

It can be said that there exists an intimate relationship between values and customary law: one informs the other while at the same time reinforcing its own importance within any given culture or society (Snyder, 1984; Sprankling, 2014; Sun, 2010; Syaufi & Zahra, 2021; Tan, 1993, 2018; Tegnan, 2015). This connection helps ensure continuity across generations while allowing for flexibility when needed so as to accommodate changing circumstances over time without sacrificing core principles upon which all members agree upon living together harmoniously under one roof – regardless of race, religion etc. Ultimately this symbiotic relationship ensures both stability and progressiveness simultaneously – something essential for any successful civilization.

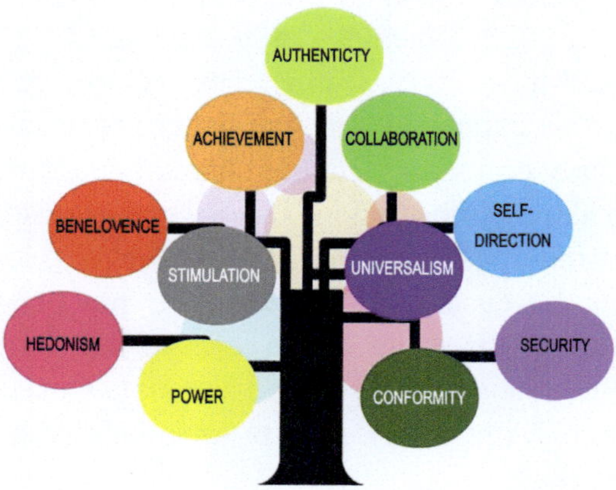

Figure 5.4. Organizational values as human values.

Source: Pulse via LinkedIn.

When we consider organizations that are subject to a range of rules and regulations, then it becomes clear that these organizational values are ultimately human values. That is why values can never be completely divorced from humanity. This is an approach that is used when creating institutions that support customary law (Worugji et al., 2019; Wu, 2018; Young, 2019; Zamir, 2015; Zarea, 2022; Zenker & Höhne, 2018; Zerner, 1994). Figure 5.4 makes this point graphically with reference to organizations, yet the same principles can be applied at the societal level.

Organizational values are often seen as a set of principles that guide the behavior and actions of an organization. However, these values can also be viewed as human values, which have been around for centuries in the form of customary law (Tripp, 2004; Tsai, 2015; Tucker, 1972; Tunkin, 1993; Tupper, 1881; Ubink, 2016; Ubink & Weeks, 2017). Customary law is based on traditions and customs that have been passed down through generations, providing guidance to individuals and communities on how to live their lives. Customary law has long been used to regulate social interactions between people within a community or society. It provides guidelines for acceptable behavior and helps maintain order by setting out rules for resolving disputes without resorting to violence or other forms of coercion. This type of law is still relevant today, especially when it comes to organizational values.

Organizations need clear sets of values in order to ensure that everyone involved understands what is expected from them and how they should behave towards each other (Merry, 1991; Meyer, 2012; Milanovic, 2011; Mnisi & Claassens, 2009; Moore, 1986; Morrison, 2016; Morudu & Maimela, 2021). These values provide direction for employees so they know what kind of conduct is appropriate in different situations, such as dealing with customers or colleagues. They also help create a sense of unity among staff members by establishing common goals and objectives that everyone can work towards together.

The same principles apply when it comes to organizational values – they should reflect the core beliefs held by those who make up the organization's culture, while at the same time being consistent with traditional laws like customary law which may already exist within certain societies or cultures where organizations operate globally (Barrie, 2016; Baxi, 2020; Beavers, 2019; Beer, 2022; Bennett, 2008, 2009, 2015; Benson & Siddiqui, 2014). By doing this, organizations can ensure their policies are not only effective but also respectful towards local customs and traditions wherever possible.

Organizational values should be seen not just as business practices but rather as human ones too – reflecting both modern-day expectations while remaining true to traditional laws like customary law which have stood the test of time over many generations (Menski, 1988; Meron, 1987, 1991; Meron et al., 1987; Merry, 1991; Meyer, 2012; Milanovic, 2011; Mnisi & Claassens, 2009). By taking this approach, organizations will be able to foster strong relationships with all stakeholders, including customers, employees, suppliers, partners etc., creating an environment where everyone feels respected regardless of background or culture. A related and important concept is that of folkways.

5.3. WHAT ARE FOLKWAYS?

Folkways, also known as customary law, are a set of unwritten rules that govern the behavior of members within a particular society (Vanboven, 1991; Vergouwen, 2013; Vines, 2017; Watson, 1984; Webber, 2009; Weinberg, 2016; Williams & Klusener, 2013). These laws are based on tradition and have been passed down through generations.

They can be seen in many aspects of everyday life, from how people dress to how they interact with one another. Customary law is an important part of any culture because it helps maintain order and stability within the community. It provides guidelines for acceptable behavior and sets expectations for individuals to follow. This type of law is often enforced by social pressure rather than formal legal action; however, if someone violates these norms there may be consequences such as ostracism or ridicule from their peers.

Customary law can vary greatly between different cultures and societies; what might be considered acceptable in one place may not be so in another (Sheleff, 1994, 2013; Shingleton, 1983; Sibisi, 2020; Siegel, 2015; Sierra, 1995; Singer, 1972; Skomerska-Muchowska, 2017). For example, some cultures may frown upon public displays of affection while others embrace them openly. Similarly, certain religious practices or dietary restrictions could also differ depending on where you live.

It is important to remember that folkways should always be respected regardless of whether you agree with them or not – after all, they are part of a larger cultural identity which should never be taken lightly. By understanding and respecting these customs we can ensure that our communities remain harmonious places to live in harmony with each other despite our differences.

Folkways are an important part of any culture, providing a set of norms and expectations that guide behavior (Ndulo, 2011; Ngira, 2018, 2021; Nhlapo, 2017; Nnona, 2018; Norr, 1973; Nwapi, 2016; Nyane, 2019). As such, it is essential to understand the various theories that explain their function in order to gain insight into how they shape our lives.

To better understand folkways, it is pertinent to critically evaluate, compare, and contrast three prominent theories: functionalism, symbolic interactionism, and conflict theory as well as their influences on the emergence and operationalization of folkways. As a starting point, Figure 5.5 defines folkways. This definitions then opens the possibility of laying a theoretical basis for folkways.

DEFINITIONS OF FOLKWAYS

- According to Reuter and Hart (1933), "The folkways are simple habits of action common to the members of the group; they are the ways of the folks that are somewhat standardised and have some degree of traditional sanction for their persistence".
- Maclver and Page (1949) defined it as: "The folkways are the recognized or accepted ways of behaving in the society.'

Figure 5.5. Definition of folkways.

Source: Dr. Bandana Baishya via YouTube.

Functionalism is a sociological perspective which views society as composed of interdependent parts working together for the benefit of all members (Diala, 2017, 2019; Diala & Bagni, 2019; Dubner, 1994; Dubois, 1992; Dupont, 2013; Duxbury, 2017). According to this view, folkways serve an important role in maintaining social stability by providing shared values and beliefs that help define group identity and promote cooperation among members. This theory suggests that folkways are beneficial because they provide structure and guidance for individuals within a given society or culture.

Symbolic interactionism takes a different approach to understanding folkways by focusing on how individuals interact with one another through symbols like language or gestures (Fletcher, 2007; Frulli, 2015; Gadzo, 2018; Gagnon-Bergeron, 2018; Gal-Or, 2015; Galindo & Yip, 2017; Gao, 2013; Gillespie & Tran, 2022). This theory argues that people use these symbols to create meaning out of their experiences; thus folkways can be seen as tools used by individuals to communicate with each other about what is expected from them in terms of behavior or attitude towards certain topics or situations.

Contrastingly, conflict theory proposes that power dynamics between groups play an important role in shaping social structures like folkways (De Wet, 2004; Debelva & De Broe, 2022; Dekoster, 2019; Demian, 2014; Diala, 2017, 2019). According to this view, those who have more power tend to impose their own values onto others through laws or customs which then become accepted as "normal" within the larger society over time; thus creating inequality between those who have access to resources versus those who do not have access due to lack of privilege or status within the system itself.

While all three theories offer valuable insights into why folkways exist and how they function within societies around the world today – each has its own unique strengths when it comes explaining why certain behaviors become accepted norms over time while others remain marginalized outside mainstream acceptance (Quane, 2013; Rautenbach, 2020; Rose, 1989; Rubin, 1990; Russo, 1988; Sarbah, 1904; Seidman, 1983; Sheleff, 1994). By critically evaluating these perspectives side-by-side we can gain greater insight into how cultural practices evolve over time – ultimately helping us better understand our own place within them too.

Because some literature uses the terms synonymously, it is necessary to highlight the subtle distinctions between customary law and folkways (Snyder, 1984; Sprankling, 2014; Sun, 2010; Syaufi & Zahra, 2021; Tan, 1993, 2018; Tegnan, 2015). When discussing the differences between folkways and customary law, it is important to understand what each term means. Folkways are informal norms of behavior that exist within a society or culture. They are not enforced by any legal authority but rather accepted as part of the social fabric of a community. Customary law, on the other hand, is an established set of rules and regulations that have been recognized by a court system or government body as legally binding.

The primary difference between folkways and customary law lies in their source of origin (Debelva & De Broe, 2022; Dekoster, 2019; Demian, 2014; Diala, 2017, 2019; Diala & Bagni, 2019). Folkways originate from tradition and custom while customary laws come from formal legislation passed by governments or courts. This distinction has implications for how these two types of norms are enforced in society; folkways rely on peer pressure and social acceptance while customary laws can be enforced through fines or imprisonment if violated.

Another key difference between folkways and customary law is their scope; whereas customs tend to be localized to specific communities, countries, or regions, laws apply universally across all jurisdictions where they have been enacted into legislation (Gal-Or, 2015; Galindo & Yip, 2017; Gao, 2013; Gillespie & Tran, 2022; Golo et al., 2022; Gradoni, 2019). Additionally, customs may change over time depending on cultural shifts while laws remain relatively static until amended through legislative action. There are several distinct differences between folkways and customary law which should be taken into consideration when discussing either concept separately or together: their source of origin (tradition vs legislation), enforcement mechanisms (peer pressure vs fines/imprisonment), scope (localized vs universal), and longevity (changeable vs static). Understanding these distinctions can help us better appreciate both concepts' roles in shaping our societies today.

We should then consider the impact of folkways (Pratiwi et al., 2020; Qerimi, 2020; Quane, 2013; Rautenbach, 2020; Rose, 1989; Rubin, 1990; Russo, 1988; Sarbah, 1904). One of those effects is the creation or mitigation of inequality and inequity. Customary law, also known as folkways, is a set of unwritten rules and regulations that are passed down from generation to generation. These laws are often based on tradition and culture rather than written statutes or legal codes. While these laws can be beneficial in some cases, they can also be harmful or discriminatory in others.

In many societies, customary law dictates the roles of men and women within the family structure (Fleck, 2013; Fletcher, 2007; Frulli, 2015; Gadzo, 2018; Gagnon-Bergeron, 2018; Gal-Or, 2015; Galindo & Yip, 2017; Gao, 2013). This type of gender-based discrimination has been used to limit the rights of women for centuries. Women may not have access to education or employment opportunities due to traditional beliefs about their role in society. In addition, they may face restrictions on their ability to own property or make decisions regarding marriage and childbearing without male approval.

Customary law can also lead to unequal treatment under the law when it comes to issues such as inheritance rights or criminal justice proceedings (Albakjaji, 2022; Allott, 1957, 1984; Anderson, 2003; Angelini, 2012; Armstrong, 1989; Arowolo, 2019; Asieduakrofi, 1989). For example, certain ethnic groups may be subject to harsher punishments than others due to cultural biases held by those who enforce the laws. Similarly, individuals belonging to minority religions may find themselves at a disadvantage when it comes time for them to seek justice through court systems that favor majority religious practices over minority ones.

The effects of customary law extend beyond individual cases; entire communities can suffer if discriminatory practices become entrenched within a society's legal system over time (Murphy, 2014; Mwalimu, 1988; Mwambene, 2012; Mwangi, 2022; Ndulo, 2011; Ngira, 2018, 2021; Nhlapo, 2017). This is why it is important for governments around the world to take steps towards protecting vulnerable populations from unfair treatment based on outdated customs and traditions that no longer reflect modern values of equality and justice for all citizens regardless of gender identity, ethnicity or religion.

Ultimately, while customary law has its place in many cultures around the world today, we must remain vigilant against any form of discrimination that could arise from its application (Bourgon, 2020; Budlender et al., 2011; Buss, 2010; Buxbaum, 1968; Cannizzaro & Bonafe, 2005; Carrillo-Santarelli, 2017; Castillo & Bian, 2014). By recognizing potential harms associated with folkways, we can work together towards creating more equitable societies where everyone enjoys equal protection under the rule of law.

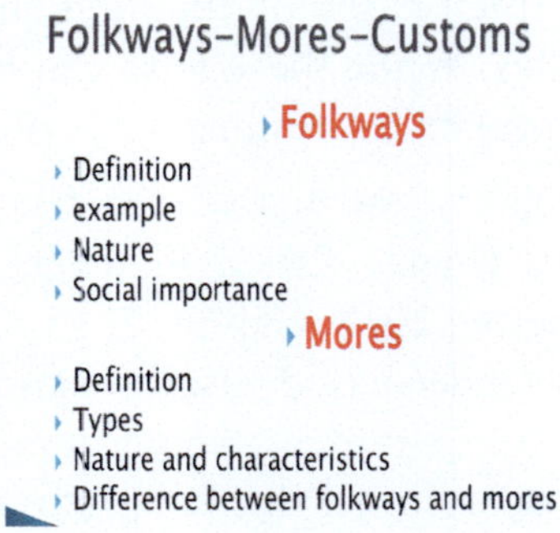

Figure 5.6. Comparing norms with mores.

Source: Study Lib

Despite their importance, folkways sometimes face misconceptions with mores and customs (Figure 5.6). Folkways, mores, and customs are all terms used to describe the unwritten rules of behavior that exist in a given society (Demian, 2014; Diala, 2017, 2019; Diala & Bagni, 2019; Dubner, 1994; Dubois, 1992; Dupont, 2013). While these three concepts may seem similar at first glance, they each have distinct characteristics that set them apart from one another. Understanding the differences between folkways, mores, and customs is essential for appreciating the unique roles they play in global cultures.

Folkways refer to everyday behaviors or habits that are considered normal within a particular culture (Nhlapo, 2017; Nnona, 2018; Norr, 1973; Nwapi, 2016; Nyane, 2019; O'Neill, 2002; Oba, 2002, 2008, 2011). These behaviors can range from simple acts such as greeting someone with a handshake or saying "please" and "thank you" when asking for something to more complex practices like religious rituals or traditional dress codes.

Folkways do not carry any moral implications; rather, they simply reflect what is accepted as normal within a certain cultural context.

Mores are norms of behavior that carry moral significance within a given culture (Carrillo-Santarelli, 2017; Castillo & Bian, 2014; Cataldi & Titu Maiorescu, 2015; Chang, 2022; Chanock, 1989; Cheng, 2012). They often involve issues related to right and wrong conduct such as honesty, respect for authority figures, sexual morality, etc., and violations of these norms can result in serious consequences ranging from social disapproval to legal punishment depending on the severity of the offense. Mores tend to be much stricter than folkways since they involve matters of morality rather than just etiquette or tradition.

Finally, customs refer specifically to traditions associated with special occasions such as holidays or weddings which vary greatly across different cultures around the world (Oba, 2002, 2008, 2011; Obatusin, 2018; Olaf & Markus, 2018; Omidire, 1990; Orebech et al., 2005; Osman, 2019). Customs typically involve specific activities like gift-giving during Christmas time or wearing white dresses at weddings but also encompass broader aspects such as language use (e.g., speaking Spanish during Cinco de Mayo celebrations) and food preparation (e.g making tamales for Day of Dead festivities). Unlike folkways and mores which tend to be relatively consistent over time due their importance in maintaining social order within societies, customs can change significantly over generations due their association with specific events.

Overall, folkways, mores, and customs all serve important functions in global cultures by providing guidelines on how people should behave both inside and outside their own communities (Damato, 1973; Damato et al., 1993; Dancer, 2017; Danilenko, 1988; Davis & Klare, 2010; De ruysscher, 2008). Although there may be some overlap between these three concepts, it is important to recognize their distinct roles so we can better appreciate how different societies operate around the world. Perhaps, these intricacies are best explored by considering the role of human and social anthropology.

5.4. HUMAN AND SOCIAL ANTHROPOLOGY

Human and social anthropology is an ongoing exploration of the true meaning and implications of customary law (Tan, 2018; Tegnan, 2015; Thipe & Buthelezi, 2014; Thirlway, 1972, 2015, 2017; Tobin, 2014). Fundamentally, customary law is a type of legal system that is based on the customs and traditions of a particular society. Customary law has been around for centuries, and it still plays an important role in many cultures today. But what exactly is customary law, and how does it relate to human anthropology and social anthropology?

Human anthropology is the study of humans as biological organisms. This includes examining physical characteristics such as height, weight, skin color, hair texture, etc., as well as behavior patterns like language use or mating habits. Social anthropology focuses more on cultural aspects such as beliefs about religion or family structure. Both fields are closely related because they both involve studying people's behaviors and beliefs in order to understand them better (Ottley, 2016; Parisi, 2001; Pedersen, 2014; Pelizzon, 2015; Perreau-Saussine & Murphy, 2007; Petersen, 2007, 2017).

Customary law can be seen as a bridge between these two disciplines since it involves understanding both the biological aspects (such as physical traits) and cultural aspects (such as religious practices) of a given society (Gradoni, 2019; Graves, 2017; Gray, 2021; Griffiths, 1998; Hager, 2020; Haggenmacher, 2021; Hammond, 2019; Harmathy, 2016). For example, some societies may have laws that dictate who can marry whom based on their respective families' backgrounds or wealth levels; this would be considered part of their customary law system. Similarly, certain tribes may have specific rules regarding hunting rights or land ownership; again this would fall under their customary laws.

In short, customary law provides us with insight into how different societies function by looking at both the biological makeup of its members along with its cultural norms and values – something which neither human nor social anthropology could do alone (Russo, 1988; Sarbah, 1904; Seidman, 1983; Sheleff, 1994, 2013; Shingleton, 1983; Sibisi, 2020; Siegel, 2015). By combining these two disciplines we gain valuable insights into why certain groups behave in certain ways – information which can help us better understand our own culture. The tenets of anthropology are useful in harnessing this understanding.

Anthropology is a field of study that seeks to understand the human experience through an interdisciplinary approach (Kane, 1972; Kassoti, 2017; Kelly & Windia, 2019; Kilian, 2019; Kim, 2009, 2020; Kingwill, 2016). This includes examining social, cultural, and biological aspects of humanity in order to gain insight into how people interact with each other and their environment. One area of anthropology that has been studied extensively is customary law – the unwritten laws and regulations that govern behavior within a particular society or culture. It is pertinent to discuss the tenets and methods used by anthropologists when studying customary law.

The first tenet of anthropology when studying customary law is understanding context (Maunatlala & Maimela, 2020; Maxim & Titu Maiorescu, 2015; McAuslan, 2015; McCarthy, 1971; McLachlan, 1988; Menski, 1988). Anthropologists must take into account the historical, political, economic, religious, and environmental factors that shape a given society's legal system in order to accurately interpret its customs. Additionally, they must consider how these factors have changed over time as well as any external influences on the system such as colonialism or globalization.

The second tenet is recognizing diversity among societies' legal systems (Benson & Siddiqui, 2014; Bianchi, 2009; Bond, 2009, 2010; Botha & Bekink, 2018; Bourgon, 2020; Budlender et al., 2011; Buss, 2010). Customary laws vary greatly from one culture to another due to differences in values and beliefs about justice and morality; therefore it is important for anthropologists to be aware of these variations when conducting research on them. Furthermore, they should also be mindful of power dynamics between different groups within a society which can affect access to resources or influence decision-making processes related to legal matters.

When it comes to methods used by anthropologists for researching customary law there are several approaches available depending on what type of information needs gathering (Kilian, 2019; Kim, 2009, 2020; Kingwill, 2016; Koskenniemi, 1990; Kreso, 2010; Krieger, 2006; Kumar, 2020; Lagji, 2019). For example, participant observation (involving living with members of a community), interviews (conducting conversations with individuals), and archival research (examining written records such as court documents), surveys (collecting data from large numbers of people) have all invariably been utilized over time. All these techniques allow researchers not only collect data but also gain insights into how people perceive their own legal systems which can provide valuable information about why certain rules exist or why certain behaviors are accepted/rejected by members within a given society.

Overall, it is important for anthropologists who study customary law not just describe what they observe but also relate those observations back to broader themes like power structures, gender roles, religion, and others (Worugji et al., 2019; Wu, 2018; Young, 2019; Zamir, 2015; Zarea, 2022; Zenker & Höhne, 2018; Zerner, 1994; Zilberman, 1996; Zitzke, 2022; Zwalve, 2012). This helps create more meaningful interpretations rather than simply providing surface level descriptions. It also allows researchers to draw connections between different cultures' legal systems so patterns can be identified across multiple societies.

Anthropology provides an invaluable perspective when studying customary law due its focus on contextualizing findings while taking into account diverse perspectives (Bond, 2010; Botha & Bekink, 2018; Bourgon, 2020; Budlender et al., 2011; Buss, 2010; Buxbaum, 1968). By utilizing various methods such as participant observation, interviews, archival research etc., anthropologists can uncover unique insights about how communities view their own laws which would otherwise remain hidden if traditional approaches were taken instead. Ultimately this knowledge contributes towards our overall understanding of humanity's complex relationship with justice & morality throughout history and around the world.

Anthropology is a field of study that has been used to examine customary law for centuries (Marasinghe, 1978; Masengu, 2016; Mastura, 1994; Maunatlala & Maimela, 2020; Maxim & Titu Maiorescu, 2015; McAuslan, 2015). Customary law, also known as indigenous or traditional law, is the set of rules and regulations that are passed down from generation to generation within a particular culture or society. Anthropologists have long sought to understand how these laws shape social behavior and influence decision-making in different societies.

The primary goal of anthropology when studying customary law is to gain an understanding of the cultural context in which it exists (Shingleton, 1983; Sibisi, 2020; Siegel, 2015; Sierra, 1995; Singer, 1972; Skomerska-Muchowska, 2017; Snyder, 1984). This involves examining the history, values, beliefs, and practices associated with each particular culture's legal system. Anthropologists may use qualitative methods such as interviews and participant observation to collect data on how people interact with their legal systems on a daily basis. They may also employ quantitative methods such as surveys or statistical analysis to measure changes over time in attitudes towards certain laws or behaviors related to them (figure 5.7).

In addition, anthropologists often seek out ways in which customary law can be adapted for modern contexts while still preserving its core principles and values (Morudu & Maimela, 2021; Murphy, 2014; Mwalimu, 1988; Mwambene, 2012; Mwangi, 2022; Ndulo, 2011). For example, they might look at how traditional dispute resolution mechanisms could be incorporated into contemporary court systems so that individuals can access justice without having to resort solely to Western-style litigation processes. By doing this kind of work, anthropologists help bridge gaps between cultures by finding common ground between different legal systems while respecting their unique differences at the same time.

- Social anthropology then takes this further and is the study of human society and cultures, of our local and international communities and of our wider world

- Social anthropologists seek to understand how societies are created or built, how people live in or outside of those societies and how they make their lives meaningful.

Figure 5.7. Understanding the tenets of anthropology.

Source: Reach Cambridge.

Overall, anthropology provides valuable insights into customary law by helping us better understand its historical roots and current applications across various cultures around the world today (Parisi, 2001; Pedersen, 2014; Pelizzon, 2015; Perreau-Saussine & Murphy, 2007; Petersen, 2007, 2017; Pocar, 2016). Through careful research techniques such as ethnography and comparative analysis, anthropologists are able to identify patterns in behavior related to specific laws while also exploring potential solutions for adapting them for more modern contexts where necessary. In this way they provide invaluable contributions not only towards our knowledge about customary law but also towards creating more equitable societies overall through greater cross-cultural understanding and collaboration among diverse groups of people worldwide.

Human anthropology is the study of humans and their behavior, culture, and physical characteristics (Diala, 2017, 2019; Diala & Bagni, 2019; Dubner, 1994; Dubois, 1992; Dupont, 2013; Duxbury, 2017; Edmundson, 2015). It is a holistic approach to understanding human beings in all aspects of life. Social anthropology is an area of study within human anthropology that focuses on the social relationships between people and how they interact with each other in different societies. The two disciplines are closely related as both involve studying humans from a variety of perspectives. Human anthropology looks at biological factors such as genetics, evolution, and adaptation while social anthropology examines cultural practices such as language, religion, customs, values, norms, beliefs systems etc. Both fields also look at how these elements shape individuals' lives and influence their behavior in society. One important aspect of social anthropology is the study of customary law which refers to laws or regulations that have been established by custom rather than by statute or written law (Jonas & Gunda, 2015; Kadens, 2012; Kammerhofer, 2012; Kane, 1972; Kassoti, 2017; Kelly & Windia, 2019; Kilian, 2019; Kim, 2009). Customary law has been used throughout history to regulate various aspects of society including marriage ceremonies; inheritance rights; land ownership; trade agreements; religious rituals; criminal justice systems etc., often without any formal legal system being present. This type of law can be seen across many cultures around the world today and provides insight into how different societies functioned before modern legal systems were developed. Customary law plays an important role in understanding human behavior because it helps us understand why certain behaviors are accepted or rejected within particular communities based on shared values or beliefs about what constitutes acceptable conduct for members living within those communities (Corrin & Mulitalo, 2015; Costa, 1998; Craik, 2020; Crawford, 2012; Criddle, 2013; Cuskelly, 2011; Dahlitz, 1991; Damato, 1973). By looking at customary laws we can gain insight into how people interacted with one another historically which can help us better understand our own contemporary societies today.

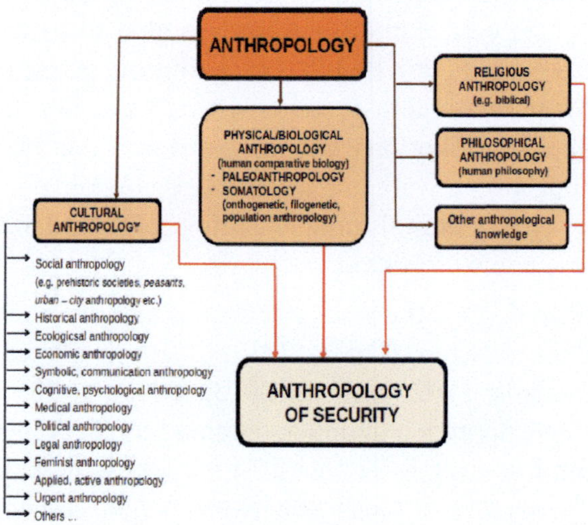

Figure 5.8. Anthropology of security among anthropological sciences.

Source: Jarmoszko (2020).

Human anthropologists use their knowledge about biology, evolution, adaptation, language, religion, customs, values, and norms to gain insights into past societies through the examination of customary laws (Fleck, 2009, 2013; Fletcher, 2007; Frulli, 2015; Gadzo, 2018; Gagnon-Bergeron, 2018; Gal-Or, 2015; Galindo & Yip, 2017). This information then allows them to make informed decisions about current issues facing humanity today. Understanding this relationship between human anthropology and social anthropology gives us valuable tools for navigating our complex world more effectively.

One of the examples of this in practice is an analysis of the anthropology of security among societies (Figure 5.8). The anthropology of societal security is a field of study that examines the ways in which societies protect themselves from external threats (Woodman, 1969, 2001; Worugji et al., 2019; Wu, 2018; Young, 2019; Zamir, 2015; Zarea, 2022; Zenker & Höhne, 2018). It looks at how different cultures and nations respond to perceived dangers, as well as how they develop strategies for mitigating risk. By using theoretical paradigms, we can critically describe and evaluate this area of research in order to gain a better understanding of its implications. One such paradigm is the concept of "security culture," which refers to the shared beliefs and practices that shape an individual or group's approach to security issues (Sheleff, 2013; Shingleton, 1983; Sibisi, 2020; Siegel, 2015; Sierra, 1995; Singer, 1972; Skomerska-Muchowska, 2017). This includes both physical measures (such as fortifications) and psychological ones (such as fear-mongering). Security culture has been studied extensively by anthropologists who have sought to understand why certain groups are more likely than others to take extreme measures when faced with potential danger.

Another important theoretical framework used in the anthropology of societal security is "risk perception" (Morrison, 2016; Morudu & Maimela, 2021; Murphy, 2014; Mwalimu, 1988; Mwambene, 2012; Mwangi, 2022). This involves examining how individuals perceive risks associated with particular situations or events, and what factors influence their decisions about whether or not those risks should be taken seriously. Risk perception studies have revealed interesting insights into why some people may be more willing than others to accept certain levels of risk when it comes to protecting their communities from harm.

Finally, there is also the concept of "resilience" – which focuses on how societies adapt and recover after experiencing traumatic events such as natural disasters or terrorist attacks. Resilience studies look at both short-term responses (e.g., emergency relief efforts) and long-term strategies (e.g., rebuilding infrastructure) (Thirlway, 1972, 2017; Tobin, 2014; Tomuschat, 2021; Treasure et al., 2016; Tripp, 2004; Tsai, 2015). Anthropologists have found that resilience often depends on social networks within communities; these networks provide support during difficult times but can also lead to increased vulnerability if they become too dependent on one another for protection against external threats.

By utilizing these various theoretical paradigms, we can gain a deeper understanding of the anthropology of societal security – including its implications for our own lives today – so that we can make informed decisions about our own safety and wellbeing in an increasingly uncertain world (Sibisi, 2020; Siegel, 2015; Sierra, 1995; Singer, 1972; Skomerska-Muchowska, 2017; Snyder, 1984; Sprankling, 2014). Through critical analysis based on these frameworks, we can identify areas where further research needs to be done in order for us all to benefit from improved security measures.

The study of customary law anthropology is a fascinating field that explores the complex ways in which diverse societies sustain security (Sheleff, 2013; Shingleton, 1983; Sibisi, 2020; Siegel, 2015; Sierra, 1995; Singer, 1972; Skomerska-Muchowska, 2017). Customary law, also known as traditional or indigenous law, is an unwritten set of rules and regulations that are passed down from generation to generation within a particular community. It is based on customs and practices that have been developed over time by members of the society in order to maintain social order and harmony.

Customary law has been used for centuries by many different cultures around the world, including those living in rural areas where there may be no formal legal system or government structure (Howell, 2018; Hu, 2017; Huizenga, 2018, 2022; Hulme, 2010; Hutchison, 2020; Hutchison & Sibanda, 2017; Iyi, 2016). In these cases, customary laws provide a means for resolving disputes between individuals without resorting to violence or other forms of coercion. This type of informal justice system can be seen as an alternative form of dispute resolution when compared with more formal systems such as courts or tribunals.

Customary laws vary greatly from one culture to another depending on their history and values (Harmathy, 2016; Henry, 2017; Hernández, 2012; Holleman, 1969, 1972; Horii, 2019; Howell, 2018; Hu, 2017). However, they all share certain common features such as being based on shared beliefs about right and wrong behavior. Another commonality is having sanctions for violations (such as fines or ostracism). They are also known for providing mechanisms for resolving conflicts peacefully rather than through violence. Additionally, these systems rely heavily on consensus-based decision making processes rather than top-down authority structures.

In recent years anthropologists have begun studying how customary laws are applied in various contexts around the world in order to gain insight into how different societies manage conflict resolution without resorting to violence or other coercive measures (Gadzo, 2018; Gagnon-Bergeron, 2018; Gal-Or, 2015; Galindo & Yip, 2017; Gao, 2013; Gillespie & Tran, 2022; Golo et al., 2022; Gradoni, 2019).

By understanding how these systems work it can help us better understand why some communities are able to remain peaceful while others experience high levels of crime and unrest despite similar economic conditions. Additionally, this research can help inform policy makers who seek solutions for reducing violent crime rates across different countries by looking at what works best within each unique context instead of trying to impose universal standards upon them all at once.

Overall, studying customary law anthropology provides valuable insights into how diverse societies sustain security without relying solely on external forces like governments or police forces but instead using internal methods rooted deeply within their own cultural traditions and values (Tunkin, 1993; Tupper, 1881; Ubink, 2016; Ubink & Weeks, 2017; Ubink, 2008; Utama, 2021; van Caenegem, 2014). A key component of some societal controls such as the ones described above is the legitimacy of outcomes. The next section will specifically explore the legitimacy of judicial decisions.

5.5. THE LEGITIMACY OF JUDICIAL DECISIONS

The legitimacy of judicial decisions is a complex and multifaceted issue (Mwangi, 2022; Ndulo, 2011; Ngira, 2018, 2021; Nhlapo, 2017; Nnona, 2018; Norr, 1973; Nwapi, 2016). It involves the consideration of various factors, including the legal system in which the decision was made, the quality of evidence presented, and even public opinion. In particular, customary law decisions are often seen as being less legitimate than those made by formal courts or tribunals. This raises questions about how to increase their legitimacy and effectiveness.

Customary law is an informal system of justice that has been used for centuries in many parts of the world. It relies on local customs and traditions to resolve disputes between individuals or groups without resorting to formal court proceedings (Jentoft & Bavinck, 2019; John-Hopkins, 2010; Johnson, 1986; Joireman, 2008; Jonas & Gunda, 2015; Kadens, 2012; Kammerhofer, 2012). While it can be effective in resolving certain types of conflicts, its lack of structure makes it difficult to ensure that all parties receive fair treatment under this system. As such, there is a need for greater oversight over customary law decisions if they are to be considered legitimate by society at large.

One way to increase the legitimacy of customary law decisions is through increased transparency and accountability measures within these systems (Qerimi, 2020; Quane, 2013; Rautenbach, 2020; Rose, 1989; Rubin, 1990; Russo, 1988; Sarbah, 1904; Seidman, 1983). For example, having clear rules regarding who can participate in dispute resolution processes would help ensure that all parties have access to justice regardless of their social status or economic resources. Additionally, providing more detailed records about each case could help provide insight into why certain outcomes were reached so that any potential biases can be identified and addressed accordingly. Another way to improve the legitimacy of customary law decisions is through better training for those involved in dispute resolution processes such as mediators or arbitrators who may not have received adequate instruction on how best to handle cases fairly and impartially according to established laws or regulations governing these matters (Thipe & Buthelezi, 2014; Thirlway, 2015, 2017; Thirlway, 1972; Tobin, 2014; Tomuschat, 2021; Treasure et al., 2016). Furthermore, introducing mechanisms for appealing unfavorable rulings could also help reduce instances where people feel like they have been treated unfairly due to cultural differences or other forms discrimination based on gender identity or ethnicity among others.

Finally, engaging with communities affected by disputes before making any final judgments could also go a long way towards increasing trust between citizens, government officials, and traditional leaders when it comes time for them to make binding rulings (Magnusson, 2013, 2017; Manaka & Corrin, 2021; Manullang, 2021; Marasinghe, 1978; Masengu, 2016; Mastura, 1994). By taking steps like these, we can work towards creating a more equitable environment where everyone feels confident that their rights will be respected no matter what type of judicial process they choose. Ultimately, ensuring fairness across all levels of justice requires us to take seriously our responsibility to create systems which prioritize impartiality above all else. Only then will we be able truly say that our judicial decisions are both legitimate effective.

The notion of judicial activism can threaten impartiality and has been the subject of intense debate (Holleman, 1969, 1972; Horii, 2019; Howell, 2018; Hu, 2017; Huizenga, 2018, 2022; Hulme, 2010). Judicial activism is a term used to describe the actions of judges who go beyond their traditional role in interpreting and applying laws. It involves making decisions that are based on personal or political beliefs, rather than on established legal principles. Judicial activism has become increasingly common in recent years, with some courts taking an active role in shaping public policy and social change.

In customary law, judicial activism can take many forms (Gagnon-Bergeron, 2018; Gal-Or, 2015; Galindo & Yip, 2017; Gao, 2013; Gillespie & Tran, 2022; Golo et al., 2022; Gradoni, 2019; Graves, 2017). For example, a court may interpret existing laws more broadly than they were originally intended to be applied; it may create new rules or standards for resolving disputes; or it may even make rulings that contradict existing legislation. In all cases, judicial activism can have far-reaching consequences for individuals and society as a whole (Figure 5.9).

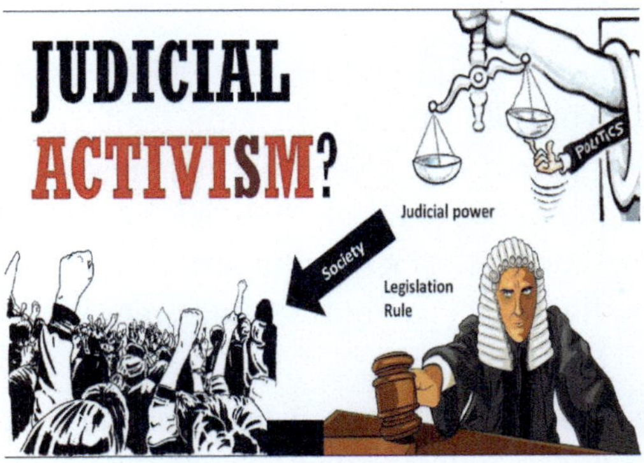

Figure 5.9. The notion of judicial activism.

Source: Target GS via YouTube.

One example of judicial activism in customary law is the decision by the Supreme Court of India in 2018 to recognize transgender people as a "third gender" under Indian law. This ruling was seen as an important step forward for LGBTQ rights in India, but also raised questions about how this recognition would be implemented across different states and communities within India where there are varying levels of acceptance towards transgender people. Another example is the decision by the High Court of Botswana to decriminalize same-sex relationships between consenting adults in 2019 – overturning colonial-era laws which had criminalized such behavior since 1965. This ruling was widely celebrated by human rights activists around the world but also sparked debate over whether such changes should be made through legislative action instead of through judicial intervention.

To prevent judicial activism from having unintended consequences on individuals and society at large, it is important that governments ensure that their judiciary systems are independent from political interference and operate according to established legal principles and procedures when making decisions related to customary law matters (Kelly & Windia, 2019; Kilian, 2019; Kim, 2009, 2020; Kingwill, 2016; Koskenniemi, 1990; Kreso, 2010; Krieger, 2006).

Additionally, governments should strive to provide adequate resources for training judges so they can better understand local customs and traditions when making rulings related to them – ensuring that any interventions into these areas are done with sensitivity towards cultural norms while still upholding fundamental human rights protections enshrined within international treaties like the Universal Declaration of Human Rights (UDHR).

Finally, governments should work closely with civil society organizations who specialize in advocating for minority groups affected by discriminatory practices embedded within customary law systems – helping ensure that any changes brought about through judicial intervention benefit those most vulnerable members of society without infringing upon anyone else's basic freedoms or liberties guaranteed under international human rights instruments like UDHR.

Overall, judicial activism has been instrumental in advancing certain causes related to minority groups protected under international human rights conventions (Milanovic, 2011; Mnisi & Claassens, 2009; Moore, 1986; Morrison, 2016; Morudu & Maimela, 2021; Murphy, 2014). However, it must always remain mindful not only of its potential impacts on individuals but also its implications for broader societal values.

-By following these guidelines, governments can help ensure that any interventions into customary law matters do not lead down paths which could potentially undermine long standing traditions while still protecting fundamental individual freedoms. Judicial restraint (Figure 5.10) may support some of these ideals.

Type of Issue/Category	What has been labelled as Judicial 'Activism'	What has been labelled as Judicial 'Passivity'/'Conservativism'/'Restraint'
Constitutional Interpretive Methodology[116]	- Liberal - Purposive - Conceptual/contextual	- Conservative (more appropriately 'non-liberal')[117] - Ordinary, plain or natural meaning - Originalism, legal positivism
Law-making	- makes law - invalidates legislation	- do not make law (leaves that to legislatures) - declines to invalidate legislation
Policy choices	- where appropriate willing to adjudicate on matters of policy	- unwilling to adjudicate on matters of policy since considers questions of policy strictly the ambit of other branches of government not the judiciary
Political disputes	- entertains political decisions in their courts	- do not entertain political decisions in their courts
Creativity	- creative/innovative (develops new concepts)	- not creative/innovative (unwilling to develop new concepts)
Sensitivity to social realities	- are sensitive to social realities (concerns themselves with the ends of the law)	- are not sensitive to social realities (do not concern themselves with the ends of the law)

Figure 5.10. Judicial activism and restraint in Malawi.

Source: Chifundo Jairus Kachale (2012).

The notion of judicial restraint has been advanced as helping to maintain the integrity of customary law (Willms, 2009; Wilson, 1961; Wolff, 2016; Woodman, 1988, 1969, 2001; Worugji et al., 2019; Wu, 2018). The concept of judicial restraint is an important one in the context of customary law. It refers to a judge's ability to remain impartial and unbiased when making decisions based on traditional laws and customs. This is especially relevant in countries where customary law still plays a major role in legal proceedings, such as many African nations. It is therefore pertinent to critically examine the ways in which judicial restraint can ensure impartiality in customary law.

First, it is essential that judges understand the cultural context within which they are operating when applying customary law (Arowolo, 2019; Asieduakrofi, 1989; Barnabas, 2022; Barrie, 2016; Baxi, 2020; Beavers, 2019; Beer, 2022; Bennett, 2008; Bennett, 2015). Judges must be aware of any potential biases or preconceived notions they may have about certain cultures or traditions before making their rulings. This requires them to take into account all available evidence and consider different perspectives before coming to a decision. Additionally, judges should strive for consistency by adhering strictly to established rules and procedures while also being open-minded enough to recognize new interpretations or applications of existing laws if necessary.

Second, judges must be willing to challenge long-held beliefs or practices if they believe these are not consistent with modern values or principles of justice and fairness (McAuslan, 2015; McCarthy, 1971; McLachlan, 1988;

Menski, 1988; Meron, 1987, 1991; Meron et al., 1987). For example, some traditional practices may discriminate against certain groups such as women or minorities. Thus, it is important for judges to be able to identify these issues and make appropriate changes accordingly without compromising their own sense of impartiality or objectivity.

Finally, it is crucial that judges maintain an attitude of respect towards those who practice traditional customs even if they disagree with them personally (Danilenko, 1988; Davis & Klare, 2010; De ruysscher, 2008; de Vries, 2021; De Wet, 2004; Debelva & De Broe, 2022; Dekoster, 2019). This helps foster trust between parties involved in legal proceedings involving customary law as well as ensuring that judgments are made fairly without bias towards either side's beliefs or values systems. Furthermore, judges should also strive for transparency by providing clear explanations for their decisions so that everyone involved understands why particular rulings were made.

Overall, judicial restraint plays an integral role in ensuring impartiality when dealing with matters related to customary law (Williams, 2022; Willms, 2009; Wilson, 1961; Wolff, 2016; Woodman, 1988, 1969, 2001; Worugji et al., 2019). By understanding the cultural context within which they operate, challenging outdated beliefs, and maintaining respectful attitudes towards all parties involved, judges can help ensure fair outcomes regardless of personal opinions. Ultimately, this helps promote justice while preserving tradition at the same time.

CHAPTER 5 SUMMARY

This chapter highlighted the possibility of perceiving customary laws as an expression of norms. The chapter developed working definitions of norms, values, and folkways. These are the anthropological tools that are often used to describe and predict human behavior. The desire to control human behavior is explained by the discussion surrounding judicial restraint and activism in decision-making. In the next chapter, we will consider the embedding of customary laws in existing judicial structures.

CHAPTER 6

Embedding Customary Law in Existing Legal Structures

Contents

Customary law is typically included in structures that are already existing and that is the topic that will be explored in this chapter. We will consider the repertoire of norms under the flexibility thesis. The chapter will also interrogate the notion of skepticism in judicial processes. A critique of the legal codification process will allow us to understand why certain seemingly practical laws and rules are left off the statute book. Going back to medieval custumals, this chapter will demonstrate the evolution of the law across time. We commence the chapter by discussing Comaroff and Robert's flexibility thesis which led to the development of a repertoire of norms.

6.1. COMAROFF AND ROBERTS' FLEXIBILITY THESIS OF A "REPERTOIRE OF NORMS"

In their book Rules and Processes: The Cultural Logic of Dispute in an African Context, Jean Comaroff and John L. Roberts propose a "flexibility thesis" that suggests the existence of a "repertoire of norms" within any given society. This idea is based on the notion that societies are not static entities but rather dynamic ones, constantly adapting to changing circumstances (Lewis, 1983, 2016; Liakopoulos, 2019; Lijnzaad, 2022; Lingaas, 2022; Lita et al., 2017; Liu, 2019; Loja, 2014; Lon & Widyawati, 2021). As such, they argue that there is no single set of rules or laws governing all aspects of life; instead, different sets of norms exist side by side in order to accommodate various situations.

The flexibility thesis has been used to explain how certain cultures have managed to survive despite drastic changes over time (Meron, 1991; Meron et al., 1987; Merry, 1991; Meyer, 2012; Milanovic, 2011; Mnisi & Claassens, 2009; Moore, 1986). For example, it can be seen in how some traditional African societies have adapted their customs and beliefs as new technologies become available or when faced with external pressures from other cultures or governments. In this way, these societies are able to maintain their core values while also incorporating elements from outside sources into their own culture. This is particularly important when analyzing leadership across cultures.

Leadership is a complex concept that has been studied and discussed for centuries (Osman, 2019; Osman & Baase, 2022; Osman & Himonga, 2017; Ottley, 2016; Parisi, 2001; Pedersen, 2014). It is often defined as the ability to influence, motivate, and inspire others to achieve a common goal. However, in recent years there has been an increased focus on understanding leadership from a cross-cultural perspective. It is therefore pertinent to critically examine how flexibility leadership can explain leadership using this lens.

Flexibility leadership is based on the idea that leaders must be able to adapt their approach depending on the context they are operating in (Engel & Kurschilgen, 2013; Farran, 2019; Fenrich et al., 2011; Fleck, 2009, 2013; Fletcher, 2007; Frulli, 2015; Gadzo, 2018). This means being aware of cultural differences between countries or regions and adjusting one's style accordingly. For example, if working with people from different cultures it may be necessary to adjust communication styles or decision-making processes so that everyone feels comfortable participating in the process (Figure 6.1).

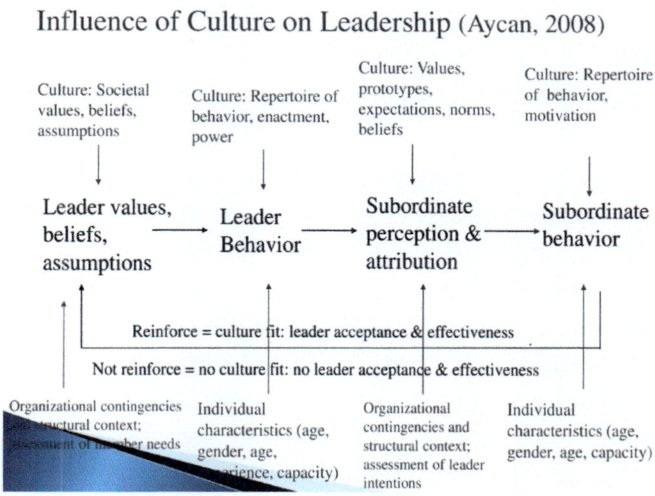

Figure 6.1. Leadership across various cultures.

Source: Kenneth Burns.

The key element of flexibility leadership is its emphasis on collaboration rather than top-down control structures which are more commonly associated with traditional forms of leadership such as autocratic or bureaucratic models. By encouraging open dialog between all stakeholders involved in a project, leaders can ensure that everyone's perspectives are taken into account when making decisions which ultimately leads to better outcomes for all parties involved. Additionally, by taking into consideration cultural norms and values when leading teams across borders it allows for greater understanding among team members which helps foster trust and respect within the group dynamic – something essential for successful teamwork regardless of culture or location (Fenrich et al., 2011; Fleck, 2009, 2013; Fletcher, 2007; Frulli, 2015; Gadzo, 2018; Gagnon-Bergeron, 2018; Gal-Or, 2015).

Overall, flexibility leadership provides an effective way of explaining how leaders should operate when working across cultures by emphasizing collaboration over control structures while also taking into account cultural norms and values when making decisions or communicating with team members from different backgrounds (Dubois, 1992; Dupont, 2013; Duxbury, 2017; Edmundson, 2015; Elias, 1956; Enabulele & Bazuaye, 2019; Engel & Kurschilgen, 2013). By doing so it ensures that everyone feels included in the process while also allowing for better outcomes due to improved understanding among those involved in any given project or initiative. Ultimately, this type of approach enables organizations to maximize their potential by leveraging diversity both within their own ranks as well as externally through partnerships with other entities around the world.

Comaroff and Roberts suggest that this ability for adaptation is key for any society's survival because it allows them to remain flexible enough to respond quickly and effectively when confronted with change without sacrificing too much of its identity in the process (Dupont, 2013; Duxbury, 2017; Edmundson, 2015; Elias, 1956; Enabulele & Bazuaye, 2019; Engel & Kurschilgen, 2013; Farran, 2019). They further argue that this type of flexibility should be encouraged as it helps ensure social stability by allowing people from different backgrounds and perspectives to come together under one shared set of norms without having to completely abandon their individual identities in the process.

Ultimately, Comaroff and Roberts' flexibility thesis provides an interesting perspective on how societies can adapt over time while still maintaining a sense of continuity throughout generations (Osman & Baase, 2022; Osman & Himonga, 2017; Ottley, 2016; Parisi, 2001; Pedersen, 2014; Pelizzon, 2015). By recognizing the importance of having multiple sets of norms coexisting alongside each other within any given culture, we can better understand why certain traditions persist even after centuries while others fade away more quickly due to external influences or technological advancements. It also serves as an important reminder about our need for cultural diversity if we want our communities—and ultimately our world—to continue thriving well into the future. In recent years, there has been an increased focus on human-centered cultural designs as part of global practice of customary law (Nhlapo, 2017; Nnona, 2018; Norr, 1973; Nwapi, 2016; Nyane, 2019; O'Neill, 2002; Oba, 2002, 2008). It is useful to explore how these designs can be applied to customary law and what implications they may have for its implementation. Human-centered design (HCD) is an approach to problem solving that puts people at the center by understanding their needs, motivations, and experiences. It involves creating solutions that are tailored to meet those needs while also taking into account other factors such as culture, environment, technology, economics etc. HCD seeks to create products or services that are both useful and desirable from the user's perspective (Figure 6.2).

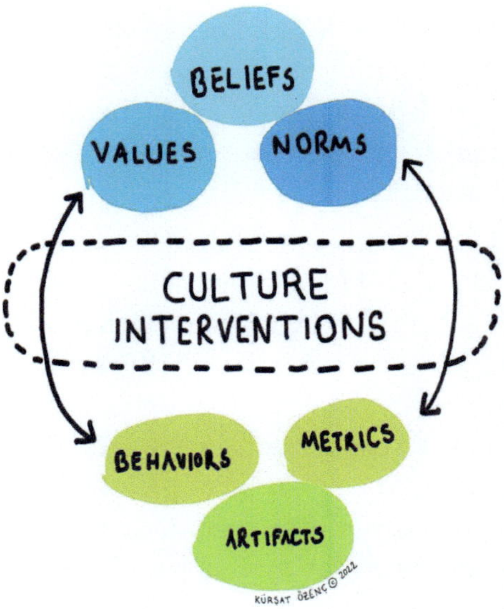

Figure 6.2. Human-centered cultural designs.

Source: Kursat Ozenc (2022) via Medium.

When it comes to applying HCD principles to customary law practice there are several considerations which must be taken into account (Nyane, 2019; O'Neill, 2002; Oba, 2002, 2008, 2011; Obatusin, 2018; Olaf & Markus, 2018; Omidire, 1990). These include understanding local context; respecting traditional values; ensuring access for all stakeholders; promoting collaboration between different groups; encouraging participation in decision making processes; providing clear communication channels between parties involved in dispute resolution proceedings; developing effective enforcement mechanisms; and finally evaluating outcomes against predetermined goals or objectives. These are issues and considerations that all practitioners of customary law should be aware of and include in their own activities when embedding this form of justice.

The use of HCD principles can help ensure that customary laws remain relevant within modern contexts by allowing them to evolve with changing times while still preserving their core values and beliefs (John-Hopkins, 2010; Johnson, 1986; Joireman, 2008; Jonas & Gunda, 2015; Kadens, 2012; Kammerhofer, 2012; Kane, 1972). For example, when designing new systems or procedures related to dispute resolution it is important not only consider existing legal frameworks but also take into account local customs so as not alienate any members of the community who may feel excluded due lack familiarity with formal legal structures or language barriers which could prevent them from participating fully in proceedings. Additionally, incorporating elements such as visual aids, simplified language, online platforms etc can make information more accessible thus increasing engagement among stakeholders.

Ultimately, human-centered cultural designs provide an opportunity for communities around the world to embrace change without sacrificing their traditional values (Weinberg, 2016; Williams & Klusener, 2013; Williams, 2022; Willms, 2009; Wilson, 1961; Wolff, 2016; Woodman, 1988). By recognizing individual perspectives within a collective framework we can ensure that our laws remain relevant across generations while still protecting fundamental rights. As such, this approach should be considered when implementing global practices of customary law. The tone of sensitivity and inclusiveness that is advocated for by this paradigm can be challenged by the notion of rule skepticism.

6.2. SKEPTICISM IN THE LAW OR "RULE SKEPTICISM"

The legal system is built on the foundation of trust and respect for the rule of law (Cannizzaro & Bonafe, 2005; Carrillo-Santarelli, 2017; Castillo & Bian, 2014; Cataldi & Titu Maiorescu, 2015; Chang, 2022; Chanock, 1989). However, in recent years there has been a growing trend towards "rule skepticism" – an attitude that questions the legitimacy of laws and regulations. This type of skepticism can be seen in many areas, from criminal justice to environmental protection. Rule skeptics often argue that laws are too restrictive or outdated, or that they do not adequately address current issues (Nhlapo, 1997; Nhlapo, 2017; Nnona, 2018; Norr, 1973; Nwapi,

2016; Nyane, 2019; O'Neill, 2002; Oba, 2002, 2008). They may also point out inconsistencies between different statutes or suggest that certain rules are overly complex and difficult to understand. In some cases, rule skeptics may even challenge the constitutionality of certain laws or regulations.

This type of skepticism can have both positive and negative effects on society as a whole (Krieger, 2006; Kumar, 2020; Lagji, 2019; Lavalle, 2014; Laylin, 1976; Lewis, 1983, 2016; Liakopoulos, 2019; Lijnzaad, 2022; Lingaas, 2022). On one hand, it encourages people to think critically about existing laws and push for reforms when necessary. On the other hand, it can lead to confusion among citizens who are not sure which rules apply in any given situation – leading to potential violations due to ignorance rather than intent.

It is important for lawyers and lawmakers alike to take into account this growing trend towards rule skepticism when crafting new legislation or interpreting existing ones (Nwapi, 2016; Nyane, 2019; O'Neill, 2002; Oba, 2002, 2008, 2011; Obatusin, 2018; Olaf & Markus, 2018). By taking into consideration public opinion on various topics such as privacy rights or gun control, legislators can ensure their decisions reflect current values while still protecting individual freedoms within reasonable limits set by law enforcement agencies like police departments across America. Additionally, attorneys should strive to make sure their clients understand all relevant legal matters so they do not inadvertently break any rules due to lack of knowledge. Figure 6.3 highlights the three levels of skepticism and the resultant concessions that they may inspire.

Level	Type of Case	Concession to Skeptic
1	Naïve Student-2 (i.e., motivated reasoning leads us astray)	*Minimal*; the concession to the skeptic does not go beyond those beliefs that we'd already be inclined to regard as unjustified.
2	Naïve Student-1 (i.e., motivated reasoning nudges us in the right direction)	*Substantial*; the concession to the skeptic includes some beliefs that we'd be inclined to regard as justified. Crucially, this includes cases where one bases (true) beliefs on good reasons.
3	Enlightened Student (Parts I and II) (i.e., one does not believe via motivated reasoning, but reflects on the empirical literature and cannot rule out that one did reason this way)	*Critical:* the concession to the sceptic includes some beliefs that we'd be inclined to regard as epistemically impeccable. Crucially, this includes cases where the subject doesn't actually engage in motivated reasoning.

Figure 6.3. Three levels of skepticism and resultant concessions.

Source: Cambridge University Press & Assessment.

Ultimately, understanding how rule skepticism affects our legal system is essential if we want our society to remain fair, just, and safe. It allows us all – lawyers, lawmakers, citizens – to work together to create effective solutions without sacrificing civil liberties. The concept of "rule skepticism" has been gaining traction in the legal world, particularly with regards to customary law (Cataldi & Titu Maiorescu, 2015; Chang, 2022; Chanock, 1989; Cheng, 2012; Chirayath et al., 2005; Claassens & Mnisi, 2009). This notion suggests that traditional rules and customs should be viewed skeptically, as they may not always reflect current values or norms. While this perspective can be beneficial in some cases, it is important to consider the potential drawbacks of such an approach before embracing it fully. At its core, rule skepticism implies a certain level of distrust towards established laws and customs (Lewis, 2016; Liakopoulos, 2019; Lijnzaad, 2022; Lingaas, 2022; Lita et al., 2017; Liu, 2019; Loja, 2014; Lon & Widyawati, 2021). It assumes that these rules are outdated or no longer applicable to modern society and thus should be questioned or disregarded altogether. While this attitude can lead to positive changes in certain areas – for example, allowing more flexibility when interpreting existing laws – it also carries risks.

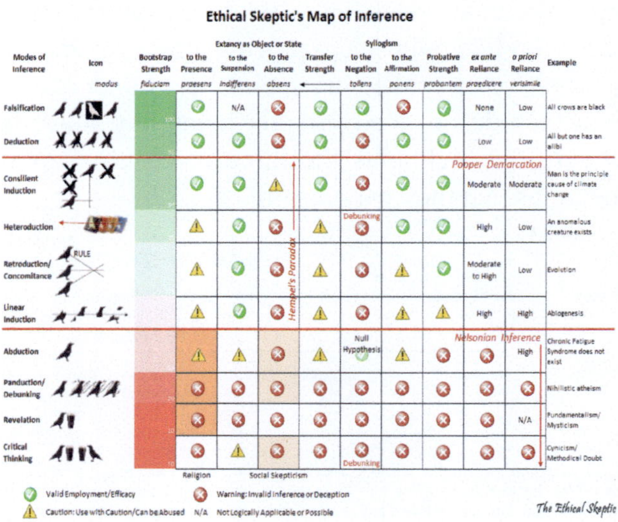

Figure 6.4. Example of a map of ethical skepticism thinking.

Source: TES – the ethical skeptic.

For instance, if taken too far, rule skepticism could lead to a disregard for long-standing traditions which have served communities well over time.

Figure 6.4 attempts to conceptually map the notion of ethical thinking. This map demonstrates the complexity of skepticism beyond merely disagreeing with the established way of doing things.

It is notable there is a danger that rule skepticism could become overly politicized if used as a tool by those who wish to push their own agendas at the expense of others' rights and beliefs (Tan, 1993, 2018; Tegnan, 2015; Thipe & Buthelezi, 2014; Thirlway, 1972, 2015, 2017). In addition, relying on subjective interpretations rather than objective facts could create confusion among members of the public about what is legally permissible under customary law. Ultimately then, while there are certainly benefits associated with viewing traditional rules through a skeptical lens from time-to-time; caution must be exercised when doing so in order to ensure that any changes made do not undermine fundamental principles or cause unnecessary disruption within communities governed by customary law systems. As such, it is essential that any decisions regarding rule skepticism are made carefully after considering all relevant factors involved in each particular case before arriving at an informed conclusion about how best proceed going forward.

This then raises an important consideration whether rule skepticism defeats the purposes of common law in ordering society (Tomuschat, 2021; Treasure et al., 2016; Tripp, 2004; Tsai, 2015; Tucker, 1972; Tunkin, 1993). There has been an increasing trend towards rule skepticism in recent years which could potentially be harmful to societal harmony under customary law. Rule skepticism can be defined as questioning or doubting established laws or norms within a given society. This type of attitude can lead to individuals disregarding certain aspects of customary law which may have previously been respected and followed by their ancestors for generations. As such, it can create tension between different groups within a society who may disagree about how certain laws should be interpreted or enforced. Furthermore, it can also lead to confusion among members of the same group who may not agree on what constitutes acceptable behavior according to their shared customs and traditions.

In addition to creating tensions between different groups within a society, rule skepticism can so undermine respect for authority figures such as elders or religious leaders who are responsible for upholding traditional values and enforcing customary laws (Perreau-Saussine & Murphy, 2007; Petersen, 2007, 2017; Pocar, 2016; Poespasari, 2020; Polanski, 2017). Without this respect from younger generations, these authority figures will find it difficult to ensure that everyone follows the same set of rules which could ultimately result in chaos and disorder within communities where they were once able to maintain peace through adherence to traditional values and practices.

While some degree of rule skepticism is necessary in order for societies to progress over time with changing needs and circumstances; too much doubt regarding established laws could prove detrimental both socially as well as economically if left unchecked due its potential impact on societal harmony under customary law across societies worldwide (Claassens & Mnisi, 2009; Cooter, 1991; Corrin & Mulitalo, 2015; Costa, 1998; Craik, 2020; Crawford, 2012; Criddle, 2013). Therefore, it is important that governments take steps towards educating citizens about why respecting traditional values is important so that they understand why following certain rules even when they do not necessarily agree with them might still be beneficial in terms of maintaining peace amongst all members regardless of age or background. Only then will we truly see lasting change when it comes to preserving social harmony under customary law across societies worldwide. Understanding traditional processes is a critical part of this equation.

6.3. TRADITIONAL CULTURAL JUDICIAL PROCESSES

In many cultures, traditional judicial processes are still used to resolve disputes and conflicts (Singer, 1972; Skomerska-Muchowska, 2017; Snyder, 1984; Sprankling, 2014; Sun, 2010; Syaufi & Zahra, 2021). These systems of justice have been in place for centuries, providing a way for communities to settle disagreements without resorting to violence or other forms of aggression. Traditional cultural judicial processes vary from culture to culture but typically involve the use of elders or respected members of the community as mediators. The process is often based on principles such as respect, fairness, and equity rather than legalistic rules and regulations. This allows for more flexibility when it comes to resolving disputes while also ensuring that all parties involved feel heard and respected.

The primary goal of these traditional systems is not necessarily punishment but rather reconciliation between those involved in the dispute (Meyer, 2012; Milanovic, 2011; Mnisi & Claassens, 2009; Moore, 1986; Morrison, 2016; Morudu & Maimela, 2021). In some cases, this may mean finding a mutually agreeable solution that both sides can accept; in others, it could involve an apology or even compensation being offered by one party to another. Regardless of what form it takes, the aim is always resolution through dialog rather than retribution through force or coercion.

These traditional methods are still widely used today in many parts of the world where access to formal legal systems may be limited due to poverty or lack of resources (Loja, 2014; Lon & Widyawati, 2021; Magnusson, 2013, 2017; Manaka & Corrin, 2021; Manullang, 2021). They provide an effective means for people living within these communities to seek justice without having recourse outside their own society's norms and values – something which can be invaluable when dealing with sensitive matters such as family feuds or land disputes between neighbors.

It is important that we recognize the value that traditional cultural judicial processes bring both locally and globally (Beer, 2022; Bennett, 2008, 2009, 2015; Benson & Siddiqui, 2014; Bianchi, 2009; Bond, 2009). This is because they offer a unique approach towards conflict resolution which has stood the test of time over generations and continues to serve its purpose today just as effectively as ever before. By understanding how these systems work we can better appreciate their importance within our societies while also learning valuable lessons about how best handle difficult situations peacefully instead of relying solely on punitive measures alone.

The traditional cultural judicial processes have been in existence for centuries, and they are still used today in many parts of the world (Bennett, 2015; Bennett, 2009; Benson & Siddiqui, 2014; Bianchi, 2009; Bond, 2009, 2010; Botha & Bekink, 2018; Bourgon, 2020). These systems of justice provide an alternative to the formal legal system, and can be beneficial in certain circumstances. However, there are also some drawbacks associated with these types of proceedings that should be considered before deciding whether or not to use them. A case of African traditional dispute resolution is instructive in this respect.

A case in point is the traditional justice system that is used in South Africa (Figure 6.5). The rainbow nation has been built on truth and reconciliation after a period of apartheid. However, there are many other forms of traditional conflict resolution mechanisms in Africa. Although not entirely well respected or widespread due to eurocentrism, they are nonetheless important examples of how tradition can resolve disputes (Adebola, 2021; Akande, 2004; Albakjaji, 2022; Allott, 1957, 1984; Anderson, 2003; Angelini, 2012).

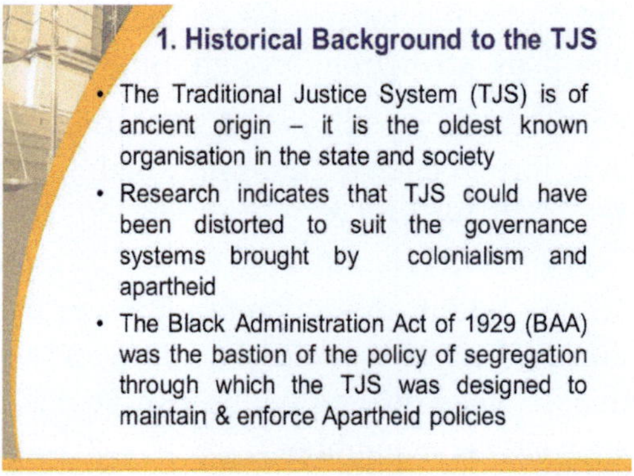

Figure 6.5. Background to traditional justice system in South Africa.

Source: Justice and Constitutional Development.

Conflict resolution is an important part of any society, and African cultures have developed a variety of approaches to resolving disputes. These traditional methods are still relevant today, as they provide valuable insight into how we can better manage conflicts in our own lives (Budlender et al., 2011; Buss, 2010; Buxbaum, 1968; Cannizzaro & Bonafe, 2005; Carrillo-Santarelli, 2017; Castillo & Bian, 2014). They also speak of the rich cultural diversities that characterize judicial processes across the globe. Nothing is more authentic when we speak of cross cultural respect and understanding in the judicial process.

One common approach to conflict resolution in Africa is the use of mediation (Pocar, 2016; Poespasari, 2020; Polanski, 2017; Pratiwi et al., 2020; Qerimi, 2020; Quane, 2013). This involves bringing together two or more parties who are involved in a dispute and having them discuss their differences with the help of a neutral third party. The mediator helps each side understand the other's perspective and encourages them to come up with mutually beneficial solutions that will satisfy both sides. Mediation has been used for centuries by African societies, and it remains an effective way to resolve conflicts even today.

Another popular method of conflict resolution among African cultures is arbitration (Vanboven, 1991; Vergouwen, 2013; Vines, 2017; Watson, 1984; Webber, 2009; Weinberg, 2016; Williams & Klusener, 2013). In this process, one or more arbitrators listen to both sides present their case before making a decision on how best to settle the dispute. Arbitration allows for greater flexibility than mediation since it does not require all parties involved in the dispute to agree on a solution; instead, it relies on an impartial third-party opinion which may be more objective than what either side would propose themselves.

Many African societies also rely heavily on negotiation when attempting to resolve conflicts between individuals or groups (Farran, 2019; Fenrich et al., 2011; Fleck, 2009, 2013; Fletcher, 2007; Frulli, 2015; Gadzo, 2018; Gagnon-Bergeron, 2018). Negotiation involves both sides discussing their issues openly until they reach an agreement that satisfies everyone involved without resorting to violence or coercion tactics such as threats or intimidation techniques often seen elsewhere around the world. Negotiations allow people from different backgrounds and perspectives to come together peacefully while still respecting each other's rights and interests – something that is essential for successful conflict resolution efforts anywhere in the world today.

Traditional African approaches towards conflict resolution offer valuable lessons about how we can better handle disagreements within our own communities today (Pedersen, 2014; Pelizzon, 2015; Perreau-Saussine & Murphy, 2007; Petersen, 2007, 2017; Pocar, 2016). By understanding these methods, we can learn from past generations' wisdom while adapting them appropriately so that they remain relevant even now. With careful consideration, open dialog, mutual respect, and creative problem solving, we can create peaceful resolutions no matter where we live.

Overall, there are numerous traditional approaches used by Africans throughout history when dealing with conflicts between individuals or groups within their communities – from mediation and arbitration processes through restorative justice practices – that remain highly relevant today despite being hundreds (or even thousands) years old. By understanding these various methods we can gain valuable insights into how we can better manage our own personal disputes while also learning about different ways people have dealt with disagreements throughout history – ultimately helping us create healthier relationships now and into the future.

One advantage of traditional cultural judicial processes is that they often involve a more holistic approach than what is found in the formal legal system (Hu, 2017; Huizenga, 2018, 2022; Hulme, 2010; Hutchison, 2020; Hutchison & Sibanda, 2017; Iyi, 2016; Jentoft & Bavinck, 2019). This means that all aspects of a dispute may be taken into account when making decisions about how it should be resolved. For example, rather than simply looking at who was right or wrong according to the law, judges may consider factors such as community values and customs when determining outcomes. This can lead to fairer results for those involved since their individual circumstances will be taken into consideration instead of just relying on rigid rules and regulations set out by the state or other authorities.

Another benefit is that these proceedings tend to take less time than going through a court case would require (Thirlway, 1972, 2015, 2017; Tobin, 2014; Tomuschat, 2021; Treasure et al., 2016; Tripp, 2004). Since there are fewer steps involved and no need for lengthy paperwork or complex procedures, disputes can usually be settled much faster using this method compared to taking it through official channels. Additionally, costs associated with traditional cultural judicial processes tend to be lower since there's no need for lawyers or expensive court fees like you would find in regular courts.

One major disadvantage is that these proceedings do not always guarantee impartiality due to potential conflicts between judges' personal beliefs and interests versus what might actually constitute fair treatment under the law (Galindo & Yip, 2017; Gao, 2013; Gillespie & Tran, 2022; Golo et al., 2022; Gradoni, 2019; Graves, 2017; Gray, 2021; Griffiths, 1998; Hager, 2020). Furthermore, because these systems rely heavily on local customs which vary from place-to-place depending on culture and tradition; people living outside those areas may not receive equal protection under them if their rights are not recognized by local laws or practices. Finally, while traditional methods do offer an alternative form of justice, they lack any real enforcement power so even if someone does win their case, there's no guarantee that they will get what is owed them without having recourse elsewhere.

Many reforms are taking place in the judicial system and there is no reason why traditional judicial processes cannot consider some aspects of this reform (Gillespie & Tran, 2022; Golo et al., 2022; Gradoni, 2019; Graves, 2017; Gray, 2021; Griffiths, 1998; Hager, 2020; Haggenmacher, 2021). A case in point are the moves towards smart justice in Portugal, a modern advanced European country. In recent years, Portugal has implemented a number of smart justice reforms in an effort to reduce the country's prison population and improve public safety. These reforms have been widely praised for their innovative approach to criminal justice, but it is important to critically evaluate them in order to determine their effectiveness. It is therefore pertinent to examine the current state of smart justice reforms in Portugal and assess the extent of their usefulness. The most significant reform that Portugal has undertaken is its decriminalization of drug possession for personal use. In 2001, the Portuguese government passed legislation that removed criminal penalties for individuals caught with small amounts of drugs such as marijuana or cocaine. Instead, those found guilty are referred to treatment programs or educational courses designed to help them overcome addiction and lead healthier lives. This policy shift has had a dramatic impact on incarceration rates; since its implementation, there has been a 40% decrease in people sent to prison due solely to drug-related offenses. Figure 6.6 summarizes some of the smart justice reforms in Portugal.

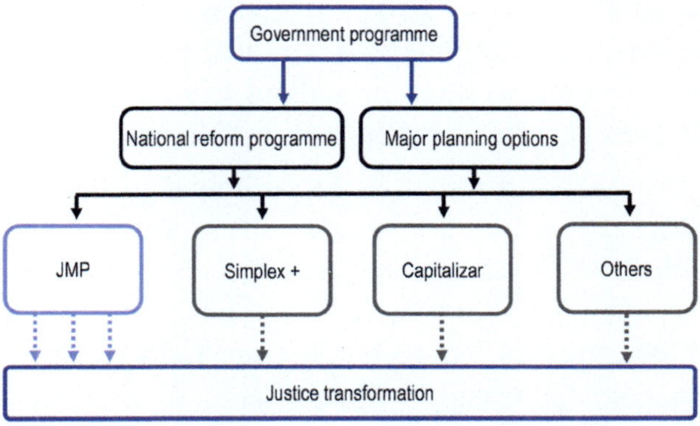

Figure 6.6. Towards smart justice in Portugal.

Source: OECD iLibrary.

Another major reform enacted by Portugal was its introduction of alternative sentencing options such as community service orders and suspended sentences for non-violent offenders who pose no threat to society at large. These measures allow judges greater discretion when deciding how best to punish criminals while also reducing overcrowding within prisons and providing more opportunities for rehabilitation outside of jail time (Beer, 2022; Bennett, 2008, 2009, 2015; Benson & Siddiqui, 2014; Bianchi, 2009; Bond, 2009, 2010). The results have been encouraging; according research conducted by Amnesty International, these alternatives have led "to fewer reoffenders being returned back into custody" which suggests they may be effective deterrents against crime overall.

Finally, Portugal has made efforts towards improving conditions within prisons themselves through initiatives like increased access mental health services and improved education programs aimed at helping inmates gain skills necessary for successful reintegration into society upon release from prison. While these changes are still relatively new, early reports suggest they may be having positive effects on inmate behavior. However, further research is needed before any definitive conclusions can be drawn.

Overall, it appears that smart justice reforms implemented by Portugal over the past two decades have had some success in reducing incarceration rates while also promoting rehabilitation rather than punishment. However, much work remains if these policies are truly going to achieve lasting change. Hence, additional resources must be allocated towards expanding existing programs so that all citizens can benefit from them equally. Moreover, continued monitoring should take place so that any potential issues can be quickly identified and addressed accordingly. With proper oversight, there is hope that smart justice reforms will continue to make progress towards creating a fairer criminal system throughout Europe. All these efforts are consistent with the restorative approach to traditional justice.

Restorative justice is an approach to criminal justice that focuses on repairing the harm caused by crime rather than punishing offenders (Kim, 2020; Kingwill, 2016; Koskenniemi, 1990; Kreso, 2010; Krieger, 2006; Kumar, 2020; Lagji, 2019; Lavalle, 2014; Laylin, 1976). It has been used in various forms for centuries, but its modern incarnation began in the 1970s and has since become increasingly popular as a way of addressing criminal behavior. While restorative justice initiatives have been successful in some cases, it is important to critically assess their applicability and rationale before implementing them more widely.

At its core, restorative justice seeks to repair relationships between victims and offenders through dialog and mediation (Ubink & Weeks, 2017; Ubink, 2008; Utama, 2021; van Caenegem, 2014; van Engelenhoven, 2021; Vanboven, 1991). This can be done through face-to-face meetings or other methods such as letters or phone calls. The goal is not only to address the immediate harm caused by a crime but also to prevent future offenses from occurring by helping both parties understand each other's perspectives and needs better. Restorative justice initiatives are often seen as an alternative to traditional punitive measures such as jail time or fines, which may not always be effective at reducing recidivism rates or rehabilitating offenders into productive members of society.

Nevertheless, there are several potential drawbacks associated with restorative justice initiatives that must be taken into account when assessing their effectiveness (Dahlitz, 1991; Damato, 1973; Damato et al., 1993; Dancer, 2017; Danilenko, 1988; Davis & Klare, 2010; De ruysscher, 2008;

de Vries, 2021). For example, they require significant resources in terms of personnel and funding; this can make them difficult for smaller communities or those with limited budgets to implement successfully. Additionally, these programs rely heavily on voluntary participation from both victims and offenders; if either party does not wish to participate then the process cannot move forward effectively. Finally, there is no guarantee that these programs will actually reduce recidivism rates; while research suggests that they may help improve outcomes for certain types of crimes (such as property offenses), further study is needed before any definitive conclusions can be drawn about their overall efficacy at preventing repeat offending behaviors across all types of crimes committed within a given jurisdiction.

Whereas traditional restorative justice initiatives offer many potential benefits over more punitive approaches towards criminal behavior, it is important for policymakers considering implementing such programs within their jurisdictions to take into account all relevant factors – including cost, availability, and effectiveness – before doing so (Sprankling, 2014; Sun, 2010; Syaufi & Zahra, 2021; Tan, 1993, 2018; Tegnan, 2015; Thipe & Buthelezi, 2014). Ultimately, restorative justice should only be pursued if it offers clear advantages over existing systems; otherwise, it could end up being ineffective at best —or even counterproductive—at worst.

Although traditional cultural judicial processes have some advantages over conventional legal systems, it is important to weigh both sides carefully before deciding which route best suits your needs (Tucker, 1972; Tunkin, 1993; Tupper, 1881; Ubink, 2016; Ubink & Weeks, 2017; Ubink, 2008). In cases where speed, cost effectiveness, and fairness are paramount considerations then this type of proceeding could prove beneficial. However, if absolute impartiality is required then another option might better serve your interests. Ultimately only you can decide which path offers you the most satisfactory outcome given your particular situation. The traditional cultural judicial processes have been in existence for centuries, and they are still used today in many parts of the world. These systems of justice provide an alternative to the formal court system, and can be beneficial in certain circumstances. However, there are also some drawbacks associated with these types of proceedings that should be considered before deciding whether or not to use them. One advantage of traditional cultural judicial processes is that they often involve a more personal approach than what is found in a typical courtroom setting. This means that people involved may feel more comfortable discussing their issues openly and honestly without fear of judgment from outsiders or legal professionals. Additionally, these proceedings tend to focus on restoring harmony between parties rather than simply punishing wrongdoers as would happen in a criminal trial.

Alternatively, there are several potential disadvantages associated with using traditional cultural judicial processes instead of relying on the formal court system (Bond, 2009, 2010; Botha & Bekink, 2018; Bourgon, 2020; Budlender et al., 2011; Buss, 2010; Buxbaum, 1968). For one thing, it can be difficult to ensure fairness when decisions are made by members of the community who may have biases or preconceived notions about how cases should be handled. Furthermore, since these proceedings do not always follow established laws and procedures like those found in courts, it can sometimes lead to outcomes that lack consistency or accuracy compared to what might occur if all parties had access to professional legal representation during their case hearings.

If we accept that traditional cultural judicial processes offer some benefits over conventional court systems such as providing a more personalized approach and focusing on reconciliation rather than punishment; we also have to accept that they also come with certain risks including potential bias among decision makers and lack of adherence to established laws which could lead to inaccurate outcomes for those involved (Enabulele & Bazuaye, 2019; Engel & Kurschilgen, 2013; Farran, 2019; Fenrich et al., 2011; Fleck, 2009, 2013; Fletcher, 2007). Therefore, it is important for individuals considering this type of proceeding to carefully weigh both its merits and demerits before making any final decisions regarding their dispute resolution process. In the next section, we explore the process of legal codification which has often eluded customary law.

6.4. THE PROCESS OF LEGAL CODIFICATION

Codification is the process of organizing laws into a systematic, organized code (Manullang, 2021; Marasinghe, 1978; Masengu, 2016; Mastura, 1994; Maunatlala & Maimela, 2020; Maxim & Titu Maiorescu, 2015). It is an important part of the legal system and helps to ensure that all citizens are aware of their rights and responsibilities under the law. Codification also makes it easier for lawyers, judges, and other legal professionals to interpret and apply laws in a consistent manner.

The codification process begins with identifying existing laws that need to be codified (John-Hopkins, 2010; Johnson, 1986; Joireman, 2008; Jonas & Gunda, 2015; Kadens, 2012; Kammerhofer, 2012). This can include statutes passed by legislatures or court decisions made by judges. Once these sources have been identified, they must be analyzed in order to determine which ones should be included in the code. The analysis typically involves looking at how similar or different each source is from one another as well as considering any potential conflicts between them. Once this analysis has been completed, the next step is drafting a code that incorporates all relevant sources into one comprehensive document (Maxim & Titu Maiorescu, 2015; McAuslan, 2015; McCarthy, 1971; McLachlan, 1988; Menski, 1988; Meron, 1987, 1991). This document will then need to go through several rounds of review before it can become official law. During this review period, experts may suggest changes or additions based on their understanding of current legal trends or developments in related areas of law. After all suggested changes have been considered and incorporated if necessary, the final version will then be presented for approval by legislators or other governing bodies responsible for enacting new laws within their jurisdictions.

Once approved by those responsible for enacting new legislation within their jurisdictions, codified documents become legally binding upon publication either online or in print form depending on local regulations regarding such matters (e-publication vs paper publication) (Woodman, 2001; Worugji et al., 2019; Wu, 2018; Young, 2019; Zamir, 2015; Zarea, 2022; Zenker & Höhne, 2018). In some cases where there are multiple jurisdictions involved (such as when dealing with federal or state issues) additional steps may need to take place before full implementation occurs across all affected areas but generally speaking once published these codes become enforceable throughout whatever area they were intended for application within (i.e., state/federal level). Figure 6.7 outlines an example of a codification process.

Process of Codification

A Law Revision Counsel prepares an initial draft of a bill to restate existing law as a positive law title.

The bill is introduced in the Parliament.

After introduction of the bill, an **extensive review and comment period** ensues. The Law Revision Counsel actively seeks input from Federal agencies, congressional committees, and others with expertise in the area of law being codified.

At the conclusion of the comment period, an amendment in the nature of a substitute – reflecting corrections and comments – is prepared by the Law Revision Counsel and transmitted to the Parliament.

Figure 6.7. The process of legal codification in Switzerland.

Source: Jayson McBride.

Generally, codification plays an essential role in ensuring consistency among various sources of law while also making it easier for lawyers and other legal professionals to interpret them correctly when needed – thus helping protect citizens' rights while simultaneously providing clarity about what actions constitute violations thereof so appropriate action can be taken accordingly if necessary (Tobin, 2014; Tomuschat, 2021; Treasure et al., 2016; Tripp, 2004; Tsai, 2015; Tucker, 1972). Legal codification is a process by which laws are organized, structured, and made accessible to the public.

It is an important part of any legal system as it helps ensure that citizens have access to the law and can understand their rights and obligations under it (Masengu, 2016; Mastura, 1994; Maunatlala & Maimela, 2020; Maxim & Titu Maiorescu, 2015; McAuslan, 2015; McCarthy, 1971). Different countries around the world have different processes for codifying their laws, each with its own advantages and disadvantages. It is worthwhile to evaluate these processes in terms of their relevance to modern society.

The first type of legal codification process is statutory law, which involves creating statutes or acts that set out specific rules or regulations on certain topics (van Engelenhoven, 2021; Vanboven, 1991; Vergouwen, 2013; Vines, 2017; Watson, 1984; Webber, 2009; Weinberg, 2016). This type of codification has been used for centuries in many countries around the world and remains popular today due to its ability to quickly create new laws without having to go through lengthy legislative procedures. However, some critics argue that this method does not provide enough flexibility when dealing with complex issues such as human rights or environmental protection since statutes tend to be rigidly enforced without taking into account changing circumstances or social values over time.

Figure 6.8. Difference between consolidation and codification in legislation.

Source: Carmella Meagan Tate.

One of the critical distinctions that has been explored in existing literature is that which exists between consolidation and codification (Figure 6.8). The legal systems of many countries are based on a combination of common law and statutory law. Common law is the body of laws that have been developed over time through court decisions, while statutory law is created by legislatures or other governing bodies. Consolidation and codification are two processes used to organize these laws into a more manageable form. While both involve organizing existing laws, there are important practical and philosophical differences between them.

Consolidation involves combining multiple statutes into one document in order to make it easier for lawyers, judges, and citizens to access the relevant information quickly (Kadens, 2012; Kammerhofer, 2012; Kane, 1972; Kassoti, 2017; Kelly & Windia, 2019; Kilian, 2019; Kim, 2009, 2020; Kingwill, 2016). This process does not change any of the underlying principles or rules; rather, it simply makes them easier to find and understand. The main advantage of consolidation is that it reduces confusion by making all related statutes available in one place instead of scattered throughout different documents.

Codification takes consolidation a step further by actually changing the language used in existing statutes so as to clarify their meaning or update outdated terminology (Castillo & Bian, 2014; Cataldi & Titu Maiorescu, 2015; Chang, 2022; Chanock, 1989; Cheng, 2012; Chirayath et al., 2005). Codified versions may also include additional provisions that were not present in earlier versions but which reflect current societal values or norms. Unlike consolidation, codification can result in changes to existing laws – though this should be done with caution since such changes could potentially affect people's rights or obligations under those laws.

From a philosophical perspective, consolidation reflects an emphasis on stability while codification reflects an emphasis on progressiveness and adaptability within the legal system (Tripp, 2004; Tsai, 2015; Tucker, 1972; Tunkin, 1993; Tupper, 1881; Ubink, 2016). Consolidation seeks to preserve existing legal principles without making any major changes; its goal is essentially just organization rather than reformulation or modernization of those principles themselves. On the other hand, codification allows for greater flexibility when dealing with new situations because it enables lawmakers to adjust old rules as needed without having to create entirely new ones from scratch each time something arises that was not addressed before or at least not adequately.

Although both processes involve organizing existing laws into more accessible forms they differ significantly when viewed from practical and philosophical perspectives alike: whereas consolidation focuses primarily on ease-of-access without altering underlying principles too much (if at all), codification goes beyond mere organization by allowing for modernizations OR adjustments where necessary so as better address contemporary issues within society today (McCarthy, 1971; McLachlan, 1988; Menski, 1988; Meron, 1987, 1991; Meron et al., 1987; Merry, 1991; Meyer, 2012). As such, understanding these distinctions can help ensure that our legal systems remain up-to-date yet still maintain their core foundations intact.

Another form of legal codification is case law, which relies on judicial decisions from courts rather than legislation passed by legislatures (Cuskelly, 2011; Dahlitz, 1991; Damato, 1973; Damato et al., 1993; Dancer, 2017; Danilenko, 1988; Davis & Klare, 2010; De ruysscher, 2008). This approach allows judges more freedom in interpreting existing laws based on current facts and circumstances while also providing precedent for future cases involving similar issues. The downside of relying solely on case law is that it can lead to inconsistencies between rulings from different courts if they interpret a particular issue differently. However, this risk can be mitigated by establishing clear guidelines for how judges should interpret relevant statutes or precedents when making decisions about a given case. There are also systems where both statutory law and case law are combined together into one unified body of code known as "codified" or "unified" codes (such as those found in civil-law countries) (Cheng, 2012; Chirayath et al., 2005; Claassens & Mnisi, 2009; Cooter, 1991; Corrin & Mulitalo, 2015; Costa, 1998; Craik, 2020). These codes typically contain both general principles derived from court decisions as well as specific rules created through legislation; thus allowing them greater flexibility than either statute-based systems alone or common-law systems relying only on court rulings would allow them individually. Additionally, unified codes often include detailed commentaries written by experts explaining how various provisions should be interpreted – something which may help reduce confusion among members of the public who need access to information about their rights under the code but do not necessarily possess specialized knowledge about legal matters themselves.

All three types of legal codification processes discussed here offer distinct advantages depending upon what kind of situation they're being applied to – though none are perfect solutions unto themselves (Rautenbach, 2020; Rose, 1989; Rubin, 1990; Russo, 1988; Sarbah, 1904; Seidman,

1983; Sheleff, 1994, 2013). Statutory Law provides quick results but lacks flexibility, Case Law offers more nuanced interpretations but risks inconsistency between rulings, while Unified Codes combine elements from both approaches while adding additional commentary designed specifically for lay people. As such, each country must decide what mix best suits its needs before embarking upon any sort of formalized codification process. Ultimately though, no matter what route chosen – ensuring easy accessibility and understanding amongst citizens remains paramount if any legal system hopes remain relevant within our ever-changing societies. The final part of this chapter focuses on medieval custumals as an exemplar of how things change in some respects but remain the same in others.

6.5. THE TRADITION OF MEDIEVAL CUSTUMALS

The medieval period was a time of great change and development in many areas, including the customs and traditions that were observed by people living during this era (Lavalle, 2014; Laylin, 1976; Lewis, 1983, 2016; Liakopoulos, 2019; Lijnzaad, 2022; Lingaas, 2022; Lita et al., 2017; Liu, 2019). Custumals, or customary laws, were an important part of life during the Middle Ages. These laws provided guidance on how to conduct oneself in society and helped to maintain order within communities. Custumals originated from ancient Roman law which was adopted by Germanic tribes as they moved into Europe after the fall of Rome (Buxbaum, 1968; Cannizzaro & Bonafe, 2005; Carrillo-Santarelli, 2017; Castillo & Bian, 2014; Cataldi & Titu Maiorescu, 2015; Chang, 2022). Over time these laws evolved to become more specific to each region or country as local customs developed over centuries. In England for example, custumal law became known as 'common law' due to its widespread use throughout the kingdom. In addition to providing guidance on social behavior, custumal law also regulated economic activities such as trade and commerce between different regions or countries. This allowed merchants from different parts of Europe to do business with one another without fear of being cheated or taken advantage of due to unfamiliarity with local customs and regulations. Figure 6.9 is a satirical representation of the custumal.

Custumal law also played an important role in resolving disputes between individuals or groups who could not agree on a particular issue themselves (Wu, 2018; Young, 2019; Zamir, 2015; Zarea, 2022; Zenker & Höhne, 2018; Zerner, 1994; Zilberman, 1996). Disputes would be brought before a court where judges would decide based upon what was considered fair according to custom rather than relying solely upon written statutes which may have been outdated at the time when judgment needed to be made quickly in order for justice to prevail swiftly.

Figure 6.9. Satirical illustration of medieval custumals.

Source: History Today.

The importance placed upon custumal law began declining towards the end of the Middle Ages however it still remains influential today in some parts of Europe where traditional practices are still observed even if they no longer hold legal authority over modern day citizens (Armstrong, 1989; Arowolo, 2019; Asieduakrofi, 1989; Barnabas, 2022; Barrie, 2016; Baxi, 2020; Beavers, 2019; Beer, 2022; Bennett, 2008). It is clear that while much has changed since then, certain aspects remain unchanged – namely our need for rules, regulations, and guidelines that help us live together peacefully. The relationship between medieval custumals and customary law is an important one that has been studied for centuries. Custumals are documents from the Middle Ages that contain information about local customs, laws, and regulations. Customary law is a body of unwritten rules based on tradition or custom which have been accepted as legal principles by society over time.

In many cases, these two sources of law were closely intertwined in the Middle Ages (Allott, 1984; Anderson, 2003; Angelini, 2012; Armstrong, 1989; Arowolo, 2019; Asieduakrofi, 1989; Barnabas, 2022; Barrie, 2016). Medieval custumals often contained detailed descriptions of local customs and laws that had developed over time through common practice. This was especially true in rural areas where there was no formal written code of laws to follow. In such cases, people relied heavily on their own traditions and customs to govern their behavior and resolve disputes among themselves.

At the same time, some custumals also included references to more formalized systems of justice such as those found in royal charters or other official documents issued by kings or lords (Ndulo, 2011; Ngira, 2018, 2021; Nhlapo, 2017; Nnona, 2018; Norr, 1973; Nwapi, 2016; Nyane, 2019). These references could provide additional guidance when it came to interpreting local customs or resolving disputes between parties who did not agree with each other's interpretation of a particular custom or rule. Today, scholars continue to study both medieval custumals and customary law in order to gain insight into how societies functioned during this period in history as well as how they evolved over time into modern-day legal systems we know today. By examining these two sources together, researchers can better understand how different cultures interacted with each other during this era and what role traditional practices played in shaping our current understanding of justice around the world today.

It is clear that there is a strong connection between medieval custumals and customary law which continues to be explored even today by historians seeking greater insight into our past legal systems and cultural norms throughout history up until now (Hutchison, 2020; Hutchison & Sibanda, 2017; Iyi, 2016; Jentoft & Bavinck, 2019; John-Hopkins, 2010; Johnson, 1986; Joireman, 2008). The Middle Ages were a period of great change and development in Europe, with many customs and traditions being established that would shape the societies of today. One such tradition is the medieval custumal, which was an important source of law during this time. While these laws may seem outdated to modern eyes, they still have relevance to our current society.

A custumal was a collection of customary laws that governed everyday life in medieval times (Vergouwen, 2013; Vines, 2017; Watson, 1984; Webber, 2009; Weinberg, 2016; Williams & Klusener, 2013; Williams, 2022). These laws covered everything from marriage and inheritance rights to land ownership and taxation. They were based on local custom rather than written statutes or royal decrees, making them unique to each region or town. Custumals also provided guidance for resolving disputes between individuals or groups without resorting to violence or other forms of coercion. Though these laws are no longer enforced today, they still provide valuable insight into how people lived during the Middle Ages and can help us understand why certain aspects of our society are structured as they are now (Bennett, 2009; Benson & Siddiqui, 2014; Bianchi, 2009; Bond, 2009, 2010; Botha & Bekink, 2018; Bourgon, 2020; Budlender et al., 2011). For example, some elements of English common law can be traced back to medieval custumals. Likewise, many European countries' property rights systems owe their origins to these ancient documents. Furthermore, studying custumals can give us an understanding of how different cultures interacted with one another at this time – something which is particularly relevant given the increasing globalization we see today.

Figure 6.10. Illustration of a barbaric medieval justice system.

Source: Brewminate.

Although some of the custumal processes seem strange and inappropriate today, there is still research interest into the rich cultural heritage that they represent (Lewis, 1983, 2016; Liakopoulos, 2019; Lijnzaad, 2022; Lingaas, 2022; Lita et al., 2017; Liu, 2019). In addition to providing historical context for modern legal systems, studying medieval custumals can also offer useful lessons about conflict resolution techniques that could be applied in contemporary settings too – such as arbitration instead of litigation when settling disputes between parties involved in business transactions or international relations negotiations. This knowledge could prove invaluable for those seeking peaceful solutions in difficult situations where traditional methods have failed before now.

Overall, it is clear that while much has changed since the days when Medieval Custumals were first created, there is still much we can learn from them (Henry, 2017; Hernández, 2012; Holleman, 1969, 1972; Horii, 2019; Howell, 2018; Hu, 2017; Huizenga, 2018). By examining these ancient documents, we gain a better understanding not only about our past but also about how best to approach conflicts both within our own societies and beyond them. In doing so, we ensure that history does not repeat itself but instead serves as a guide towards creating more harmonious futures for all.

CHAPTER 6 SUMMARY

This chapter has explored the various ways in which customary law is embedded into structures that are already existing. Starting with a discussion about a repertoire of norms, this chapter included brief outlines of the principles underpinning rule skepticism in law as well as the incorporation of traditional cultural judicial processes. We critically reviewed the legal codification process and highlighted some of the contradictions in a case study of medieval custumals. The penultimate chapter in this book will consider the fundamentals necessary to understand and integrate customary law.

CHAPTER 7

Fundamentals to be addressed in Customary Law

Contents

The seventh chapter in this book highlights some fundamentals to be addressed in our understanding and integration of customary law. Hence, the chapter will explore the meaning of peremptory norms and their application to areas such as crimes against humanity. We will explore how customary law can explain the laws against genocide as well as the enduring gender inequalities that exist in most societies. Other potentially problematic areas in which customary law may intervene include xenophobia, bigotry, and racism. Peremptory norms form an important background to these discussions.

7.1. WHAT ARE PEREMPTORY NORMS?

Peremptory norms are a set of rules that govern international law (van Caenegem, 2014; van Engelenhoven, 2021; Vanboven, 1991; Vergouwen, 2013; Vines, 2017; Watson, 1984). They are also known as jus cogens, which is Latin for "compelling law." These norms have been established by the international community and they cannot be changed or modified by any state or individual. The purpose of peremptory norms is to protect fundamental human rights and ensure that all states abide by certain standards of behavior in their dealings with one another. This includes prohibiting genocide, slavery, torture, racial discrimination, and other forms of inhuman treatment. It also prohibits the use of force against another state without justification and requires states to settle disputes peacefully through negotiation or arbitration rather than resorting to war.

In addition to protecting basic human rights, peremptory norms also serve as a check on the power of governments over their citizens (Akande, 2004; Albakjaji, 2022; Allott, 1957, 1984; Anderson, 2003; Angelini, 2012; Armstrong, 1989; Arowolo, 2019). For example, they prohibit arbitrary arrest and detention without due process; guarantee freedom from cruel punishment; require fair trials; protect property rights; provide access to education; promote gender equality; and more generally uphold the rule of law within each country's borders. Peremptory norms are binding on all countries regardless of whether they have ratified them or not because these rules reflect universal values shared by all nations around the world. As such, any violation can be challenged before an international court or tribunal if necessary in order to seek justice for those affected by it.

It could be argued that peremptory norms play an important role in ensuring that everyone enjoys basic human rights no matter where they live in the world while at the same time providing a framework for peaceful relations between states so that conflicts can be resolved without resorting to violence or war whenever possible (Dancer, 2017; Danilenko, 1988; Davis & Klare, 2010; De ruysscher, 2008; de Vries, 2021; De Wet, 2004; Debelva & De Broe, 2022). Peremptory norms are a set of rules that have been established to govern the behavior of individuals in certain situations. These norms are often used as a way to ensure that people act in accordance with accepted social standards and expectations. While peremptory norms can be beneficial, they can also be problematic if not applied correctly or if they become too restrictive. In this section, we will discuss the creation and application of peremptory norms and how they should be evaluated for their effectiveness. Figure 7.1 summarizes the notion of jus cogens, a key element of peremptory norms.

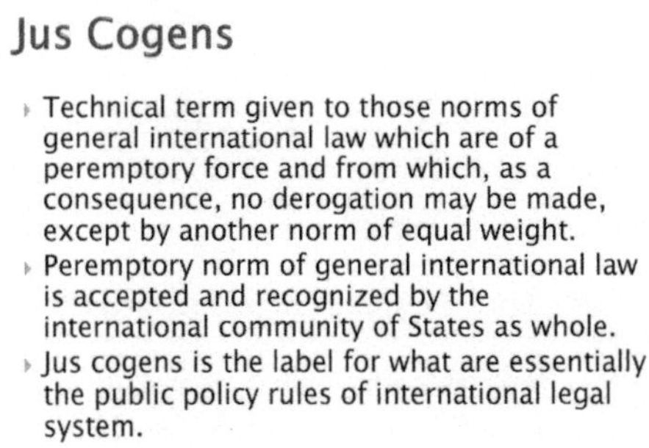

Figure 7.1. The notion of jus cogens.

Source: Susanti Hardja.

The first step in creating effective peremptory norms is determining what behaviors need to be regulated (Buss, 2010; Buxbaum, 1968; Cannizzaro & Bonafe, 2005; Carrillo-Santarelli, 2017; Castillo & Bian, 2014; Cataldi & Titu Maiorescu, 2015). This requires an understanding of the context in which these rules will apply, as well as an assessment of what types of behaviors would benefit from regulation. Once these factors have been identified, it is important to consider how best to enforce them so that everyone involved understands their purpose and follows them accordingly.

Once created, it is essential for those responsible for enforcing peremptory norms to do so consistently and fairly across all members of society who may come into contact with them (Frulli, 2015; Gadzo, 2018; Gagnon-Bergeron, 2018; Gal-Or, 2015; Galindo & Yip, 2017; Gao, 2013; Gillespie & Tran, 2022; Golo et al., 2022). This means ensuring that any punishments or consequences associated with breaking these rules are applied equally regardless of gender, race, religion or other characteristics unrelated to the violation itself. Additionally, those responsible for enforcing such regulations must remain open-minded when assessing potential violations; while some infractions may seem minor on the surface level but could still warrant serious repercussions depending on the circumstances surrounding them.

Finally, it is important for those responsible for evaluating peremptory norms to periodically assess whether or not they are achieving their intended goals effectively enough without becoming overly restrictive or oppressive towards certain groups within society at large (Diala & Bagni, 2019; Dubner, 1994; Dubois, 1992; Dupont, 2013; Duxbury, 2017; Edmundson, 2015; Elias, 1956; Enabulele & Bazuaye, 2019). If changes need to be made then this should occur through a process involving input from both experts knowledgeable about relevant laws/regulations as well as representatives from affected communities who can provide insight into how different regulations might impact their lives directly. In Figure 7.1.62 we see how jus cogens is applied to the USA context.

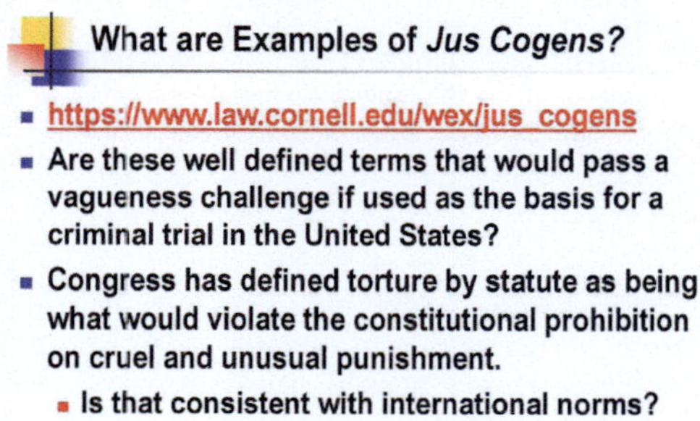

Figure 7.2. Examples of criterion for defining jus cogens in the USA.

Source: Samantha McCoy.

Creating and applying effective peremptory norms requires careful consideration, thoughtful evaluation, and ongoing monitoring (Sun, 2010; Syaufi & Zahra, 2021; Tan, 1993, 2018; Tegnan, 2015; Thipe & Buthelezi, 2014; Thirlway, 2015). By taking all necessary steps during each stage, we can ensure that our efforts result in positive outcomes rather than furthering existing inequalities within our societies. In recent years, the concept of peremptory norms has been widely discussed in legal circles. Peremptory norms are a set of principles that have been established by international law and which all countries must adhere to. These norms are considered to be fundamental rights and obligations that cannot be violated or disregarded by any nation. This raises the question: do these peremptory norms still have relevance in today's modern legal systems?

The answer is yes, they do. Although many aspects of international law have changed over time, the core principles behind peremptory norms remain relevant today (Golo et al., 2022; Gradoni, 2019; Graves, 2017; Gray, 2021; Griffiths, 1998; Hager, 2020; Haggenmacher, 2021; Hammond, 2019). For example, one such norm is jus cogens – a Latin term meaning "compelling law" – which states that certain rules of international law are so fundamental that no country can ignore them or override them with their own laws. This principle remains as important now as it did when it was first established centuries ago.

Another example is the prohibition on genocide, which has become an increasingly important part of international human rights law since its adoption in 1948 following World War II (Huizenga, 2018, 2022; Hulme, 2010; Hutchison, 2020; Hutchison & Sibanda, 2017; Iyi, 2016; Jentoft & Bavinck, 2019). The prohibition against genocide serves as an essential reminder to nations around the world about their responsibility to protect vulnerable populations from mass atrocities and other forms of violence and discrimination based on race, religion or ethnicity. Finally, there is also the principle known as non-interventionism – another key element of contemporary international relations theory – which holds that each state should respect the sovereignty and territorial integrity of other states without interference from outside forces or actors. This norm helps ensure peace between nations by preventing one state from interfering in another's internal affairs for political gain or economic advantage.

In general, some aspects of international law may have evolved over time due to changing geopolitical realities and technological advances (Poespasari, 2020; Polanski, 2017; Pratiwi et al., 2020; Qerimi, 2020; Quane, 2013; Rautenbach, 2020; Rose, 1989; Rubin, 1990). However, many core principles embodied within peremptory norms remain just as relevant today as they were when they were first established centuries ago. Indeed, these principles continue to serve an essential role in protecting human rights around the world and promoting peaceful coexistence among nations large and small alike. As such, it is clear that these timeless standards still hold great importance for contemporary legal systems worldwide. The next section considers customary law perspectives on crimes against humanity.

7.2. CUSTOMARY LAW PERSPECTIVES ON CRIMES AGAINST HUMANITY

Crimes against humanity are some of the most heinous acts that can be committed, and they have been recognized as such for centuries (Griffiths, 1998; Hager, 2020; Haggenmacher, 2021; Hammond, 2019; Harmathy, 2016; Henry, 2017; Hernández, 2012). In recent years, there has been an increased focus on international criminal law to address these crimes. However, customary law perspectives on crimes against humanity remain largely unexplored. Customary law is a form of unwritten legal tradition based on long-standing practices in a particular society or culture. It is often used to supplement written laws when those laws do not provide sufficient guidance or protection for certain issues. Customary law may also be used to fill gaps in existing legislation or even replace it altogether if it is deemed outdated or inadequate by the community at large.

When it comes to crimes against humanity, customary law provides important insights into how societies view and respond to these offenses (Ubink, 2016; Ubink & Weeks, 2017; Ubink, 2008; Utama, 2021; van Caenegem, 2014; van Engelenhoven, 2021). For example, many cultures have traditionally viewed torture as abhorrent and unacceptable behavior regardless of whether it was codified in any written laws at the time. This perspective has been reflected in various forms throughout history including religious texts and folk tales which condemn torture as immoral and unjustifiable under any circumstances.

In addition, customary law can help inform our understanding of what constitutes a crime against humanity today by providing insight into how different societies perceive such offenses historically and culturally speaking (Kammerhofer, 2012; Kane, 1972; Kassoti, 2017; Kelly & Windia, 2019; Kilian, 2019; Kim, 2009, 2020; Kingwill, 2016; Koskenniemi, 1990). For instance, while genocide may now be widely accepted as one of the worst possible atrocities imaginable due to its widespread recognition through international criminal tribunals like The Hague's International Criminal Court (ICC), this was not always so clear cut from a traditional standpoint; some cultures had their own definitions for what constituted genocide prior to modern times which could differ significantly from current interpretations depending on context and circumstance. A case in point is the tenets of GC12.

The Global Challenge 12 (GC12) is an international initiative that seeks to prevent crimes against humanity. It was launched in 2018 by the United Nations Office on Drugs and Crime (UNODC), with the aim of strengthening global efforts to combat impunity for such crimes. The GC12 focuses on four key areas: prevention, prosecution, protection, and reparation. Prevention is a key component of GC12's strategy, as it seeks to reduce the risk of future atrocities through education and awareness-raising campaigns. This includes initiatives such as training law enforcement personnel in human rights standards; providing legal advice to victims; and developing public information materials about international criminal justice mechanisms. In addition, GC12 has established a network of experts who can provide technical assistance when needed. In terms of prosecution, GC12 aims to strengthen national judicial systems so they are better equipped to investigate and prosecute cases involving crimes against humanity. This includes supporting countries in their efforts to ratify relevant treaties or conventions related to these issues; providing capacity building support for prosecutors; and encouraging states parties to cooperate with each other in bringing perpetrators of such crimes before justice systems at all levels – from local courts up through international tribunals like the ICC.

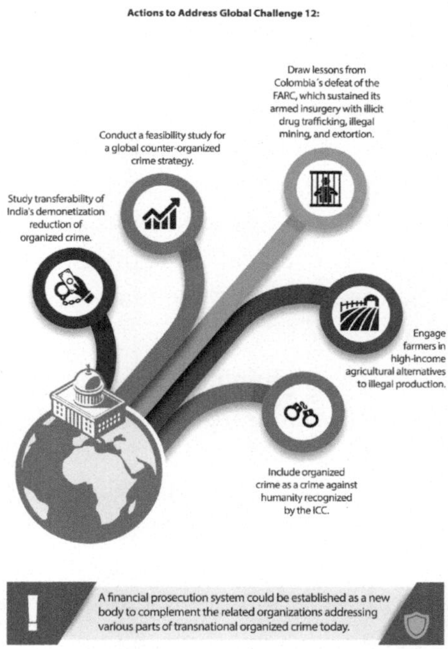

Figure 7.3. Crimes against humanity were part of global challenge 12.

Source: The millennium project.

Protection is another important element within GC12's framework (Figure 7.3), as it seeks to ensure that victims have access to appropriate services throughout their recovery process. This includes measures such as establishing safe havens for survivors; providing medical care; offering psychological counseling services; creating economic opportunities for those affected by violence or displacement due war or conflict situations; and ensuring access rights are respected during investigations into alleged violations of human rights laws or humanitarian law principles.

Finally, reparation forms part of this initiative too – aiming not only at restoring dignity but also promoting reconciliation between communities affected by atrocity crimes committed against them. Reparations may include financial compensation for damages suffered due war or conflict situations but also symbolic acts like apologies from governments involved in perpetrating these acts or memorialization ceremonies honoring victims' memory among others things. While there have been some successes since its launch two years ago – including increased cooperation between state parties regarding prosecutions – much more needs to be done if we want real progress towards preventing further atrocities from occurring around the world (Watson, 1984; Webber, 2009; Weinberg, 2016; Williams & Klusener, 2013; Williams, 2022; Willms, 2009; Wilson, 1961). For instance, greater investment should be made into research projects aimed at understanding why certain individuals commit these types of heinous acts; stronger partnerships need be forged between civil society organizations working on similar issues; and more resources must be allocated towards implementing effective strategies designed specifically to address root causes underlying mass violence. Only then will we truly see tangible results stemming from this ambitious endeavor.

The case study above has highlighted some of the principles that were once attributed to custumals (Cannizzaro & Bonafe, 2005; Carrillo-Santarelli, 2017; Castillo & Bian, 2014; Cataldi & Titu Maiorescu, 2015). Ultimately, examining customary law perspectives on crimes against humanity can provide valuable insight into how different societies view these offenses both historically and currently – something that should not be overlooked when considering ways to prevent future atrocities from occurring around the world today. By taking into account cultural norms alongside more formalized approaches, we can gain greater clarity about what constitutes an atrocity according to global standards while still respecting local customs where appropriate.

The prosecution of crimes against humanity under international law is a complex and challenging process (Duxbury, 2017; Edmundson, 2015; Elias, 1956; Enabulele & Bazuaye, 2019; Engel & Kurschilgen, 2013; Farran, 2019; Fenrich et al., 2011). It requires an understanding of the legal framework, as well as the ability to recognize and address any potential biases that may arise during the course of proceedings. It is pertinent to explore some of the common biases that can occur when prosecuting crimes against humanity under international law.

One bias that often arises in these cases is a tendency to focus on certain types of victims over others (Utama, 2021; van Caenegem, 2014; van Engelenhoven, 2021; Vanboven, 1991; Vergouwen, 2013; Vines, 2017). For example, there may be an inclination to prioritize prosecutions for those who have suffered physical or sexual violence over those who have experienced psychological trauma or economic deprivation due to their victimization. Additionally, there may be a preference for prosecuting perpetrators from certain countries or regions rather than others, which could lead to unequal treatment among victims based on their nationality or ethnicity.

Another bias that can arise in these cases is related to gender dynamics (Seidman, 1983; Sheleff, 1994, 2013; Shingleton, 1983; Sibisi, 2020; Siegel, 2015; Sierra, 1995; Singer, 1972). In many instances, women are more likely than men to experience violations such as rape and other forms of sexual violence during conflicts; however, they are also less likely to receive justice due to cultural norms and stereotypes about gender roles within society. Furthermore, female survivors may face additional barriers when seeking redress through legal channels due to lack of access resources or fear of reprisal from perpetrators if they come forward with allegations.

Finally, it is important for prosecutors handling cases involving crimes against humanity under international law to not only consider issues related directly with the case at hand but also take into account broader systemic factors such as poverty and inequality which can contribute towards perpetuating cycles of violence in affected communities around the world (Baxi, 2020; Beavers, 2019; Beer, 2022; Bennett, 2008, 2009, 2015; Benson & Siddiqui, 2014; Bianchi, 2009). By recognizing how these underlying conditions shape people's experiences with conflict-related abuses and taking steps towards addressing them accordingly throughout proceedings can help ensure greater accountability for all involved parties while promoting long-term peacebuilding efforts in affected areas going forward. This is pertinent at a time when there is a democratic decline (Figure 7.4).

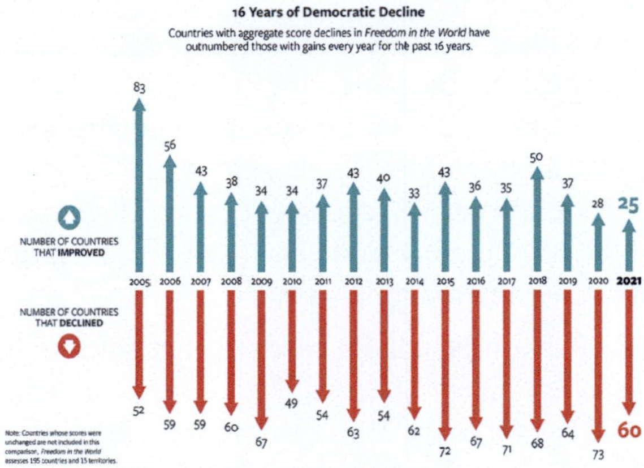

Figure 7.4. Global expansion of authoritarianism.

Source: Freedom House.

In conclusion, it is essential for prosecutors working on cases involving crimes against humanity under international law to remain aware of potential biases so they can effectively identify them before proceeding further with investigations (Laylin, 1976; Lewis, 1983, 2016; Liakopoulos, 2019; Lijnzaad, 2022; Lingaas, 2022; Lita et al., 2017; Liu, 2019; Loja, 2014). Doing so will help ensure fair outcomes by ensuring equal treatment among all victims regardless their background, gender identity, etc., while helping promote lasting peacebuilding initiatives worldwide. The next section is a study of the role of customary law when preventing and prosecuting genocide.

7.3. A CASE STUDY OF GENOCIDE AND CUSTOMARY LAW

Genocide is a term used to describe the intentional destruction of an entire people or nation (Thipe & Buthelezi, 2014; Thirlway, 1972, 2015, 2017; Tobin, 2014; Tomuschat, 2021; Treasure et al., 2016). It is considered one of the most heinous crimes against humanity and has been recognized as such by international law since 1948. The United Nations Convention on the Prevention and Punishment of Genocide defines genocide as "any act committed with intent to destroy, in whole or in part, a national, ethnic, racial or religious group." Figure 7.5 is a comparative analysis of the potential hot spots for genocide.

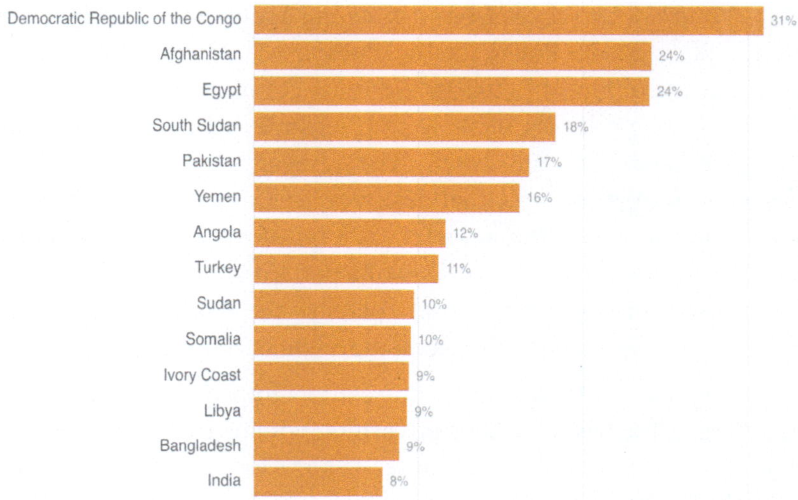

Figure 7.5. Possibility of predicting genocide hotspots across the globe.

Source: Colorado Public Radio.

The term was first coined by Raphael Lemkin in 1944 when he wrote Axis Rule in Occupied Europe: Laws of Occupation – Analysis of Government – Proposals for Redress. In his book he described how Nazi Germany had systematically destroyed Jewish communities throughout Europe during World War II. He argued that this systematic destruction constituted genocide and should be recognized as such under international law. Since then, there have been numerous instances where genocide has occurred around the world including Cambodia (1975–1979), Rwanda (1994) and Darfur (2003-present). These acts are often perpetrated by governments but can also be carried out by non-state actors such as rebel groups or militias.

Genocide is not only limited to physical violence; it can also include psychological tactics like forced displacement, cultural assimilation, and economic deprivation which all contribute to destroying a particular group's identity and way of life (Magnusson, 2017; Manaka & Corrin, 2021; Manullang, 2021; Marasinghe, 1978; Masengu, 2016; Mastura, 1994; Maunatlala & Maimela, 2020). This makes it difficult for survivors to rebuild their lives after experiencing such atrocities because they no longer have access to their traditional resources or support networks within their community.

It is important that we recognize genocide for what it truly is – an abhorrent crime against humanity – so that we can take steps towards preventing future occurrences from happening again anywhere in the world (Petersen, 2007, 2017; Pocar, 2016; Poespasari, 2020; Polanski, 2017; Pratiwi et al., 2020; Qerimi, 2020). We must continue working together at both local and global levels if we want to ensure that these horrific events never happen again on our watch. The relevance of customary law to genocide is an important topic that deserves attention. Customary law, also known as traditional or indigenous law, is a set of rules and regulations that are based on the customs and practices of a particular community or society. It has been used for centuries in many parts of the world to regulate social behavior and resolve disputes between individuals or groups.

Customary law can be seen as having a direct impact on genocide because it often serves as the basis for laws governing how people interact with each other within their communities (Moore, 1986; Morrison, 2016; Morudu & Maimela, 2021; Murphy, 2014; Mwalimu, 1988; Mwambene, 2012). In some cases, these laws may even provide justification for acts of violence against certain groups deemed "undesirable" by those in power. This type of legal framework can create an environment where discrimination and hatred towards certain populations become normalized, leading to increased tensions between different ethnicities or religions which can eventually lead to mass atrocities such as genocide.

In addition, customary law can also play an indirect role in facilitating genocide by providing legal cover for oppressive regimes who use it to justify their actions against minority populations (Robert W Tucker, 1972; Tunkin, 1993; Tupper, 1881; Ubink, 2016; Ubink & Weeks, 2017; Ubink, 2008; Utama, 2021). For example, during the Rwandan Genocide in 1994, Hutu extremists used existing customary laws regarding land ownership rights to target Tutsi civilians who were perceived as encroaching upon Hutu-controlled territory. By using this type of legal framework they were able to legitimize their actions while avoiding international condemnation from human rights organizations like Amnesty International and Human Rights Watch.

Finally, customary law can also be used after a conflict has ended in order to help rebuild societies affected by genocide through reconciliation processes such as truth commissions and reparations programs aimed at restoring justice and healing wounds caused by past atrocities committed against vulnerable populations (Kane, 1972; Kassoti, 2017; Kelly & Windia, 2019; Kilian, 2019; Kim, 2009, 2020; Kingwill, 2016; Koskenniemi, 1990; Kreso, 2010). These efforts rely heavily on local knowledge about traditional customs which helps ensure that any new policies implemented are culturally appropriate and accepted by all members of society regardless of ethnicity or religion affiliation. Unfortunately, genocide is a historical crime that is deeply embedded in human conditions (Figure 7.6).

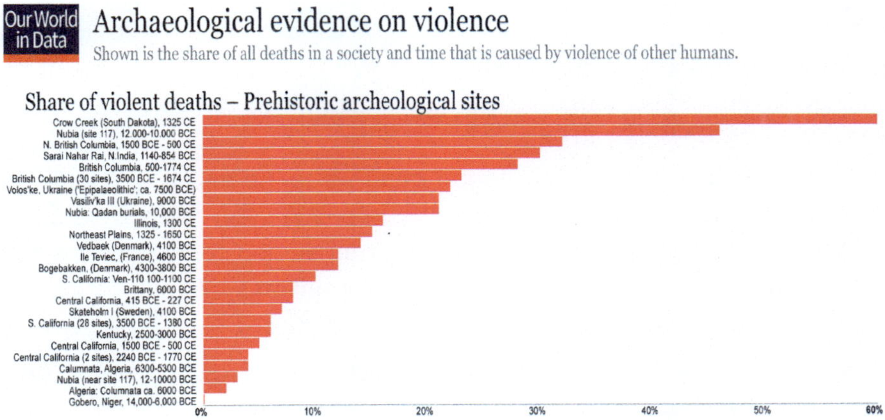

Figure 7.6. Archeological evidence of historical community and societal violence.

Source: Our world in data.

Overall, it is clear that customary law plays an important role when it comes to understanding how genocides occur both directly through its potential influence over discriminatory behaviors within communities but also indirectly through its ability to provide legal cover for oppressive regimes seeking legitimacy for their actions abroad (Botha & Bekink, 2018; Bourgon, 2020; Budlender et al., 2011; Buss, 2010; Buxbaum, 1968; Cannizzaro & Bonafe, 2005; Carrillo-Santarelli, 2017). As such, it should not be overlooked when discussing ways we might prevent future genocides from occurring around the world. Genocide is one of the most heinous crimes that can be committed against humanity. It involves the intentional destruction of a group based on their ethnicity, race, religion or other characteristics. As such, it is important to ensure that those responsible for committing genocide are held accountable and prosecuted accordingly. However, there are certain limitations when prosecuting genocide under customary law.

Customary law refers to laws which have been established through long-standing practice rather than by written legislation or judicial decisions

(Pedersen, 2014; Pelizzon, 2015; Perreau-Saussine & Murphy, 2007; Petersen, 2007, 2017). In some cases, this type of law may be used in order to prosecute individuals who have committed acts of genocide. However, there are several drawbacks associated with using customary law in these situations.

One limitation is that customary law does not always provide clear definitions for what constitutes an act of genocide and how it should be punished (Rubin, 1990; Russo, 1988; Sarbah, 1904; Seidman, 1983; Sheleff, 1994, 2013; Shingleton, 1983; Sibisi, 2020). This makes it difficult to determine whether a particular action qualifies as an act of genocide and if so, what kind of punishment should be imposed upon the perpetrator(s). Additionally, since customary laws vary from region to region and even within countries themselves, they may not always provide consistent standards for prosecution across different jurisdictions.

Another limitation is that many countries lack adequate legal systems which would allow them to effectively enforce customary laws related to prosecuting acts of genocide (Woodman, 1988, 1969, 2001; Worugji et al., 2019; Wu, 2018; Young, 2019; Zamir, 2015; Zarea, 2022). Without proper enforcement mechanisms in place, perpetrators may go unpunished despite having committed serious crimes against humanity due to a lack of resources or political will on behalf of governments or international organizations tasked with enforcing justice in these cases. While some countries do have well-established legal systems capable of enforcing customary laws related to prosecuting acts of genocide (such as Rwanda), others still rely heavily on traditional methods such as tribal councils or village elders who may not necessarily adhere strictly enough to international standards when determining guilt and sentencing perpetrators appropriately according their actions' severity. In conclusion, while customary law can play an important role in bringing perpetrators of genocide to justice, it has its own set of limitations which must be taken into account when considering how best to prosecute those responsible for committing these horrific crimes against humanity (Webber, 2009; Weinberg, 2016; Williams & Klusener, 2013; Williams, 2022; Willms, 2009; Wilson, 1961; Wolff, 2016). It is therefore important that governments and international organizations work together to develop stronger legal mechanisms which can effectively enforce customary laws and ensure that the perpetrators are held accountable for their actions accordingly. The next section analyzes how customary law addresses issues of gender equality.

7.4. GENDER EQUALITY AND CUSTOMARY LAW

Gender inequality is a term used to describe the unequal treatment of individuals based on their gender (Polanski, 2017; Pratiwi et al., 2020; Qerimi, 2020; Quane, 2013; Rautenbach, 2020; Rose, 1989; Rubin, 1990; Russo, 1988). It can manifest itself in many different ways, from unequal access to education and employment opportunities, to discrimination in the workplace or even violence against women. Gender inequality has been an issue for centuries, but it remains a major problem today.

The United Nations defines gender equality as "the equal rights, responsibilities and opportunities of women and men and girls and boys." This means that everyone should have the same access to resources such as education, healthcare services, economic opportunities, and political participation regardless of their gender identity or expression (Cooter, 1991; Corrin & Mulitalo, 2015; Costa, 1998; Craik, 2020; Crawford, 2012; Criddle, 2013; Cuskelly, 2011; Dahlitz, 1991). Unfortunately, this is not always the case in many parts of the world where there are still significant disparities between genders when it comes to these areas.

In some countries around the world, women are denied basic human rights such as freedom of movement or choice over marriage partners due to cultural norms that favor male dominance over female autonomy (Beavers, 2019; Beer, 2022; Bennett, 2008, 2009, 2015; Benson & Siddiqui, 2014; Bianchi, 2009; Bond, 2009). In other places like India or Pakistan for example, girls may be prevented from attending school because they are seen as less valuable than boys who will eventually become breadwinners for their families while girls will only marry into another family at best. Gender inequality also exists within certain professions where women often face pay gaps compared with men doing similar jobs despite having comparable qualifications and experience levels; this is known as occupational segregation which occurs when people are assigned roles based on traditional ideas about what constitutes appropriate work for each sex rather than individual merit alone.

Additionally, sexual harassment continues to be a pervasive problem across all industries with victims facing stigma if they speak out against perpetrators due to fear of retribution or lack of support from employers who may prioritize protecting reputations over justice for those affected by abuse at work environments. This is part of wider inequalities (Figure 7.7 for an example of this phenomenon in land and housing). This is a systemic issue that ought to be tackled holistically including when customary law is utilized as an intervention (Thirlway, 1972; Tobin, 2014; Tomuschat, 2021; Treasure et al., 2016; Tripp, 2004; Tsai, 2015; Tucker, 1972).

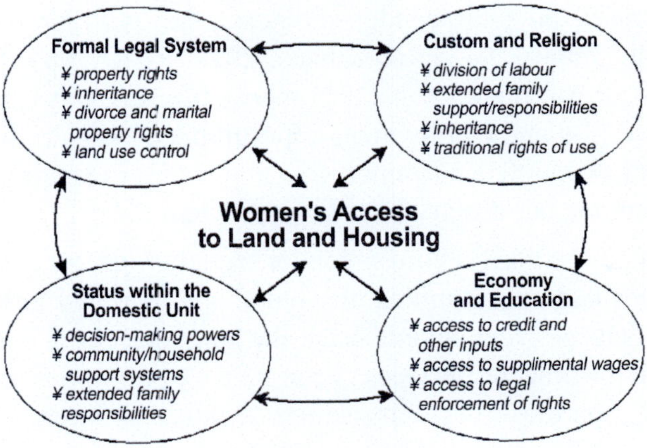

Figure 7.7. Gendered housing to land and housing under customary law.

Source: Food and Agriculture Organization of the United Nations.

It is clear that much more needs to be done in order for us achieve true gender equality worldwide – governments must take action by introducing laws that protect vulnerable populations from discrimination while also providing adequate resources so that everyone can benefit equally from society's offerings regardless of their sex or gender identity/expression (Anderson, 2003; Angelini, 2012; Armstrong, 1989; Arowolo, 2019; Asieduakrofi, 1989; Barnabas, 2022; Barrie, 2016; Baxi, 2020). We must continue advocating for change until we reach a point where no one feels disadvantaged simply because they were born into a particular group.

In many societies around the world, customary laws are still used as a form of governance for family matters such as marriage, divorce, inheritance rights and other issues related to women's rights (Iyi, 2016; Jentoft & Bavinck, 2019; John-Hopkins, 2010; Johnson, 1986; Joireman, 2008; Jonas & Gunda, 2015; Kadens, 2012). In some countries where these laws exist they may not be legally binding but they still have an impact on how people live their lives. For example, in some parts of Africa women may not have access to education or employment opportunities due to traditional beliefs about gender roles which are enforced through customary law.

Customary laws can also limit women's ability to own property or make decisions regarding their own bodies such as whether or not they should get married at a certain age or if they should bear children at all (Damato et al.,

1993; Dancer, 2017; Danilenko, 1988; Davis & Klare, 2010; De ruysscher, 2008; de Vries, 2021; De Wet, 2004). These restrictions prevent them from having control over their own lives and limit their economic opportunities which further contributes to gender inequality within those communities.

Furthermore, customary laws often prioritize men when it comes to inheritance rights which means that even if a woman has worked hard her entire life she will likely receive less than her male counterparts upon death due to traditional beliefs about who deserves what share of an estate after someone passes away (Morrison, 2016; Morudu & Maimela, 2021; Murphy, 2014; Mwalimu, 1988; Mwambene, 2012; Mwangi, 2022). This perpetuates existing power imbalances between genders by ensuring that men remain in positions of authority while women remain subordinate regardless of any progress made towards equality elsewhere in society. Overall, it is clear that while there are benefits associated with using customary law for governing social relationships within certain communities it can also lead to significant levels of gender inequality depending on its implementation and enforcement within those societies.

Therefore, it is important for governments and civil society organizations alike work together towards creating more equitable legal systems so that everyone has equal access justice regardless of their sex or background (Koskenniemi, 1990; Kreso, 2010; Krieger, 2006; Kumar, 2020; Lagji, 2019; Lavalle, 2014; Laylin, 1976). Customary law is an important part of many societies, providing a framework for social and economic relationships. However, it has often been criticized for its lack of gender sensitivity. This can lead to women being disadvantaged in terms of access to resources, rights, and opportunities. In order to ensure that customary law is more equitable and just, there are several steps that can be taken towards reform. These discussions are pertinent in an age when violence against women is rife (Figure 7.8).

First and foremost, it is essential that the voices of women are heard when discussing changes to customary law (Angelini, 2012; Armstrong, 1989; Arowolo, 2019; Asieduakrofi, 1989; Barnabas, 2022; Barrie, 2016; Baxi, 2020; Beavers, 2019). Women should be consulted on how they would like the laws to be reformed so as to better reflect their needs and interests. This could involve creating forums or other spaces where women can discuss their experiences with existing laws and suggest ways in which they could be improved upon.

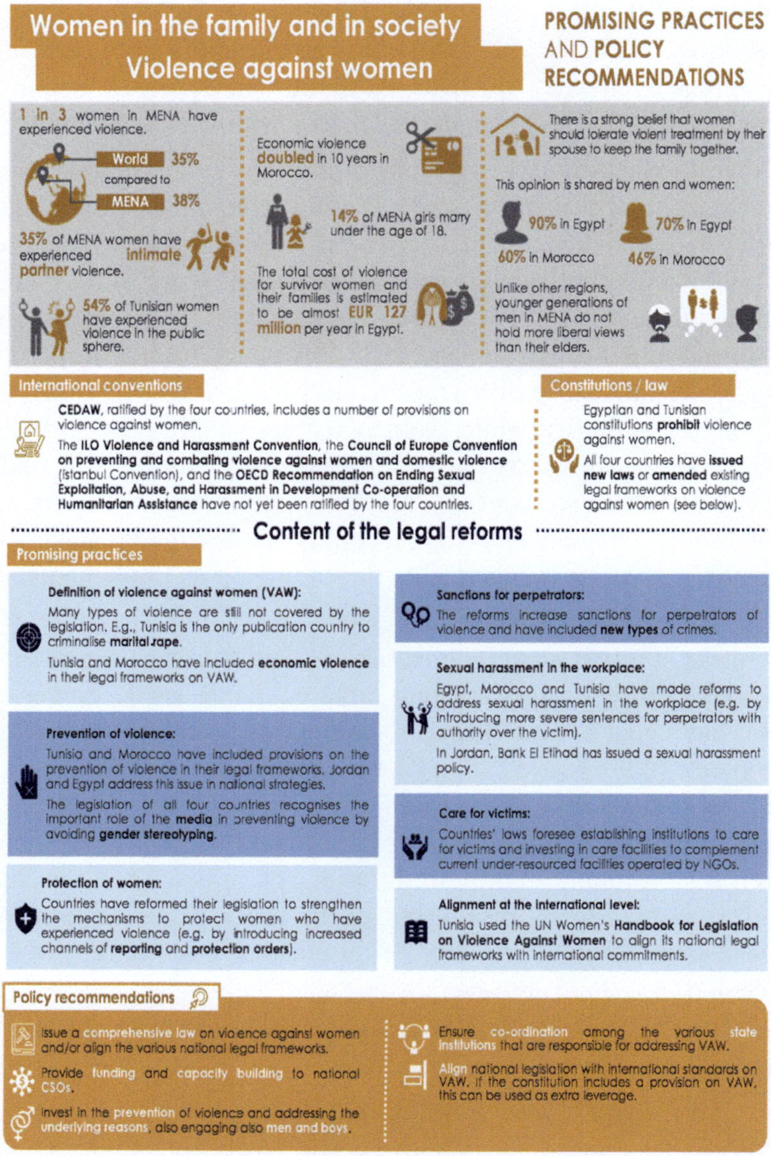

Figure 7.8. Violence against women in society.

Source: OECD iLibrary.

In addition, governments should take steps towards ensuring that customary laws are gender-sensitive by introducing legislation which explicitly prohibits discrimination against women based on their sex or gender identity (Mwalimu, 1988; Mwambene, 2012; Mwangi, 2022; Ndulo, 2011;

Ngira, 2018, 2021; Nhlapo, 2017; Nnona, 2018). Such legislation should also provide clear guidance on what constitutes discriminatory practices under the law so as to ensure compliance with international standards such as those set out in CEDAW (the Convention on the Elimination of All Forms of Discrimination Against Women). Finally, education initiatives must also play a role in reforming customary law so that it is more gender sensitive.

These initiatives should focus not only on raising awareness about existing legal frameworks but also encouraging dialog between men and women about how these frameworks might need changing in order for them to become fairer for all genders involved (Pocar, 2016; Poespasari, 2020; Polanski, 2017; Pratiwi et al., 2020; Qerimi, 2020; Quane, 2013; Rautenbach, 2020). Education programs could include workshops or seminars aimed at teaching people about different aspects of customary law from a gender perspective as well as providing practical advice on how individuals can challenge any discriminatory practices they may encounter within their communities or workplaces. By taking these measures into account we can begin working towards making sure that our legal systems are fair and just for everyone regardless of sex or gender identity – something which will ultimately benefit all humanity. This chapter will close by considering the role of customary law when dealing with the enduring challenges of xenophobia, bigotry, and racism.

7.5. RACISM, BIGOTRY, AND XENOPHOBIA IN CUSTOMARY LAW

The concept of customary law has been around for centuries, and it is still a major part of many societies today (Asieduakrofi, 1989; Barnabas, 2022; Barrie, 2016; Baxi, 2020; Beavers, 2019; Beer, 2022; Bennett, 2008, 2009, 2015). Unfortunately, this traditional form of justice often contains elements of bigotry which are deeply rooted in outdated beliefs about gender roles, race, religion, sexuality and more. This type of discrimination can manifest itself in various ways such as unequal access to resources or services; exclusion from certain activities; or even physical violence against those who do not conform to the accepted norms within a given society.

It is important to recognize that these forms of prejudice exist within customary law systems so that we can work towards eliminating them from our communities (Obatusin, 2018; Olaf & Markus, 2018; Omidire, 1990; Orebech et al., 2005; Osman, 2019; Osman & Baase, 2022). We must strive to create an inclusive legal system where everyone's rights are respected regardless of their background or identity. This means challenging any laws which discriminate against individuals based on factors such as gender, race, religion or sexual orientation – something which should never be tolerated under any circumstances. At the same time, we must also acknowledge the importance of preserving cultural heritage while ensuring equal protection under the law for all citizens regardless of their background or identity. To achieve this balance between tradition and progressiveness requires careful consideration by lawmakers when crafting legislation related to customary law systems across different countries and regions worldwide.

Generally, it is essential that we recognize bigotry in customary law systems so that we can take steps towards creating an equitable legal framework for all members within our societies – one which respects diversity while upholding fundamental human rights at its core values (Ubink & Weeks, 2017; Ubink, 2008; Utama, 2021; van Caenegem, 2014; van Engelenhoven, 2021). Only then will true justice prevail globally. Racism is a pervasive issue in many societies, and customary law is no exception. Unfortunately, racism has been embedded into some of these traditional practices for centuries. Recording events and complaints (Figure 7.9 for an example of complaints statistics in Portugal).

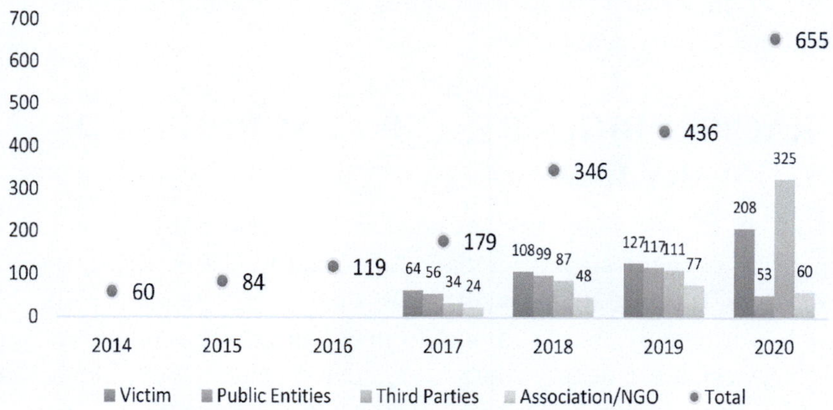

Figure 7.9. Evolution of participation, complaints or denunciations received by the CICDR in Portugal 2014–2020.

Source: Inês Casquilho-Martins, et al., (2022).

Customary law often dictates how people interact with each other within their communities. This includes rules about marriage, inheritance rights, land ownership and more. In some cases, these laws have been used as tools of oppression against certain racial or ethnic groups by denying them access to resources or opportunities available to others in the same society (Rautenbach, 2020; Rose, 1989; Rubin, 1990; Russo, 1988; Sarbah, 1904; Seidman, 1983; Sheleff, 1994). For example, in South Africa during apartheid (1948–1994), black citizens were denied basic human rights such as freedom of movement due to discriminatory customary laws that favored white citizens over black ones.

In addition to this institutionalized racism found in customary law systems around the world today, there are also subtle forms of discrimination present in everyday interactions between members of different races or ethnicities within a given community (Bennett, 2008, 2009, 2015; Benson & Siddiqui, 2014; Bianchi, 2009; Bond, 2009, 2010; Botha & Bekink, 2018). These can include language barriers or cultural misunderstandings that lead to unequal treatment based on race or ethnicity rather than merit alone. It is important for us all to be aware of how racism manifests itself through our legal systems so we can work together towards eliminating it from our societies altogether.

We must recognize when customs are being used as tools for oppression and take steps towards creating an equitable system where everyone has equal access regardless of race or ethnicity (Ngira, 2021; Nhlapo, 2017; Nnona, 2018; Norr, 1973; Nwapi, 2016; Nyane, 2019; O'Neill, 2002; Oba, 2002). By doing so we will create a better future for generations yet unborn who should not have to suffer under oppressive regimes like those seen throughout history due to racist customs still present today in many parts of the world. Xenophobia is a fear or hatred of people from other countries, and it has been an issue in many societies for centuries. In some cases, this fear manifests itself in the form of customary law – laws that are based on traditional beliefs and practices rather than formal legislation. This type of xenophobic behavior can have serious consequences for those who are targeted by it.

Customary law is often used to regulate social interactions between members of different ethnic groups or nationalities. It may be used to restrict access to certain resources, such as land or water rights, or even limit marriage opportunities between individuals from different backgrounds. In some cases, these laws may also be used to discriminate against immigrants and refugees who seek asylum in a new country (Meron, 1987, 1991; Meron et al., 1987; Merry, 1991; Meyer, 2012; Milanovic, 2011; Mnisi & Claassens, 2009).

The effects of xenophobia expressed through customary law can be devastating for those affected by it (Chanock, 1989; Cheng, 2012; Chirayath et al., 2005; Claassens & Mnisi, 2009; Cooter, 1991; Corrin & Mulitalo, 2015; Costa, 1998). For example, if someone is denied access to resources due to their nationality or ethnicity, they may not have the means necessary to survive in their new environment. Additionally, discriminatory marriage laws can lead to isolation and alienation within communities where inter-ethnic marriages are prohibited.

It is important that we recognize the dangers posed by xenophobia expressed through customary law and take steps towards eliminating it wherever possible (Graves, 2017; Gray, 2021; Griffiths, 1998; Hager, 2020; Haggenmacher, 2021; Hammond, 2019; Harmathy, 2016). We must ensure that all individuals regardless of their background have equal access to resources and opportunities so that everyone can live with dignity and respect no matter where they come from or what language they speak. Furthermore, we should strive towards creating more inclusive environments where diversity is celebrated instead of feared so that everyone feels welcome regardless of their origin story or cultural identity. In Figure 7.10, we see how racism can penetrate something as universal as healthcare.

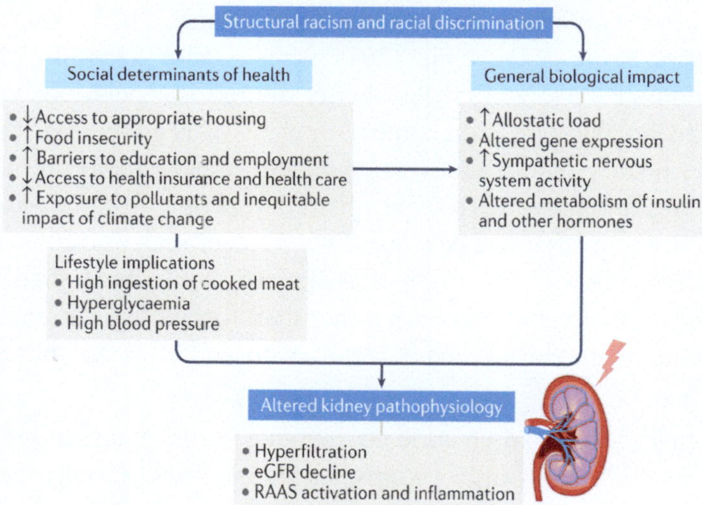

Figure 7.10. Health inequities and the inappropriate use of race in nephrology.

Source: Nature Reviews Nephrology.

By taking action against xenophobia expressed through customary law we will create a more equitable society where everyone's rights are respected regardless of race, religion, gender, sexual orientation, etc. (Dekoster, 2019; Demian, 2014; Diala, 2017, 2019; Diala & Bagni, 2019; Dubner, 1994). Only then will we truly achieve true equality among all people.

CHAPTER 7 SUMMARY

This penultimate chapter of the book has addressed the fundamentals of customary law which predetermine the possibility of integrating it into any existing legal framework. We considered the role and limitations of peremptory norms. This led to discussions about how customary law can help to conceptualize legal notions such as crimes against humanity, genocide, equality, and bigotry. The final chapter will look ahead at the prospects of customary law.

CHAPTER 8

Prospects of Customary Law in Community Life

Contents

As we close this book, we will outline the prospects of customary law in community life. For instance, the chapter will discuss how customary law can contribute to civil law and legal pluralism. We will also critique the limitations and possibilities of canonical jurisprudence in a modern context. The chapter will show how we can learn from English Common Law as well as oral law traditions. Let us open the final chapter in the book by looking for links between civil and customary law.

8.1. INCORPORATING CUSTOMARY LAWS INTO CIVIL LAW

The legal system of any country is a complex and intricate web of laws, regulations, and customs (Bond, 2010; Botha & Bekink, 2018; Bourgon, 2020; Budlender et al., 2011; Buss, 2010; Buxbaum, 1968; Cannizzaro & Bonafe, 2005). In many countries around the world, customary law has been an integral part of civil law for centuries. In recent years, there has been an increased focus on incorporating customary laws into civil law systems (Figure 8.1) in order to better reflect the needs and interests of local populations. This approach recognizes that different cultures may have different ways of resolving conflicts or addressing certain issues, which should be taken into account when crafting legislation or adjudicating cases. By recognizing these differences, it allows for more equitable outcomes while also respecting cultural norms and traditions.

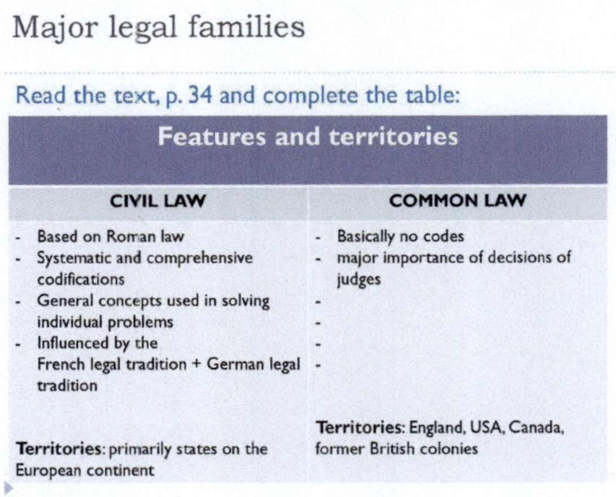

Features and territories	
CIVIL LAW	COMMON LAW
- Based on Roman law - Systematic and comprehensive codifications - General concepts used in solving individual problems - Influenced by the French legal tradition + German legal tradition Territories: primarily states on the European continent	- Basically no codes - major importance of decisions of judges - - - - Territories: England, USA, Canada, former British colonies

Figure 8.1. The major legal families of the world.

Source: Yuliani Pranata.

There are several benefits to incorporating customary laws into civil law systems:

- It provides greater access to justice for marginalized communities who may not otherwise have access due to language barriers or lack of resources;
- It helps ensure that decisions are made with respect for local culture;
- It encourages dialog between different stakeholders by providing a platform where they can discuss their respective views;
- And it promotes social cohesion by allowing people from diverse backgrounds to come together under one set of rules that everyone understands and respects.

However, there are some challenges associated with this approach as well:

Customary laws vary widely across regions so it can be difficult to create uniform standards;

- Some customs may conflict with existing civil laws so finding a balance between them can be tricky;
- And enforcing compliance with customary laws can prove challenging if they are not properly codified in national legislation.

Despite these challenges, incorporating customary laws into civil law systems is essential if we want our legal frameworks to remain relevant in today's increasingly globalized world. By taking this approach we will ensure fairer outcomes while also preserving cultural diversity within our societies – something which should always be encouraged rather than discouraged (de Vries, 2021; De Wet, 2004; Debelva & De Broe, 2022; Dekoster, 2019; Demian, 2014; Anthony C Diala, 2017). In many countries, customary laws are an integral part of the legal system. These laws have been passed down through generations and often reflect the values and beliefs of a particular culture or community. However, when it comes to incorporating these laws into civil law, there can be some challenges that must be addressed.

One challenge is ensuring that all parties involved in a dispute understand the applicable customary law (Ubink, 2008; Utama, 2021; van Caenegem, 2014; van Engelenhoven, 2021; Vanboven, 1991; Vergouwen, 2013). This can be difficult because customary laws vary from one region to another and may not always be written down or easily accessible. Additionally, if there is no clear consensus on how certain aspects of the law should be interpreted, this could lead to confusion among those who are unfamiliar with them. Another challenge is making sure that any changes made to incorporate customary laws do not conflict with existing civil law regulations or international human rights standards. It is important for governments to ensure that any new legislation does not violate fundamental rights such as freedom of expression or religious liberty while still respecting traditional customs and practices within their jurisdiction.

It is essential for governments to provide adequate resources for implementing any changes they make in order to ensure compliance with both local and international standards (Liu, 2019; Loja, 2014; Lon & Widyawati, 2021; Magnusson, 2013, 2017; Manaka & Corrin, 2021; Manullang, 2021). This includes providing training for judges so they can properly interpret applicable customary laws as well as funding programs designed to educate citizens about their rights under these systems of justice. In Figure 8.2, we see that there are commonalities and divergences between civil and common law.

Characteristic	Civil Law	Common Law
Independence of Judiciary from State	State controlled	Independent
Professional Status of Judge	Professional judges	Lay judges
Use of Juries	Less frequent	Frequent
Role of Judge in Trial Process	Inquisitorial	Adverserial
Legal Instruction	Legal codes	Broad legal principles
Precendent	Less important	Important
Appeal / re-litigation	Less important	Important
Certainty of Law?	Legal standards	Rules

Figure 8.2. Juxtaposing civil and common law traditions.

Source: Cassey Lee (2005).

Incorporating customary laws into civil law presents numerous challenges but also offers great potential benefits by allowing communities access to justice systems more closely aligned with their cultural values and traditions than what might otherwise exist under state-enforced legal codes alone (Tupper, 1881; Ubink, 2016; Ubink & Weeks, 2017; Ubink, 2008; Utama, 2021; van Caenegem, 2014; van Engelenhoven, 2021). By addressing each of these issues carefully, governments can create effective solutions which respect both local customs and universal human rights principles alike. The relationship between customary laws and civil law is complex, with both systems having their own distinct advantages and disadvantages. Customary laws are based on the customs of a particular community or group, while civil law is based on written statutes enacted by governments. In many countries, these two legal systems exist side-by-side but often conflict with each other. This can lead to confusion for those who must abide by both sets of rules.

In order to ensure that both customary laws and civil law complement each other rather than clash, it is important to understand how they interact in different contexts (Maiorescu, 2015; McAuslan, 2015; McCarthy, 1971; McLachlan, 1988; Menski, 1988; Meron, 1987, 1991). One way this can be done is through harmonization – the process of bringing together different legal systems so that they work together more effectively. Harmonization involves finding common ground between the two systems and creating a unified approach which takes into account the needs of all parties involved.

One example of harmonizing customary laws and civil law could involve recognizing certain aspects of traditional practices as legally binding within a given jurisdiction (Haggenmacher, 2021; Hammond, 2019; Harmathy, 2016; Henry, 2017; Hernández, 2012; Holleman, 1969, 1972; Horii, 2019). For instance, some communities may have long-standing traditions regarding land ownership or marriage rights which could be recognized under local legislation if appropriate safeguards were put in place to protect vulnerable individuals from exploitation or abuse. Similarly, certain cultural norms such as dispute resolution processes could be incorporated into existing court procedures where appropriate so that people have access to justice without having to resort solely to formal legal proceedings.

Harmonizing customary laws and civil law also requires an understanding of how these two systems interact at an international level – particularly when it comes to issues such as human rights protection or environmental conservation efforts which cross borders or affect multiple jurisdictions simultaneously (Sierra, 1995; Singer, 1972; Skomerska-Muchowska, 2017; Snyder, 1984; Sprankling, 2014; Sun, 2010; Syaufi & Zahra, 2021). Here too there may be opportunities for collaboration between states in order to create mutually beneficial solutions which take into account local customs while still adhering to global standards set out by international organizations like the United Nations (UN). Ultimately, harmonizing customary laws and civil law requires careful consideration from all sides in order for it to succeed. However, if done correctly it has great potential for improving access justice across societies while respecting cultural diversity at the same time. By taking steps towards greater harmony between these two legal frameworks we can ensure that everyone's rights are respected regardless of their background or beliefs. In the next section, we consider the notion of legal pluralism.

8.2. EMBEDDING THE NOTION OF LEGAL PLURALISM

Legal pluralism is a concept that refers to the presence of multiple legal systems within one geographic area (Mnisi & Claassens, 2009; Moore, 1986; Morrison, 2016; Morudu & Maimela, 2021; Murphy, 2014; Mwalimu, 1988). It is an important concept in law, as it allows for different laws and regulations to coexist in the same space. This can be seen in countries with federal systems of government, where each state or province has its own set of laws and regulations. The concept of legal pluralism also applies to societies with diverse cultural backgrounds, such as those found in many parts of Africa and Asia. In these societies, there may be several distinct legal systems operating at once – including customary law (based on traditional customs), religious law (based on religious beliefs) and statutory law (enacted by governments). All three types of laws are recognized by the courts and have equal standing under the rule of law.

Legal pluralism can lead to conflicts between different sets of laws when they come into contact with each other (Meron et al., 1987; Merry, 1991; Meyer, 2012; Milanovic, 2011; Mnisi & Claassens, 2009; Moore, 1986; Morrison, 2016). For example, if two people from different cultures enter into a contract governed by their respective customary laws but then find themselves subject to a court ruling based on statutory law, this could create confusion about which set of rules should apply. To address this issue, some countries have adopted hybrid approaches that combine elements from both customary and statutory laws so that all parties involved understand what is expected from them legally speaking.

In addition to providing greater flexibility for individuals living within multicultural societies, legal pluralism also helps promote social cohesion by allowing people from different backgrounds to interact more easily without fear or prejudice towards one another's culture or beliefs (Kim, 2009, 2020; Kingwill, 2016; Koskenniemi, 1990; Kreso, 2010; Krieger, 2006; Kumar, 2020; Lagji, 2019; Lavalle, 2014). By recognizing multiple sources of authority within one jurisdiction – rather than relying solely on a single source – it encourages mutual respect among citizens regardless of their background or origin while still ensuring justice is served fairly across all communities involved. Figure 8.3 summarizes the state of global legal pluralism.

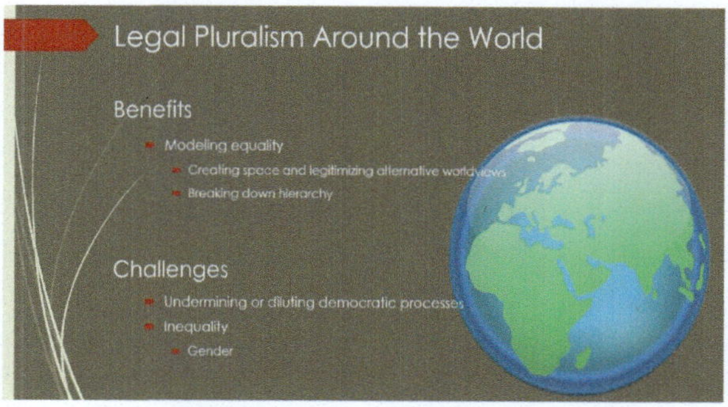

Figure 8.3. Legal pluralism across the globe.

Source: Brandi Bowers via YouTube.

Overall, understanding how legal pluralism works can help us better appreciate our differences while still finding common ground through shared values like fairness and equality before the law no matter who we are or where we come from (Orebech et al., 2005; Osman, 2019; Osman & Baase, 2022; Osman & Himonga, 2017; Ottley, 2016; Parisi, 2001). Legal pluralism is a concept that recognizes the existence of multiple legal systems within one jurisdiction.

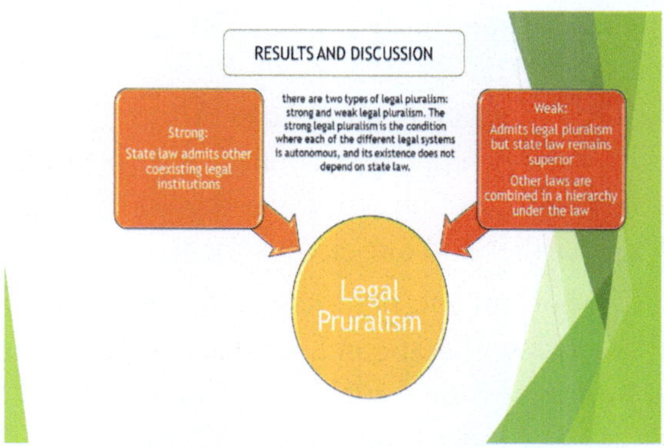

Figure 8.4. Assessing the extent of legal pluralism in jurisdictions.

Source: Suci Flambonita via YouTube.

This means that different laws may be applicable to different people, depending on their cultural or religious backgrounds. Customary law is an important part of this system, as it provides a way for individuals and communities to access justice in accordance with their own values and beliefs. Figure 8.4 shows that legal pluralism across the globe still ranges from strong to weak.

Customary law has been used throughout history by many indigenous peoples around the world as a form of dispute resolution, often in lieu of state-sanctioned courts, or other formal legal systems (Nnona, 2018; Norr, 1973; Nwapi, 2016; Nyane, 2019; O'Neill, 2002; Oba, 2002, 2008, 2011; Obatusin, 2018). In recent years, customary law has become increasingly recognized by governments as an alternative source of justice for certain groups who may not have access to more mainstream forms of dispute resolution due to language barriers or lack of resources. The role that customary law plays in legal pluralism is twofold: firstly, it allows individuals from diverse backgrounds to access justice according to their own values; secondly, it helps ensure that all members within society are treated fairly under the rule of law regardless of their background or culture. By recognizing customary laws alongside those imposed by states, governments can provide greater protection for minority groups while also promoting social cohesion between different communities living side-by-side within one jurisdiction.

In addition to providing an alternative source of justice for marginalized populations, customary laws can also help protect traditional knowledge and practices which might otherwise be lost over time due to globalization and modernization processes taking place across the globe today (Chang, 2022; Chanock, 1989; Cheng, 2012; Chirayath et al., 2005; Claassens & Mnisi, 2009; Cooter, 1991). By preserving these ancient customs through recognition in modern legal systems we can ensure they remain alive into future generations so they continue contributing positively towards our collective understanding about how best we should live together peacefully in harmony with each other and our environment.

Customary law plays an essential role in ensuring fairness amongst all members within society while at same time protecting valuable traditions from being forgotten over time – making its inclusion into any discussion about legal pluralism pertinent (Huizenga, 2022; Hulme, 2010; Hutchison, 2020; Hutchison & Sibanda, 2017; Iyi, 2016; Jentoft & Bavinck, 2019). Legal pluralism is a concept that has been gaining traction in recent years, as it offers an alternative to the traditional legal system. It refers to the idea that multiple legal systems can exist within one jurisdiction, and each of these systems may have different rules and regulations. This allows for greater flexibility when dealing with complex issues such as family law or international trade disputes. However, there are both limitations and possibilities associated with this approach.

One limitation of legal pluralism is that it can be difficult to reconcile conflicting laws between two or more jurisdictions (Manaka & Corrin, 2021; Manullang, 2021; Marasinghe, 1978; Masengu, 2016; Mastura, 1994; Maunatlala & Maimela, 2020). For example, if two countries have different laws regarding intellectual property rights, then resolving any disputes between them could prove challenging without some form of arbitration or mediation process in place. Additionally, since each jurisdiction may have its own set of rules and regulations governing certain areas of law, it can be difficult for individuals to understand their rights under all applicable laws at once. Yet, there are also many potential benefits associated with legal pluralism (Norr, 1973; Nwapi, 2016; Nyane, 2019; O'Neill, 2002; Oba, 2002, 2008, 2011; Obatusin, 2018). By allowing multiple legal systems to coexist within one jurisdiction, individuals may be able to access justice more easily than they would otherwise be able to do so through a single unified system. Furthermore, by providing people with access to multiple sources of law they may find solutions which better suit their needs than those provided by a single source alone – something which could potentially lead to improved outcomes overall for society. While there are certainly some limitations associated with legal pluralism in modern jurisdictions – particularly when it comes reconciling conflicts between different sets of laws – there are also numerous potential benefits which should not be overlooked either; from increased access to justice for individuals right through improved outcomes for society (de Vries, 2021; De Wet, 2004; Debelva & De Broe, 2022; Dekoster, 2019; Demian, 2014; Diala, 2017). As such then it seems clear that further exploration into this area is warranted in order gain an even better understanding about how best we might make use of this concept in the future. The various forms of traditional jurisprudence that are referenced in literature have been critiqued from time to time. One of the objects of that criticism is canonical law.

8.3. CRITIQUE OF CANONICAL JURISPRUDENCE

Canonical jurisprudence is a branch of law that deals with the interpretation and application of religious laws (Hulme, 2010; Hutchison, 2020; Hutchison

& Sibanda, 2017; Iyi, 2016; Jentoft & Bavinck, 2019; John-Hopkins, 2010; Johnson, 1986). It is based on the teachings of religious texts, such as the Bible or Quran, and seeks to provide guidance for how these laws should be applied in modern society. Canonical jurisprudence has been used throughout history to resolve disputes between individuals or groups who have different interpretations of religious law.

The primary purpose of canonical jurisprudence is to ensure that all parties involved in a dispute are treated fairly and equitably according to their respective beliefs (Gao, 2013; Gillespie & Tran, 2022; Golo et al., 2022; Gradoni, 2019; Graves, 2017; Gray, 2021; Griffiths, 1998; Hager, 2020). This means that each party must be given an opportunity to present their case before a neutral third-party arbitrator who will then make a decision based on what they believe is just and fair under the circumstances. The arbitrator may also consider other factors such as public policy when making their decision.

In addition to resolving disputes, canonical jurisprudence can also help guide people's behavior by providing them with clear guidelines about what actions are acceptable within certain contexts (Criddle, 2013; Cuskelly, 2011; Dahlitz, 1991; Damato, 1973; Damato et al., 1993; Dancer, 2017; Danilenko, 1988; Davis & Klare, 2010). For example, some religions prohibit certain types of activities such as gambling or drinking alcohol while others allow it under certain conditions. By understanding these rules, individuals can better understand how they should act to remain faithful followers of their religion without breaking any laws or offending anyone else's beliefs.

Canonical jurisprudence has been used for centuries around the world and continues to play an important role today in many countries where there are multiple religions practiced side by side peacefully coexisting together despite having different views on various issues related to faith and morality (McLachlan, 1988; Menski, 1988; Meron, 1987, 1991; Meron et al., 1987; Merry, 1991; Meyer, 2012; Milanovic, 2011). While this type of legal system does not always provide perfect solutions for every situation, it does offer an effective way for people from different backgrounds and belief systems come together in order find common ground through mutual respect and understanding rather than conflict or violence which often results from misunderstanding one another's beliefs or traditions.

It could be argued that canonical jurisprudence provides an important framework for resolving conflicts between individuals who have differing interpretations regarding religious law while still allowing everyone involved maintain their own personal convictions without infringing upon those held by others around them (Corrin & Mulitalo, 2015; Costa, 1998; Craik, 2020; Crawford, 2012; Criddle, 2013; Cuskelly, 2011; Dahlitz, 1991). If all parties involved approach this process with open minds, fairness, and respect, canonical jurisprudential principles can help create peaceful resolutions even among those who disagree on matters related faith. It is tempting to dismiss canonical law as a relic of the past which has little relevance in a modern context that is imbued with egalitarianism as a founding principle. Nevertheless, as Figure 8.5 shows, canonical law is one of the branches of modern legal systems.

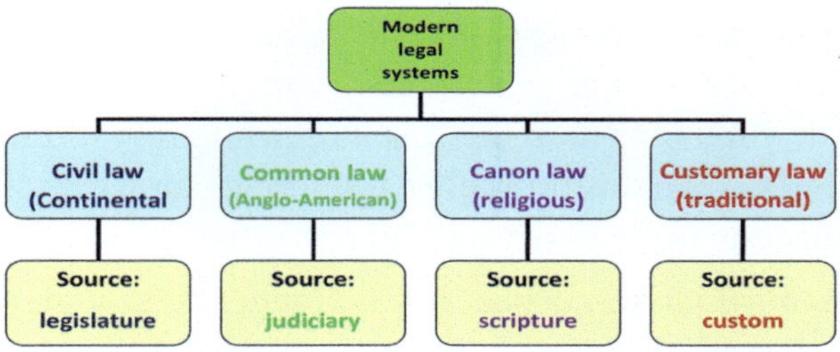

Figure 8.5. Different legal systems in the world today.

Source: Quizlet.

Canonical jurisprudence is a branch of law that has been around for centuries and is likely to exist with religious communities (Adebola, 2021; Akande, 2004; Albakjaji, 2022; Allott, 1957, 1984; Anderson, 2003; Angelini, 2012; Armstrong, 1989). It is based on the teachings of the Catholic Church and its interpretation of scripture, which was used to create laws and regulations in many countries during the Middle Ages. Today, however, it is not as widely practiced or accepted as other forms of legal systems. So, what relevance does canonical jurisprudence have today?

The answer lies in understanding how this form of law works and why it was so important historically (O'Neill, 2002; Oba, 2002, 2008, 2011; Obatusin, 2018; Olaf & Markus, 2018; Omidire, 1990). Canonical jurisprudence relies heavily on religious principles such as natural law theory, which states that certain moral truths are universal and can be derived from nature itself. This means that all people should abide by these laws regardless of their faith or beliefs. Additionally, this type of law also emphasizes justice over punishment; rather than punishing someone for breaking a rule, they would instead be encouraged to make amends with those affected by their actions through restitution or reparation payments. Despite its historical importance, there are some who argue that canonical jurisprudence has become outdated due to modern advances in technology and society's changing values and attitudes towards religion-based laws (Lita et al., 2017; Liu, 2019; Loja, 2014; Lon & Widyawati, 2021; Magnusson, 2013, 2017; Manaka & Corrin, 2021). However, there are still aspects of this system that remain relevant today – particularly when it comes to matters involving morality or ethics within business practices or international relations between countries with different religions or cultures. For example, many companies now use ethical codes based on natural law theory when making decisions about how they will conduct themselves to ensure fairness among employees and customers alike. Similarly, governments may look at canon law when negotiating treaties between nations since it provides an objective framework for resolving disputes without resorting to violence or coercion tactics often seen in more traditional forms of diplomacy like warring factions do during times conflict resolution efforts fail.

While canonical jurisprudence may no longer be as widely practiced as before due to changes in society's values over time, there are still elements from this system which remain relevant today – especially when dealing with issues related morality, ethics, business practices, AND international relations (Oba, 2008; Oba, 2011; Obatusin, 2018; Olaf & Markus, 2018; Omidire, 1990; Orebech et al., 2005; Osman, 2019). Therefore, we can say that although much less prominent than before, canonical jurisprudence still plays an important role our lives even if only indirectly. In recent years, there have been increasing calls for canonical jurisprudence to be integrated into modern judicial systems. It is worthwhile to explore how this could be achieved.

The first step towards integrating canonical jurisprudence into modern judicial systems would be to recognize its validity as a source of law (Allott, 1957, 1984; Anderson, 2003; Angelini, 2012; Armstrong, 1989; Arowolo, 2019; Asieduakrofi, 1989; Barnabas, 2022). Canonical jurisprudence should not simply be viewed as an outdated relic from the past; rather, it should be seen as a valid source of law with its own set of principles and values that are still relevant today. Once this recognition has taken place, then steps can begin to integrate canonical jurisprudence into existing legal frameworks.

One way in which this could happen is with specialized courts or tribunals that focus solely on cases involving questions related to canonical law (Henry, 2017; Hernández, 2012; Holleman, 1969, 1972; Horii, 2019;

Howell, 2018; Hu, 2017; Huizenga, 2018). These courts or tribunals would need to employ experts who understand both traditional canon law and contemporary legal principles to ensure fair outcomes for all parties involved in any given case. Additionally, these courts or tribunals could also provide guidance on how best to apply traditional canon law within the context of current laws and regulations so that justice is served appropriately according to both sets of rules simultaneously.

Another way in which integration between canonical jurisprudence and modern judicial systems could take place is through education initiatives aimed at teaching lawyers about different forms of legal reasoning including those found within traditional canon law sources such as religious texts or commentaries written by scholars over time (Edmundson, 2015; Elias, 1956; Enabulele & Bazuaye, 2019; Engel & Kurschilgen, 2013; Farran, 2019; Fenrich et al., 2011; Fleck, 2009). By providing lawyers with knowledge about different types of legal reasoning they may become more open-minded when considering cases involving questions related to religion or culture where traditional canon law might offer valuable insights into potential solutions beyond what conventional laws alone can provide them with answers for. All this is done whilst remaining that canonical law is always linked to religious institutions (Figure 8.6).

Figure 8.6. The church and canon law.

Source: Право via PPT-Online.

Governments must also play their part by creating policies that encourage greater collaboration between practitioners from both fields – those trained in conventional laws alongside those knowledgeable about traditional canon laws – so they can work together towards finding equitable solutions whenever possible without compromising either one's integrity too much along the way (Treasure et al., 2016; Tripp, 2004; Tsai, 2015; Tucker, 1972; Tunkin, 1993; Tupper, 1881). Such collaborations will help bridge gaps between two very distinct yet equally important areas within our society's overall system for delivering justice fairly across all communities regardless of if they adhere strictly only one type (i.e., either secular/modern) versus another (i.e., faith-based/traditional).

Integrating canonical jurisprudence into modern judicial systems requires careful consideration but it certainly is not impossible if done correctly with respect given towards each side's unique perspectives while striving always towards achieving just outcomes no matter what path we choose take get there eventually (Wilson, 1961; Wolff, 2016; Woodman, 1988, 1969, 2001; Worugji et al., 2019; Wu, 2018; Young, 2019). With proper planning and implementation strategies put forth now, hopefully future generations need not worry too much about whether their rights are being protected adequately under whichever forms of governance exist at any moment. However, the involvement of religious authorities and dictates remains controversial when dealing with social, political, and economic issues which may impact on the lives of those that are not necessarily adherents of specific faiths. This has been the case with the insidious criminalization of human sexuality in the developing world.

Religiosity has long been a factor in the criminalization of human sexuality (Kingwill, 2016; Koskenniemi, 1990; Kreso, 2010; Krieger, 2006; Kumar, 2020; Lagji, 2019; Lavalle, 2014; Laylin, 1976; Lewis, 1983). Historically, religious beliefs have been used to justify laws that punish people for engaging in consensual sexual activities deemed immoral by certain religions. In many countries today, these laws remain on the books and continue to be enforced despite their incompatibility with modern values of personal autonomy and freedom of expression. It is pertinent to provide an overview of how religiosity has shaped the criminalization of human sexuality throughout history and discuss its implications for contemporary society.

In ancient times, religious texts were often used as justification for punishing those who engaged in non-heteronormative sexual behavior or practices such as adultery or homosexuality (Graves, 2017; Gray, 2021; Griffiths, 1998; Hager, 2020; Haggenmacher, 2021; Hammond, 2019; Harmathy, 2016; Henry, 2017). For example, Leviticus 20:13 states "If a man lies with another man as one lies with a woman, both shall be put to death" while Deuteronomy 22:22 says "If a man is found lying with another man's wife both shall die" (NIV). These passages were interpreted literally by some societies which led to harsh punishments being imposed on those who violated them.

The influence of religion can also be seen in more recent centuries when it comes to the criminalization of sex work and contraception use (John-Hopkins, 2010; Johnson, 1986; Joireman, 2008; Jonas & Gunda, 2015; Kadens, 2012; Kammerhofer, 2012). In Europe during the 19th century, prostitution was outlawed due largely to moral objections from Christian churches which viewed it as sinful behavior that should not be tolerated within society. Similarly, birth control was illegalized in many parts of America until 1965 because it was considered immoral according to Catholic teachings at the time.

Today there are still numerous examples where religiosity continues to shape our understanding and enforcement of laws related to human sexuality including bans on same-sex marriage or abortion access in some countries based on religious grounds rather than scientific evidence or public opinion polls showing majority support for these issues among citizens living there (Galindo & Yip, 2017; Gao, 2013; Gillespie & Tran, 2022; Golo et al., 2022; Gradoni, 2019; Graves, 2017; Gray, 2021; Griffiths, 1998; Hager, 2020). This type of legal discrimination can lead to serious consequences such as unequal treatment under law or even imprisonment depending upon where you live which highlights why we must critically examine how religion influences our views about what constitutes acceptable sexual behavior if we want true equality before law regardless gender identity, orientation, or lifestyle choices.

Religiosity has played an important role throughout history when it comes to shaping attitudes towards sex and determining what types of behaviors are punishable by law (Meron, 1991; Meron et al., 1987; Merry, 1991; Meyer, 2012; Milanovic, 2011; Mnisi & Claassens, 2009; Moore, 1986). While this may have made sense hundreds of years ago, it is no longer appropriate given current social norms around personal autonomy so any laws based solely upon outdated religious beliefs should be reexamined carefully before they are enforced. Doing so would help ensure everyone enjoys equal protection under law regardless their individual preferences regarding intimate relationships. These debates and dynamics are at play in the increasing targeting of LGBT people in the developing world, especially in Africa.

The role of the USA Christian religious Right in anti-LGBT legislation in Africa has been a source of much debate and criticism. In recent years, there have been numerous reports of US-based Christian organizations providing financial support to African countries for the purpose of passing laws that criminalize same-sex relationships. This has led to an increase in discrimination against LGBT individuals across the continent, as well as a rise in violence and hate crimes targeting this community.

It is important to note that while some members of the US Christian religious Right may be motivated by genuine concern for their faith, others are driven by political agendas or personal biases. For example, many conservative Christians view homosexuality as immoral and believe it should be outlawed on moral grounds (Morrison, 2016; Morudu & Maimela, 2021; Murphy, 2014; Mwalimu, 1988; Mwambene, 2012; Mwangi, 2022). As such, they have sought to use their influence abroad to push for legislation that would restrict LGBT rights and freedoms.

Furthermore, these groups often fail to recognize or respect cultural differences between countries when advocating for anti-LGBT policies abroad. They do not take into account local customs or beliefs which may differ from those held by American Christians. Instead, they impose their own views without regard for how it might affect people living within those societies. This can lead to further marginalization and oppression of already vulnerable populations who lack access to resources or legal protection due to their sexual orientation or gender identity (Kammerhofer, 2012; Kane, 1972; Kassoti, 2017; Kelly & Windia, 2019; Kilian, 2019; Kim, 2009, 2020; Kingwill, 2016; Koskenniemi, 1990).

the role played by US Christian religious Right groups in promoting anti-LGBT legislation abroad must be critically examined if we are serious about protecting human rights around the world. It is essential that all actors involved – including governments, civil society organizations and international institutions – work together towards creating an environment where everyone can live free from fear regardless of their sexual orientation or gender identity. However, the consequences of disagreements of human sexuality are bound to be far-reaching in the future with the possibility of schism within the Anglican Church.

The Anglican Communion, a global fellowship of churches in full communion with the Church of England, is facing an unprecedented schism over human sexuality and anti-colonial emancipation hegemony. This rift has been growing for decades as different factions within the church have taken opposing stances on issues such as same-sex marriage, women bishops, and post-colonial attitudes towards former British colonies. At its core, this schism is rooted in disagreements about how to interpret scripture and doctrine. On one side are those who believe that traditional interpretations should be upheld while on the other side are those who argue for more progressive interpretations that reflect modern values. These differences have become increasingly pronounced in recent years due to changing social norms around gender identity and sexual orientation (Williams, 2022; Willms, 2009; Wilson, 1961; Wolff, 2016; Woodman, 1988; Woodman, 1969, 2001).

The divide between these two camps has also been exacerbated by declining church attendance rates across much of the Western world. As fewer people attend services or identify as members of any denomination, it becomes harder to maintain unity among believers from different backgrounds or perspectives. This lack of cohesion makes it difficult for leaders within the Anglican Communion to reach consensus on important matters such as human sexuality or post-colonial attitudes towards former British colonies. Furthermore, there is a growing sense among some members that the Church of England's influence over other denominations within the Anglican Communion is waning due to its diminished role in international affairs following Britain's exit from the European Union (EU). This feeling has only been further compounded by debates surrounding women bishops which many view as yet another example of patriarchal control being exerted over traditionally marginalized groups within society at large.

Ultimately, it remains unclear whether this schism will lead to a complete dissolution of ties between various branches within the Anglican Communion but what is certain is that tensions continue to mount with no end in sight anytime soon. If left unresolved these doctrinal disagreements could very well result in irreparable damage being done both internally and externally leading ultimately lead to an unraveling of what we know today as "the Anglican Church" worldwide. Perhaps the Church could learn the lessons of English common law in terms of pragmatism in the face of modernity.

8.4. LEARNING FROM ENGLISH COMMON LAW

English common law is a legal system that has been in place for centuries and is still used today (Lewis, 1983, 2016; Liakopoulos, 2019; Lijnzaad, 2022; Lingaas, 2022; Lita et al., 2017; Liu, 2019; Loja, 2014; Lon & Widyawati,

2021). It is based on the principles of justice, fairness, and equity. Common law originated in England during the Middle Ages and was developed over time by judges who made decisions based on precedent rather than written laws. This means that when a court makes a decision about an issue, it looks to previous cases with similar facts to determine how it should rule.

Common law has had a major influence on other legal systems around the world, including those of many former British colonies such as Canada, Australia, India, and South Africa (Liu, 2019; Loja, 2014; Lon & Widyawati, 2021; Magnusson, 2013, 2017; Manaka & Corrin, 2021; Manullang, 2021). In these countries, English common law forms part of their respective legal systems alongside local statutes or codes enacted by legislatures or governments. Figure 8.7 summarizes the tenets of English common law.

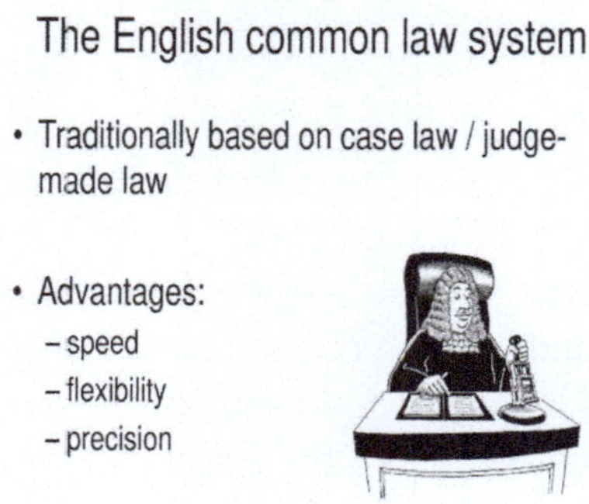

Figure 8.7. The merits of English common law.

Source: Alberta Elisabeth Marshall via Slide Player.

The main features of English common law include:

- **Precedent:** Judges make decisions based on past rulings in similar cases; this helps ensure consistency across different courts and jurisdictions (Merry, 1991; Meyer, 2012; Milanovic, 2011; Mnisi & Claassens, 2009; Moore, 1986; Morrison, 2016; Morudu & Maimela, 2021).
- **Equity:** The concept of equity ensures that justice is done even if there are no specific laws covering the situation at hand; judges can use their discretion to reach fair outcomes for all parties involved (Nhlapo, 2017; Nnona, 2018; Norr, 1973; Nwapi, 2016; Nyane, 2019; O'Neill, 2002; Oba, 2002, 2008).
- **Flexibility:** Common law allows for flexibility since it does not rely solely on written rules but also takes into account changing

social norms and values over time (Omidire, 1990; Orebech et al., 2005; Osman, 2019; Osman & Baase, 2022; Osman & Himonga, 2017; Ottley, 2016).

- **Judicial review:** Courts have the power to review legislation passed by Parliament or government bodies to ensure they comply with constitutional requirements such as human rights protections or due process guarantees (Liakopoulos, 2019; Lijnzaad, 2022; Lingaas, 2022; Lita et al., 2017; Liu, 2019; Loja, 2014; Lon & Widyawati, 2021; Magnusson, 2013, 2017).

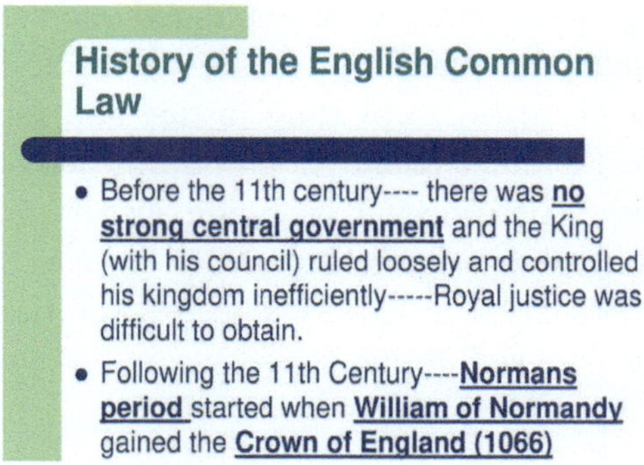

Figure 8.8. The history of English common law.

Source: Frederick long.

English common law remains an important part of many modern legal systems around the world today due its long history and ability to adapt over time (Figure 8.8) while still providing consistent results across different jurisdictions (Pocar, 2016; Poespasari, 2020; Polanski, 2017; Pratiwi et al., 2020; Qerimi, 2020; Quane, 2013; Rautenbach, 2020). It provides an effective way for courts to resolve disputes fairly while taking into account both existing laws as well as evolving social values and norms within society at large. However, there are some weaknesses associated with English common law.

Nevertheless, there are some weaknesses associated with English common law (Maxim & Titu Maiorescu, 2015; McAuslan, 2015; McCarthy, 1971; McLachlan, 1988; Menski, 1988; Meron, 1987, 1991). One of the main criticisms is that it can be slow to adapt to changing circumstances and may not always provide the most up-to-date solutions for modern problems. Additionally, since judges have a great deal of discretion when interpreting laws or applying equitable principles, outcomes can vary significantly from one court to another. This lack of consistency can lead to confusion and frustration among litigants who may feel their case was treated unfairly due to differences in judicial interpretation.

Overall, English common law has been an effective legal system for centuries, but its strengths must be balanced against its weaknesses for it remain relevant in today's world (Tobin, 2014; Tomuschat, 2021; Treasure et al., 2016; Tripp, 2004; Tsai, 2015; Tucker, 1972). It is important that courts continue to review legislation passed by Parliament or government bodies while also taking into account evolving social values and norms within society at large so as not become outdated or irrelevant over time. Modern judicial systems can learn a great deal from the English common law system. Its long history of providing justice and fairness to citizens has been an example for other countries around the world. The ability of judges to interpret laws considering changing circumstances, as well as their discretion when applying equitable principles, have allowed courts to remain flexible and responsive to society's needs. Additionally, its reliance on precedent has provided stability and consistency in legal decisions over time.

At the same time, modern judicial systems must be aware of some of the weaknesses associated with English common law such as its slow pace at adapting to new situations or its lack of uniformity between different courts (Mwangi, 2022; Ndulo, 2011; Ngira, 2018, 2021; Nhlapo, 2017; Nnona, 2018; Norr, 1973; Nwapi, 2016). For any legal system to remain effective it must be able to keep up with changes in society while also ensuring that all litigants are treated regardless of where they live or which court is hearing their case. By taking these lessons into account, modern judicial systems can ensure that justice is served now and into the future. As we close this final chapter, we go back to the very beginning of common law in the form of oral traditions.

8.5. LEARNING LESSONS FROM ORAL LAW TRADITIONS

Oral law traditions are an important part of many cultures around the world (Damato et al., 1993; Dancer, 2017; Danilenko, 1988; Davis & Klare, 2010; De ruysscher, 2008; de Vries, 2021; De Wet, 2004). They are a form of legal system that relies on oral communication rather than written documents to pass down laws and regulations from one generation to the next. This type of tradition has been used for centuries in various societies, including those in Africa, Asia, and Native American tribes.

At its core, oral law is based on storytelling to remember and transmit information about laws and customs (Manaka & Corrin, 2021; Manullang, 2021; Marasinghe, 1978; Masengu, 2016; Mastura, 1994; Maunatlala & Maimela, 2020). It is often passed down through generations by elders who have learned it from their ancestors or other respected members of society. Oral law can also be seen as a form of collective memory since it allows people to share stories with each other over time without relying on written records or books.

The oral tradition has been closely associated with religiosity as seen in the Oral Torah or Talmud (refer to Figure 8.9).

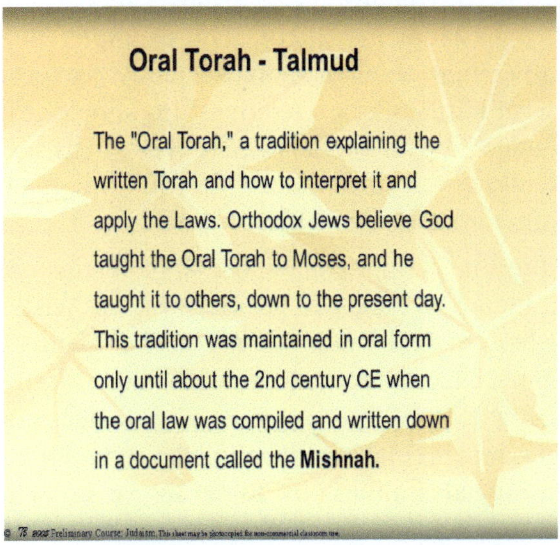

Figure 8.9. Extract explaining oral torah in Judaism.

Source: Lizbeth Hart vid slide player.

The relevance of oral Torah-Talmud in contemporary society is a topic that has been widely discussed and debated (Beer, 2022; Bennett, 2008, 2009, 2015; Benson & Siddiqui, 2014; Bianchi, 2009; Bond, 2009, 2010). Oral Torah-Talmud, which consists of the Mishnah and Gemara, are two components of Jewish law that have been passed down orally for centuries. These texts provide guidance on how to live a moral life according to Jewish tradition and values. While these teachings remain important for many Jews today, there is an increasing need to consider their relevance considering modern societal norms and expectations.

It is essential to evaluate the extent to which oral Torah-Talmud can be inclusive towards those who do not identify as part of the traditional Jewish community (Arowolo, 2019; Asieduakrofi, 1989; Barnabas, 2022; Barrie, 2016; Baxi, 2020; Beavers, 2019; Beer, 2022; Bennett, 2008; Bennett, 2015). This includes individuals from different religious backgrounds or sexual orientations who may feel excluded by certain aspects of this ancient text. It also applies to non-Jews who may wish to learn more about Judaism but find themselves unable or unwilling due to its perceived exclusivity.

To address this issue, some scholars have suggested reinterpreting certain passages within oral Torah-Talmud so they are more open and accepting towards diverse groups within society (Huizenga, 2022; Hulme, 2010; Hutchison, 2020; Hutchison & Sibanda, 2017; Iyi, 2016; Jentoft & Bavinck, 2019; John-Hopkins, 2010). For example, one interpretation suggests that rather than viewing homosexuality as forbidden behavior according to Jewish law, same sex relationships should instead be seen as permissible if conducted with mutual respect between partners (Klein). This type of approach allows for greater inclusion while still maintaining fidelity with traditional interpretations where appropriate.

At the same time, it is important not lose sight of why oral Torah-Talmud remains relevant today: its ability to provide timeless wisdom on how best we can lead our lives ethically and morally in accordance with God's will (Rosenberg) (Beer, 2022; Bennett, 2008, 2009, 2015; Benson & Siddiqui, 2014; Bianchi, 2009; Bond, 2009). As such, any changes made must ensure that core principles remain intact while allowing room for new perspectives based on current social realities. In doing so we can ensure that these ancient texts continue providing valuable guidance into the future without compromising their original intent or excluding anyone from participating in them fully regardless of background or identity.

Oral Torah – Talmud continues being highly relevant even today when considering issues related inclusiveness (Bond, 2010; Botha & Bekink, 2018; Bourgon, 2020; Budlender et al., 2011; Buss, 2010; Buxbaum, 1968; Cannizzaro & Bonafe, 2005). To make sure everyone feels included, it is necessary reinterpret certain passages accordingly while still preserving core principles. By doing so, we can guarantee that these ancient texts keep providing invaluable advice into the future without leaving anyone behind. Overall, oral law traditions offer many benefits but also come with some potential risks that should be taken into consideration before implementing such a system within any given society or culture groupings.

By understanding both the advantages and disadvantages associated with this type of legal framework we can better ensure its successful implementation while still preserving our cultural heritage for future generations (Petersen, 2007, 2017; Pocar, 2016; Poespasari, 2020; Polanski, 2017; Pratiwi et al., 2020; Qerimi, 2020). Oral law traditions have been used for centuries to govern the behavior of individuals within a given society or culture. This type of legal system relies on verbal communication between members to establish and maintain laws, regulations, and customs that are applicable to all members. The primary benefit associated with this approach is that it allows for greater flexibility when compared to written laws which can be difficult to modify or update as needed. Additionally, oral law traditions often provide an opportunity for communities to come together and discuss important issues in a more informal setting than would otherwise be possible under a formalized legal framework.

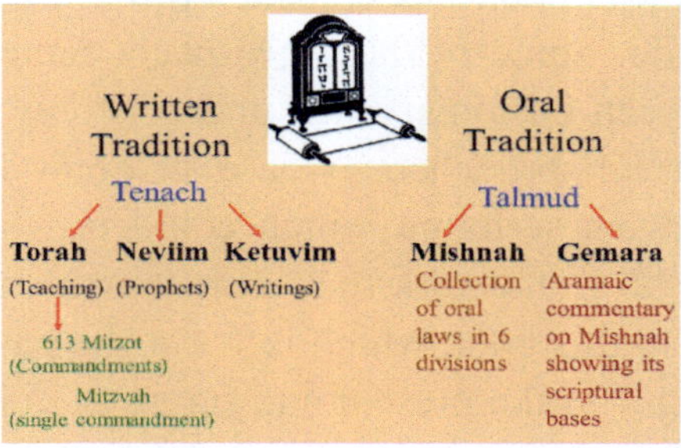

Figure 8.10. Oral and written traditions in Jewish scripture.

Source: Quran 1 Book via WordPress.

Despite these advantages however, there are some drawbacks associated with this type of legal system as well (Ndulo, 2011; Ngira, 2018, 2021; Nhlapo, 2017; Nnona, 2018; Norr, 1973; Nwapi, 2016; Nyane, 2019). For example, because there is no single authoritative source document outlining all applicable laws and regulations, disputes between parties may arise if different interpretations lead them into conflict with one another (Figure 8.10). Additionally, if not properly maintained over time through regular retelling by knowledgeable individuals within the community then certain aspects may become forgotten or distorted leading to confusion among members regarding what constitutes acceptable behavior under certain circumstances.

Oral law traditions offer many benefits but also come with some potential risks that should be taken into consideration before implementing such a system within any given society or culture groupings (Sheleff, 2013; Shingleton, 1983; Sibisi, 2020; Siegel, 2015; Sierra, 1995; Singer, 1972; Skomerska-Muchowska, 2017). By understanding both the advantages and disadvantages associated with this type of legal framework we can better ensure its successful implementation while still preserving our cultural heritage for future generations. In today's increasingly globalized world where cultures are becoming ever more intertwined it is essential that we recognize the importance of maintaining traditional practices such as those found in oral law systems so that they remain relevant even amidst rapid change. Doing so will help us create societies based on mutual respect, understanding, and cooperation rather than fear, mistrust, and division.

CHAPTER 8 SUMMARY

The final chapter in this book has considered the prospects of customary law in community life. Some of these prospects center on learning about the intersection between customary law and civil law, canonical law, and localized version of jurisprudence. A case in point is the endurance of oral traditions in Jewish scripture which could provide insights into the development of a legal framework that is sustainable for the modern age. That is a fitting end to this book which looks at the past in legal terms and finds ways of linking it to the present and future of community or societal life.

Concluding Remarks

This book has explored how customary early laws have relevance to the modern era. The first chapter introduced the notion of a customary law regime. This covered issues such as legal customs, human behavior, objectivity in the law, and the role of societal settings in determining the law. The second chapter explored some of the claims that might be made under customary law. Hence, the chapter discussed the implications of unofficial law, "*opinio juris*," community standards of behavior, the development of international law, and a case study of piracy law. In the third chapter, the book considered the practices of customary law. Some of the key areas covered include how customary law has been abused to justify societal ills including slavery. The chapter discussed the principles of "*hostis humani generis*" whilst contrasting customary law with case law as an example of the evolution of modern law from a range of sources.

In the fourth chapter, the book considered the ways in which customary law is established. Some of the key areas that were covered include the methodologies of law, Classic Western theories of jurisprudence, conceptual analyzes of customary law, social behavior, antisocial behavior, and deviancy. The fifth chapter consider how customary law is an expression of norms in a society. Hence, it was necessary to define norms before considering other related terms such as values and folkways. This was considered from a human and social anthropological perspective. The chapter then concluded with an exploration of how the legitimacy of judicial decisions is considered in contemporary legal systems.

In the sixth chapter, the book explored how customary law can be embedded in existing legal structures. The key emerging themes in this chapter were the flexibility thesis, a repertoire of norms, rule skepticism, traditional cultural judicial processes, legal codification, and a case study of medieval custumals. The seventh chapter then addressed the fundamentals of customary law. These include peremptory norms, crimes against humanity, a case study of genocide and the notion of gender equality in customary law. The chapter used a customary law perspective to address some of the modern challenges of societal living including xenophobia, bigotry, and racism.

The concluding eighth chapter looking forward to the prospects of incorporating customary law into the challenges of contemporary community life. This discussion highlighted the customary law implications for civil law as well as legal pluralism. The chapter highlighted three specific cases from which lessons and criticism can be drawn. These include canonical jurisprudence, English common law, and oral traditions. In doing so, the final chapter emphasized the overarching theme of this book that customary law can be relevant to the modern context if it is carefully embedded and integrated into current systems and expectations.

The study of customary law is an important part of legal education, and students of the law can benefit greatly from exploring it. Customary law is a set of rules that are based on long-standing traditions and customs, rather than written laws or statutes. It has been used for centuries to regulate social behavior in many societies around the world.

Customary law provides insight into how different cultures have developed their own systems for resolving disputes and regulating behavior. By studying this type of law, students gain a better understanding of how different societies functioned in the past, as well as what values were important to them at that time. This knowledge can be invaluable when considering current legal issues or trying to understand why certain laws exist today.

In addition to providing historical context, studying customary law also helps students develop critical thinking skills by forcing them to evaluate various sources and draw conclusions about which rules should apply in any given situation. Students must consider not only traditional sources such as court decisions but also other forms of evidence like oral histories or archaeological findings when making these determinations. This process encourages creative problem solving and teaches students how to think outside the box when approaching complex legal questions.

Finally, learning about customary law gives students an appreciation for cultural diversity and respect for different ways of life that may differ from their own beliefs or experiences. Understanding another culture's approach to justice can help foster empathy among people who come from diverse backgrounds while also promoting tolerance between individuals with differing opinions on matters related to the rule of law.

Overall, there are numerous benefits associated with exploring customary law during one's studies in the field of jurisprudence; it provides valuable historical context while teaching critical thinking skills and fostering respect for cultural diversity all at once! As such, it is highly recommended that all aspiring lawyers take some time out during their studies to learn more about this fascinating area within our legal system today. I hope you have enjoyed reading this book and will read the others in the series.

BIBLIOGRAPHY

1. Adebola, T., (2021). Traditional knowledge, genetic resources, customary law, and intellectual property: A global primer. *Edinburgh Law Review*, *25*(1), 141–143. https://doi.org/10.3366/elr.2021.0686.
2. Akande, D., (2004). International law immunities and the international criminal court. *American Journal of International Law*, *98*(3), 407. https://doi.org/10.2307/3181639.
3. Albakjaji, M., (2022). The responsibility for environmental damages during armed conflicts: The case of the war between Russia and Ukraine. *Access to Justice in Eastern Europe*, 82–101.
4. Allott, A. N., (1957). The judicial ascertainment of customary law in British Africa. *The Modern Law Review*, *20*(3), 244–263.
5. Allott, A. N., (1984). What is to be done with African customary law? *Journal of African Law*, *28*(1, 2), 56–71.
6. Anderson, L., (2003). The law and the desert: Alternative methods of delivering justice. *Journal of Law and Society*, *30*(1), 120–136. https://doi.org/10.1111/1467-6478.00249.
7. Angelini, P., (2012). The code of Dusan 1349–1354. *Tijdschrift Voor Rechtsgeschiedenis-Revue D Histoire Du Droit-the Legal History Review*, *80*(1, 2), 77–93. https://doi.org/10.1163/157181912x626920.
8. Armstrong, A., (1989). Zimbabwe – away from the customary law. *Journal of Family Law*, *27*(1), 339–350. <Go to ISI>://WOS:A1989T297000030.
9. Arowolo, A. L., (2019). African traditional intellectual property rights, customary law, and legal pluralism. *African Journal of Legal Studies*, *11*(4), 299–318. https://doi.org/10.1163/17087384-12340037.
10. Asieduakrofi, D., (1989). Judicial recognition and adoption of customary law in Nigeria. *American Journal of Comparative Law*, *37*(3), 571–593. https://doi.org/10.2307/840092.
11. Barnabas, S. G., (2022). Protecting land rights of indigenous peoples in Africa: The land rights of Abuja peoples of Nigeria and Ogiek peoples

of Kenya in comparative perspective. *African Journal of Legal Studies, 14*(1), 68–92. https://doi.org/10.1163/17087384-12340077.

12. Barrie, G. N., (2016). The king can do wrong: The imprisonment of the abathembu king buyelekhaya zwelibanzi dalinyebo – some comments on south African customary law and Australian parallels. *Tydskrif Vir Die Suid-Afrikaanse Reg.,* (4), 746–753. <Go to ISI>://WOS:000435364900009.
13. Baxi, U., (2020). Nevsun: A ray of hope in a darkening landscape? *Business and Human Rights Journal*, *5*(2), 241–251. https://doi.org/10.1017/bhj.2020.17.
14. Beavers, A. J., (2019). All law is customary law. *Revista General De Derecho Publico Comparado,* (26), Article 422099. <Go to ISI>://WOS:000563711400004.
15. Beer, Y., (2022). When should a lawful war of self-defense end? *European Journal of International Law*, *33*(3), 889–915. https://doi.org/10.1093/ejil/chac046.
16. Bennett, T. W., (2009). Re-introducing African customary law to the South African legal system. *American Journal of Comparative Law*, *57*(1), 1–31. <Go to ISI>://WOS:000262584400001.
17. Bennett, T., (2008). *Official vs "Living" Customary Law: Dilemmas of Description and Recognition*. Cape Town: UCT Press.
18. Bennett, T., (2015). Indigenous peoples, customary law, and human rights – why living law matters. *Journal of Legal Pluralism and Unofficial Law*, *47*(1), 140–144. https://doi.org/10.1080/07329113.2015.993878.
19. Benson, B. L., & Siddiqui, Z. R., (2014). Pashtunwali-law for the lawless, defense for the stateless. *International Review of Law and Economics*, *37*, 108–120. https://doi.org/10.1016/j.irle.2013.07.008.
20. Bianchi, A., (2009). The international regulation of the use of force: The politics of interpretive method. *Leiden Journal of International Law*, *22*(4), 651–676. https://doi.org/10.1017/s092215650999015x.
21. Bond, J. E., (2009). Gender, discourse, and customary law in Africa. *S. Cal. L. Rev.*, *83*, 509.
22. Bond, J. E., (2010). Gender, discourse, and customary law in Africa. *Southern California Law Review*, *83*(3), 509–574. <Go to ISI>://WOS:000280045500006.

23. Botha, C., & Bekink, B., (2018). Law reform in South Africa: 21 years since the establishment of a supreme constitutional dispensation. *Theory and Practice of Legislation*, *6*(2), 263–289. https://doi.org/10.1080/20508840.2018.1475904.

24. Bourgon, J., (2020). Historians at the Court: How cultural expertise in Qing law contributes to the invention of Hong Kong "Chinese customary law." *Law and History Review*, *38*(1), 85–98. https://doi.org/10.1017/s0738248019000580.

25. Brunet, A., Ouellet-Morin I., Danese A., Bowes L., & Shakoor S., (2017) Mental health problems among offenders: Prevalence estimates from a systematic review and meta-analysis. *JAMA Psychiatry, 74*(7), 721–730. doi: 10/1001/jamapsychiatry20163051.

26. Budlender, D., Mgweba, S., Motsepe, K., & Williams, L., (2011). *Women, Land and Customary Law*. https://idl-bnc-idrc.dspacedirect.org/handle/10625/47347

27. Buss, A., (2010). The Preah Vihear case and regional customary law. *Chinese Journal of International Law*, *9*(1), 111–126. https://doi.org/10.1093/chinesejil/jmp038.

28. Buxbaum, D. C., (1968). *Family Law and Customary Law in Asia: A Contemporary Legal Perspective*. Martinus Nijhoff Publishers.

29. Cannizzaro, E., & Bonafe, B., (2005). Fragmenting international law through compromissory clauses? Some remarks on the decision of the ICJ in the oil platforms case. *European Journal of International Law*, *16*(3), 481–497. https://doi.org/10.1093/ejil/chi127.

30. Carrillo-Santarelli, N., (2017). The possibilities and legitimacy of non-state participation in the formation of customary law. *International Community Law Review*, *19*(1), 98–125. https://doi.org/10.1163/18719732-12341349.

31. Castillo, N. S., & Bian, Y. M., (2014). China's obligation to conduct transboundary environmental impact assessment (TEIA) in utilizing its shared water resources. *Natural Resources Journal*, *55*(1), 105–125. <Go to ISI>://WOS:000209580900003.

32. Cataldi, G., & Titu, M., U. O. B., (2015). Jurisdictional immunities of foreign states and human rights: Which balance between domestic order's fundamental values and international customary law? [Law between modernization and tradition – implications for the legal, political, administrative, and public order organization]. *International*

Conference on Law between Modernization and Tradition – Implications for the Legal, Political, Administrative and Public Order Organization, Bucharest, Romania.

33. Chang, Y. C., (2022). Toward better maritime cooperation-a proposal from the Chinese perspective. *Ocean Development and International Law*, *53*(2, 3), 85–104. https://doi.org/10.1080/00908320.2022.2068704.
34. Chanock, M., (1989). Neither customary nor legal: African customary law in an era of family law reform. *International Journal of Law, Policy, and the Family*, *3*(1), 72–88.
35. Cheng, T. H., (2012). 'Armed attack' and article 51 of the UN charter: Evolutions in customary law and practice. *American Journal of International Law*, *106*(3), 710–715. <Go to ISI>://WOS:000307916500019.
36. Chirayath, L., Sage, C., & Woolcock, M., (2005). *Customary Law and Policy Reform: Engaging with the Plurality of Justice Systems. https://www.researchgate.net/publication/251919166_Customary_Law_and_Policy_Reform_Engaging_with_the_Plurality_of_Justice_Systems1*
37. Claassens, A., & Mnisi, S., (2009). Rural women redefining land rights in the context of living customary law. *South African Journal on Human Rights*, *25*, 491–516. <Go to ISI>://WOS:000284919500005.
38. Cooter, R. D., (1991). Inventing market property – the land courts of Papua-new-guinea. *Law & Society Review*, *25*(4), 759–801. https://doi.org/10.2307/3053869.
39. Corrin, J., & Mulitalo, L., (2015). Not 'mere window dressing': Children's rights and adoption in Samoa. *Journal of Legal Pluralism and Unofficial Law*, *47*(2), 208–225. https://doi.org/10.1080/07329113.2015.1085767.
40. Costa, A., (1998). The myth of customary law. *South African Journal on Human Rights*, *14*(4), 525–538.
41. Craik, N., (2020). The duty to cooperate in the customary law of environmental impact assessment. *International & Comparative Law Quarterly*, *69*(1), 239–259. https://doi.org/10.1017/s0020589319000459.
42. Crawford, J. R., (2012). Jurisdiction and applicable law. *Leiden Journal of International Law*, *25*(2), 471–479. https://doi.org/10.1017/s0922156512000143.

43. Criddle, E. J., (2013). Humanitarian financial intervention. *European Journal of International Law*, *24*(2), 583–615. https://doi.org/10.1093/ejil/cht037.

44. Cuskelly, K., (2011). *Customs and Constitutions: State Recognition of Customary Law Around the World.*

45. Dahlitz, J., (1991). *The Role of Customary law in Arms Limitation.* [International law of arms control and disarmament]. Symp on the International Law of Arms Control and Disarmament, Geneva, Switzerland.

46. Damato, A., (1973). International customary law and codification – Thirlway, HWA. *American Journal of International Law*, *67*(2), 357–359. https://doi.org/10.2307/2199449.

47. Damato, A., Buergenthal, T., Roth, K., Elaraby, N. A., Bolton, J. R., Gallant, K. S., Buhagiar, C. A., et al., (1993). New customary law – taking human-rights seriously. *Proceedings of the Annual Meeting – American Society of International Law*. 87th Annual Meeting of the American-Society-of-International-Law, Washington, DC.

48. Dancer, H., (2017). An equal right to inherit? Women's land rights, customary law, and constitutional reform in Tanzania. *Social & Legal Studies*, *26*(3), 291–310. https://doi.org/10.1177/0964663916677560.

49. Danilenko, G. M., (1988). The theory of international customary law. *German YB Int'l L.*, *31*, 9.

50. Davis, D. M., & Klare, K., (2010). Transformative constitutionalism and the common and customary law. *South African Journal on Human Rights*, *26*, 403–509. https://doi.org/10.1080/19962126.2010.11864997.

51. De ruysscher, D., (2008). Designing the limits of creditworthiness Insolvency in Antwerp bankruptcy legislation and practice (16th-17th centuries). *Tijdschrift Voor Rechtsgeschiedenis-Revue D Histoire Du Droit-the Legal History Review*, *76*(3, 4), 307–327. https://doi.org/10.1163/157181908x336891.

52. De Vries, B., (2021). An equivalent to article 8(2)(b)(xx) ICC statute for non-international armed conflicts? Is it warranted on the basis of international customary law? *International Criminal Law Review*, *21*(3), 561–587. https://doi.org/10.1163/15718123-bja10071.

53. De Wet, E., (2004). The prohibition of torture as an international norm

of jus cogens and its implications for national and customary law. *European Journal of International Law*, *15*(1), 97–121.

54. Debelva, F., & De Broe, L., (2022). Pillar 2: An analysis of the IIR and UTPR from an international customary law, tax treaty law, and European union law perspective. *Intertax*, *50*(12), 898–906. <Go to ISI>://WOS:000911725300005.
55. Dekoster, K., (2019). The legal foundations of post-mortem examinations in early modern Flanders. Princely legislation, custom, doctrine and judicial practice. *Tijdschrift Voor Rechtsgeschiedenis-Revue D Histoire Du Droit-the Legal History Review*, *87*(1, 2), 128–161. https://doi.org/10.1163/15718190-08712p05.
56. Demian, M., (2014). On the repugnance of customary law. *Comparative Studies in Society and History*, *56*(2), 508–536.
57. Diala, A. C., & Bagni, S., (2019). The role of customary law in the shaping of new models of pluralistic states. *Revista General De Derecho Publico Comparado,* (26), Article 422097. <Go to ISI>://WOS:000563711400002.
58. Diala, A. C., (2017). The concept of living customary law: A critique. *Journal of Legal Pluralism and Unofficial Law*, *49*(2), 143–165. https://doi.org/10.1080/07329113.2017.1331301.
59. Diala, A. C., (2019). Our laws are better than yours: The future of legal pluralism in south Africa. *Revista General De Derecho Publico Comparado,* (26), Article 422101. <Go to ISI>://WOS:000563711400006.
60. Dubner, B. H., (1994). Problem on the united-states continental-shelf – measuring the environmental effectiveness of the outer continental-shelf act (OCSA). *Natural Resources Journal*, *34*(3), 519–534. <Go to ISI>://WOS:A1994QF62800001.
61. Dubois, F., (1992). A sourcebook of African customary law for southern Africa – Bennett, TW. *International and Comparative Law Quarterly*, *41*, 742, 743. https://doi.org/10.1093/iclqaj/41.3.742.
62. Dupont, P. E., (2013). International terrorism, resistance, and the jus in bello before French courts the case of the Iranian militant opposition. *Journal of International Criminal Justice*, *11*(2), 441–462. https://doi.org/10.1093/jicj/mqt019.
63. Duxbury, N., (2017). Custom as law in English law. *Cambridge Law Journal*, *76*(2), 337–359. https://doi.org/10.1017/s0008197317000253.

64. Edmundson, W., (2015). The philosophy of customary law. *Law and Philosophy, 34*(2), 229–232. https://doi.org/10.1007/s10982-014-9223-8.

65. Elias, T. O., (1956). *The Nature of African Customary Law*. Manchester University Press.

66. Enabulele, A. O., & Bazuaye, B., (2019). Validity and enforceability of customary law in Nigeria: Towards a correct delimitation of the province of the courts. *Journal of African Law, 63*(1), 79–104. https://doi.org/10.1017/s002185531800030x.

67. Engel, C., & Kurschilgen, M., (2013). The coevolution of behavior and normative expectations: An experiment. *American Law and Economics Review, 15*(2), 578–609. https://doi.org/10.1093/aler/aht010.

68. Farran, S., (2019). The place of law in the 'blue pacific' agenda. *Revista General De Derecho Publico Comparado,* (26), Article 422108. <Go to ISI>://WOS:000563711400013.

69. Fenrich, J., Galizzi, P., & Higgins, T. E., (2011). *The Future of African Customary Law*. Cambridge University Press.

70. Fleck, D., (2009). Shortcomings of the grave breaches regime. *Journal of International Criminal Justice, 7*(4), 833–854. https://doi.org/10.1093/jicj/mqp054.

71. Fleck, D., (2013). The legal status of personnel involved in United Nations peace operations. *International Review of the Red Cross, 95*(891), 613–636. https://doi.org/10.1017/s1816383114000290.

72. Fletcher, M. L., (2007). Rethinking customary law in tribal court jurisprudence. *Mich. J. Race & L., 13*, 57.

73. Frulli, M., (2015). The contribution of international criminal tribunals to the development of international law: The prominence of opinio juris and the moralization of customary law. *Law & Practice of International Courts and Tribunals, 14*(1), 80–93. https://doi.org/10.1163/15718034-12341286.

74. Gadzo, S., (2018). The principle of 'nexus' or 'genuine link' as a keystone of international income tax law: A reappraisal. *Intertax, 46*(3), 194–209. <Go to ISI>://WOS:000428138700003.

75. Gagnon-Bergeron, N., (2018). Developments in the protection of the citizens' rights under international and European law. *Utrecht Journal of International and European Law, 34*(2), 88–91. https://doi.org/10.5334/ujiel.479.

76. Galindo, G. R. B., & Yip, C., (2017). Customary international law and the third world: Do not step on the grass. *Chinese Journal of International Law*, *16*(2), 251–270. https://doi.org/10.1093/chinesejil/jmx012.
77. Gal-Or, N., (2015). The formation of a customary international crime: Global terrorism human (in) security. *International Criminal Law Review*, *15*(4), 665–699. https://doi.org/10.1163/15718123-01504006.
78. Gao, J. J., (2013). A note on the Nicaragua v. Colombia case. *Ocean Development and International Law*, *44*(3), 219–234. https://doi.org/10.1080/00908320.2013.808934.
79. Gillespie, C. J., Hough, M., Tilley, N., & Farrington, D. P., (2019). *The Role of Revenge in Crime and Criminal Justice Criminology, 57*(2), 441–470. doi: 10/1111/1745-912512076.
80. Gillespie, J., & Tran, H. T. Q., (2022). Legal pluralism and the struggle for customary law in the Vietnamese highlands. *American Journal of Comparative Law*, *70*(1), 1–42. https://doi.org/10.1093/ajcl/avac024.
81. Golo, H. K., Ibrahim, S., & Erinosho, B., (2022). Integrating communities' customary laws into marine small-scale fisheries governance in Ghana: Reflections on the FAO Guidelines for Securing Sustainable Small-Scale Fisheries. *Review of European Comparative & International Environmental Law*, *31*(3), 349–359. https://doi.org/10.1111/reel.12478.
82. Gradoni, L., (2019). Un-procedural customary law. *Journal of International Dispute Settlement*, *10*(2), 175–199. https://doi.org/10.1093/jnlids/idz008.
83. Graves, M., (2017). Customary ivory law: Inefficient problem solving with customary international law. *Washington International Law Journal*, *26*(2), 325–347. <Go to ISI>://WOS:000424519800005.
84. Gray, S., (2021). Over-regulation of indigenous law? The burial and cremation bill 2019 (NT). *Alternative Law Journal*, *46*(1), 47–52. Article 1037969x20974796. https://doi.org/10.1177/1037969x20974796.
85. Griffiths, A., (1998). Reconfiguring law: An ethnographic perspective from Botswana. *Law and Social Inquiry-Journal of the American Bar Foundation*, *23*(3), 587–620. https://doi.org/10.1086/492646.
86. Hager, L., (2020). The dissolution of universal partnerships in South African law: Lessons to be learnt from Botswana, Zimbabwe, and Namibia. *De Jure*, *53*, 123–139. https://doi.org/10.17159/2225-7160/2020/v53a9.

87. Haggenmacher, P., (2021). An archaeological look at 'international custom as evidence of a general practice accepted as law' and article 38 of the world court's statute. *Leiden Journal of International Law*, *34*(4), 801-827, Article Pii s092215652100011x. https://doi.org/10.1017/s092215652100011x.

88. Hammond, A., (2019). Reforming the law of intestate succession in a legally plural Ghana. *Journal of Legal Pluralism and Unofficial Law*, *51*(1), 114–139. https://doi.org/10.1080/07329113.2019.1594564.

89. Harmathy, A., (2016). Customary law in Hungary: Courts, texts, and the Tripartitum. *Comparative Legal History*, *4*(1), 87–91. https://doi.org/10.1080/2049677x.2016.1176355.

90. Henry, E., (2017). Alleged acquiescence of the international community to revisionist claims of international customary law (with special reference to the jus contra bellum regime). *Melbourne Journal of International Law*, *18*(2), 260–297. <Go to ISI>://WOS:000456423800012.

91. Hernández, T. K., (2012). *Racial Subordination in Latin America: The Role of the State, Customary Law, and the New Civil Rights Response*. Cambridge University Press.

92. Hoffman, E. O., & Miller, R., (2018). *Understanding Antisocial Behavior as an Adaptive Response to Social Exclusion Frontiers in Psychology, 9*(2037), 1–14. doi: 10/3389/fpsyg201802037.

93. Holleman, J. F., (1969). *Shona Customary Law: With Reference to Kinship, Marriage, the Family, and the Estate*. Manchester University Press.

94. Holleman, J. F., (1972). Trouble-cases and trouble-less cases in the study of customary law and legal reform. *Law & Soc'y Rev.*, *7*, 585.

95. Horii, H., (2019). Pluralistic legal system, pluralistic human rights?: Teenage pregnancy, child marriage and legal institutions in Bali. *Journal of Legal Pluralism and Unofficial Law*, *51*(3), 292–319. https://doi.org/10.1080/07329113.2019.1683429.

96. Howell, P. P., (2018). *A Manual of Nuer law: Being an Account of Customary Law, its Evolution and Development in the Courts Established by the Sudan Government*. Routledge.

97. Hu, M., (2017). Orwell's 1984 and a fourth amendment cybersurveillance nonintrusion test. *Washington Law Review*, *92*(4), 1819–1904. <Go to ISI>://WOS:000540321400004.

98. Huizenga, D., (2018). Articulations of aboriginal title, indigenous rights, and living customary law in South Africa. *Social & Legal Studies*, *27*(1), 3–24. https://doi.org/10.1177/0964663917710986.

99. Huizenga, D., (2022). The right to say no to imposed development: Human rights vernacularization in reverse in South Africa. *Journal of Human Rights Practice*, *13*(2), 205–224. https://doi.org/10.1093/jhuman/huab026.

100. Hulme, K., (2010). Taking care to protect the environment against damage: A meaningless obligation? *International Review of the Red Cross*, *92*(879), 675–691. https://doi.org/10.1017/s1816383110000512.

101. Hutchison, A., & Sibanda, N., (2017). A living customary law of commercial contracting in South Africa: Some law-related hypotheses. *South African Journal on Human Rights*, *33*(3), 380–405. https://doi.org/10.1080/02587203.2017.1392430.

102. Hutchison, A., (2020). Uncovering contracting norms in Khayelitsha stokvels. *Journal of Legal Pluralism and Unofficial Law*, *52*(1), 3–27. https://doi.org/10.1080/07329113.2020.1728493.

103. Iyi, J. M., (2016). Fair hearing without lawyers? The Traditional Courts Bill and the reform of traditional justice system in South Africa. *Journal of Legal Pluralism and Unofficial Law*, *48*(1), 127–152. https://doi.org/10.1080/07329113.2015.1125188.

104. Jentoft, S., & Bavinck, M., (2019). Reconciling human rights and customary law: Legal pluralism in the governance of small-scale fisheries. *Journal of Legal Pluralism and Unofficial Law*, *51*(3), 271–291. https://doi.org/10.1080/07329113.2019.1674105.

105. John-Hopkins, M., (2010). Regulating the conduct of urban warfare: Lessons from contemporary asymmetric armed conflicts. *International Review of the Red Cross*, *92*(878), 469–493. https://doi.org/10.1017/s1816383110000391.

106. Johnson, D. H., (1986). Judicial regulation and administrative control: Customary law and the Nuer, 1898–1954. *The Journal of African History*, *27*(1), 59–78.

107. Joireman, S. F., (2008). The mystery of capital formation in Sub-Saharan Africa: Women, property rights and customary law. *World Development*, *36*(7), 1233–1246.

108. Jonas, O., & Gunda, P., (2015). Children born out of wedlock and their right to inherit from their fathers under customary law in Botswana

Baone Kealeboga & Anor v Tidimalo Mercy Kehumile & Anor. *Comparative and International Law Journal of Southern Africa-Cilsa, 48*(1), 89–97. <Go to ISI>://WOS:000217387500004.

109. Kadens, E., (2012). The myth of the customary law merchant. *Texas Law Review, 90*(5), 1153–1206. <Go to ISI>://WOS:000303139000002.
110. Kammerhofer, J., (2012). The nature of customary law. legal, historical, and philosophical perspectives. *European Journal of International Law, 23*(2), 589–594. https://doi.org/10.1093/ejil/chs026.
111. Kane, M., (1972). Status of married women under customary law in Senegal. *American Journal of Comparative Law, 20*(4), 716–723. https://doi.org/10.2307/839038.
112. Kassoti, E., (2017). The normative status of unilateral ad hoc commitments by non-state armed actors in internal armed conflicts: International legal personality and lawmaking capacity distinguished. *Journal of Conflict & Security Law, 22*(1), 67–96. https://doi.org/10.1093/jcsl/krw005.
113. Kelly, D., & Windia, W. P., (2019). Bali Mawacara: Is a quasi-common law system developing in Balinese customary law? *Indonesia Law Review, 9*(3), 296–307. https://doi.org/10.15742/ilrev.v9n3.587.
114. Kilian, P., (2019). Self-determination of peoples in the charter of the United Nations. *Revista De Estudos Constitucionais Hermeneutica E Teoria Do Direito-Rechtd, 11*(3), 341–353. https://doi.org/10.4013/rechtd.2019.113.03.
115. Kim, M. S. H., (2009). Customary law and colonial jurisprudence in Korea. *American Journal of Comparative Law, 57*(1), 205–247. https://doi.org/10.5131/ajcl.2008.0006.
116. Kim, P. Y., (2020). In, from, and to space: Safeguarding the United States of America and her interests. *University of Pennsylvania Journal of International Law, 42*(4), 1157–1199. <Go to ISI>://WOS:000718323900004.
117. Kingwill, R., (2016). En gendering the norms of customary inheritance in Botswana and South Africa. *Journal of Legal Pluralism and Unofficial Law, 48*(2), 208–237. https://doi.org/10.1080/07329113.2016.1185829.
118. Konrad, K., Schmucker, D., Gollwitzer, P. M., & Oettingen, G., (2020). *Self - Regulation Deficits Underlie Aggressive Behavior Developmental Science, 23*(5), e12988. doi: 10/1111/desc12098.

119. Koskenniemi, M., (1990). Human-rights and humanitarian norms as customary LAW – Meron, T. *Michigan Law Review*, *88*(6), 1946–1962. https://doi.org/10.2307/1289356.

120. Kreso, M., (2010). The transplant of customary law and ICTY jurisprudence to the courts in Bosnia and Herzegovina. [Assessing the legacy of the icty]. *Conference of the International-Criminal-Tribunal-for-the-former-Yugoslavia (ICTY) on Assessing the Legacy, The Hague, Netherlands*.

121. Krieger, H., (2006). A conflict of norms: The relationship between humanitarian law and human rights law in the ICRC customary law study. *Journal of Conflict and Security Law*, *11*(2), 265–291.

122. Kumar, V., (2020). On scripts and sensibility: Cold war international law and revolutionary caribbean subjects. *German Law Journal*, *21*(8), 1541–1569. https://doi.org/10.1017/glj.2020.91.

123. Lagji, A. R. W., (2019). A postcolonial perspective: Law and the literary world. *Law Culture and the Humanities*, *15*(2), 305–318. https://doi.org/10.1177/1743872116630698.

124. Lambert, N. F., & Kootstra - Rambach, S. L., (2021). *Impulsivity and Aggression in Adolescents Clinical Psychological Science*, *9*(3), 590–604. doi: 10 /1177 /2167702620968863.

125. Lavalle, R., (2014). The rights of states over low-tide elevations: A legal analysis. *International Journal of Marine and Coastal Law*, *29*(3), 457–479. https://doi.org/10.1163/15718085-12341317.

126. Laylin, J. G., (1976). Emerging customary law of sea. *International Lawyer*, *10*(4), 669–680. <Go to ISI>://WOS:A1976CW54300005.

127. Lewis, D. J., (1983). A requiem for Chinese customary law in Hong-Kong. *International and Comparative Law Quarterly*, *32*(APR), 347–379. https://doi.org/10.1093/iclqaj/32.2.347.

128. Lewis, L., (2016). Exploring the 'ecology' of laws at the interface between international rights law and subnational customary law. *African Journal of International and Comparative Law*, *24*(1), 105–141. https://doi.org/10.3366/ajicl.2016.0143.

129. Liakopoulos, D., (2019). Rough justice: Anatomy, interpretation, and exclusion of individual liability in international criminal justice. *Revista Do Curso De Direito Do Unifor*, *10*(1), 148–233. https://doi.org/10.24862/rcdu.v10i1.1013.

130. Lijnzaad, L., (2022). Going for a test drive? Some observations on the turn to informality in the laws of armed conflict. *International Review of the Red Cross, 104*(920, 921), 1930–1947, Article Pii s1816383122000807. https://doi.org/10.1017/s1816383122000807.

131. Lingaas, C., (2022). Indigenous customary law and Norwegian domestic law: Scenes of a (complementary or mutually exclusive) marriage? *Laws, 11*(2), Article 19. https://doi.org/10.3390/laws11020019.

132. Lita, H. N., Suparman, E., Supriatni, R., & Epi, D., (2017). *Application of customary Law in Improving Economic Welfare of Adat Village Community: A Case Study of Tourism Economic Potential of Adat village` in West Java.* Advances in Social Science Education and Humanities Research [Proceedings of 1st international conference of law and justice – good governance and human rights in Muslim countries: Experiences and challenges (ICLJ 2017)]. 1st International Conference of Law and Justice – Good Governance and Human Rights in Muslim Countries – Experiences and Challenges (ICLJ), Jakarta, Indonesia.

133. Liu, C. H., (2019). Regional customary international law related to China's historic rights in the South China Sea. *Korean Journal of International and Comparative Law, 7*(2), 262–276. https://doi.org/10.1163/22134484-12340128.

134. Loja, M. H., (2014). Who owns the oil that traverses a boundary on the continental shelf in an enclosed sea? Seeking answers in natural law through Grotius and Selden. *Leiden Journal of International Law, 27*(4), 893–911. https://doi.org/10.1017/s0922156514000405.

135. Lon, Y. S., & Widyawati, F., (2021). Customary law before religion and state laws regarding marriage in Manggarai, Eastern Indonesia. *Jurnal Cita Hukum-Indonesian Law Journal, 9*(1), 93–110. https://doi.org/10.15408/jch.v9i1.16510.

136. Magnusson, B. M., (2013). Outer continental shelf boundary agreements. *International & Comparative Law Quarterly, 62*(2), 345–372. https://doi.org/10.1017/s0020589313000067.

137. Magnusson, B. M., (2017). Can the United States establish the outer limits of its extended continental shelf under international law? *Ocean Development and International Law, 48*(1), 1–16. https://doi.org/10.1080/00908320.2017.1265361.

138. Manaka, M., & Corrin, J., (2021). Legal pluralism and the public solicitor's office of Solomon Islands. *Journal of Legal Pluralism and*

Unofficial Law, *53*(3), 397–406. https://doi.org/10.1080/07329113.2021.2004829.

139. Manullang, S. O., (2021). Understanding the sociology of customary law in the reformation era: Complexity and diversity of society in Indonesia. *Linguistics and Culture Review*, *5*(S3), 16–26.
140. Marasinghe, M. L., (1978). Customary law of immovable property and of succession – Kerr, AJ. *Canadian Bar Review-Revue Du Barreau Canadien*, *56*(2), 385–392. <Go to ISI>://WOS:A1978FG83200011.
141. Masengu, T., (2016). Customary law inheritance: Lessons learnt from Ramantele v. Mmusi and others. *African Journal of International and Comparative Law*, *24*(4), 582–603. https://doi.org/10.3366/ajicl.2016.0174.
142. Mastura, M. O., (1994). Legal pluralism in the Philippines. *Law & Society Review*, *28*(3), 461–475. https://doi.org/10.2307/3054065.
143. Maunatlala, K., & Maimela, C., (2020). The implementation of customary law of succession and common law of succession respectively: With a specific focus on the eradication of the rule of male primogeniture. *De Jure*, *53*, 36–53. <Go to ISI>://WOS:000582729600003.
144. Maxim, F., & Titu, M. U. O. B., (2015). *Customary International Law – a Current Concern of the International Society.* [Law between modernization and tradition – implications for the legal, political, administrative, and public order organization]. International Conference on Law between Modernization and Tradition – Implications for the Legal, Political, Administrative and Public Order Organization, Bucharest, Romania.
145. McAuslan, P., (2015). Property and empire: From colonialism to globalization and back. *Social & Legal Studies*, *24*(3), 339–357. https://doi.org/10.1177/0964663915593010.
146. McCarthy, P., (1971). Customary law – manual and jurisprudence in Zande – French – Vanderlinden, J. *American Journal of Comparative Law*, *19*(3), 595–599. <Go to ISI>://WOS:A1971J858800011.
147. McLachlan, C., (1988). The recognition of aboriginal customary law – pluralism beyond the colonial paradigm: A review article. *International and Comparative Law Quarterly*, *37*, 368–386. <Go to ISI>://WOS:A1988N399100007.
148. Menski, W. F., (1988). Social facts and fabrications – customary law on Kilimanjaro 1880-1980 – Moore, SF. *International and*

Comparative Law Quarterly, *37*, 1042–1044. https://doi.org/10.1093/iclqaj/37.4.1042-a.

149. Meron, T., (1987). The Geneva Conventions as customary law. *American Journal of International Law*, *81*(2), 348–370.
150. Meron, T., (1991). *Human Rights and Humanitarian Norms as Customary Law. https://www.corteidh.or.cr/tablas/11905.pdf*
151. Meron, T., Parks, W. H., Matheson, M. J., Gasser, H. P., Carnahan, B. M., & Solf, W., (1987). Customary law and additional protocol-I to the Geneva conventions for protection of war victims – future-directions in light of the united-states decision not to ratify. *Proceedings of the 81st Annual Meeting of the American Society of International Law.* 81st Annual Meeting of the American Soc of International Law, Boston, Ma.
152. Merry, S. E., (1991). Social facts and fabrications – customary law on Kilimanjaro, 1880-1980 – Moore, SF. *Law & Society Review*, *25*(4), 889–922. <Go to ISI>://WOS:A1991HK48000008.
153. Meyer, T., (2012). Codifying custom. *University of Pennsylvania Law Review*, *160*(4), 995–1069. <Go to ISI>://WOS:000302334500003.
154. Milanovic, M., (2011). Is the Rome statute binding on individuals? (and why we should care). *Journal of International Criminal Justice*, *9*(1), 25–52. https://doi.org/10.1093/jicj/mqq070.
155. Mnisi, S., & Claassens, A., (2009). Rural women redefining land rights in the context of living customary law. *South African Journal on Human Rights*, *25*(3), 491–516.
156. Moore, S. F., (1986). *Social Facts and Fabrications:" Customary" Law on Kilimanjaro, 1880–1980* (Vol. 1981). Cup Archive.
157. Morrison, R. D., (2016). The charter of the Kanak people: In pursuit of "cooperative and balanced legal pluralism" in New Caledonia. *Journal of Legal Pluralism and Unofficial Law*, *48*(3), 476–521. https://doi.org/10.1080/07329113.2016.1223969.
158. Morudu, N. L., & Maimela, C., (2021). The indigenization of customary law: Creating an indigenous legal pluralism within the South African dispensation: Possible or not? *De Jure*, *54*, 54–69. https://doi.org/10.17159/2225-7160/2021/v54a4.
159. Murphy, J. B., (2014). *The Philosophy of Customary Law*. Oxford University Press.

160. Mwalimu, C., (1988). A bibliographic essay of selected secondary sources on the common-law and customary law of English-speaking Sub-Saharan Africa. *Law Library Journal*, *80*(2), 241–289. <Go to ISI>://WOS:A1988P374700005.

161. Mwambene, L., (2012). Custody disputes under African customary family law in Malawi: Adaptability to change? *International Journal of Law Policy and the Family*, *26*(2), 127–142. https://doi.org/10.1093/lawfam/ebs004.

162. Mwangi, C. K., (2022). Traditional knowledge and the inclusive subordination of African customary law in Kenya: Lessons from personal law. *Journal of African Law*, *66*(1), 47–71. Article Pii s0021855321000358. https://doi.org/10.1017/s0021855321000358.

163. Ndulo, M., (2011). African customary law, customs, and women's rights. *Indiana Journal of Global Legal Studies*, *18*(1), 87–120.

164. Ngira, D. O., (2018). Re-examining burial disputes in Kenyan courts through the lenses of legal pluralism. *Onati Socio-Legal Series*, *8*(7), 1020–1040. https://doi.org/10.35295/osls.iisl/0000-0000-0000-0982.

165. Ngira, D. O., (2021). Understanding children's rights from a pluralistic legal context: Multi-legalities and the protection of the best interests of the child in rural Kenya. *Journal of Legal Pluralism and Unofficial Law*, *53*(3), 545–569. https://doi.org/10.1080/07329113.2021.1982170.

166. Nhlapo, R. T., (1997). *The Status of Customary Law in Africa: From the Age of "Law and Modernization" to the era of "Human Rights and Constitutionalism."* [Judiciary in Africa]. Seminar on the Role of the Judiciary in a Changing Africa, Cape Town, South Africa.

167. Nhlapo, T., (2017). Customary law in post-apartheid South Africa: Constitutional confrontations in culture, gender and 'living law.' *South African Journal on Human Rights*, *33*(1), 1–24. https://doi.org/10.1080/02587203.2017.1303900.

168. Nnona, C. G., (2018). Customary corporate law in common law Africa. *American Journal of Comparative Law*, *66*(3), 639–668. https://doi.org/10.1093/ajcl/avy032.

169. Norr, D., (1973). Genesis of theory of customary law. *Law and State*, *7*, 126–140. <Go to ISI>://WOS:A1973Q407400008.

170. Nwapi, C., (2016). Land grab, property rights and gender equality in pluralistic legal orders: A Nigerian perspective. *African Journal*

of Legal Studies, *9*(2), 124–146. https://doi.org/10.1163/17087384-12340005.

171. Nyane, H., (2019). A critique of the Swazi constitutional rules on succession to kingship. *De Jure*, *52*, 65–84. https://doi.org/10.17159/2225-7160/2019/v52a4.
172. Oba, A. A., (2002). Islamic law as customary law: The changing perspective in Nigeria. *International & Comparative Law Quarterly*, *51*(4), 817–850.
173. Oba, A. A., (2008). Juju oaths in customary law arbitration and their legal validity in Nigerian courts. *Journal of African Law*, *52*(1), 139–158. https://doi.org/10.1017/s0021855308000065.
174. Oba, A. A., (2011). Religious and customary laws in Nigeria. *Emory Int'l L. Rev.*, *25*, 881.
175. Obatusin, S. C., (2018). Customary law principles as a tool for human rights advocacy: Innovating Nigerian customary practices using lessons from Ugandan and South African Courts. *Columbia Journal of Transnational Law*, *56*(3), 636–679. <Go to ISI>://WOS:000451397700004.
176. Olaf, Z., & Markus, V. H., (2018). Processing the paradox: When the state has to deal with customary law. In: *The State and the Paradox of Customary Law in Africa* (pp. 1-40). Routledge.
177. Omidire, K., (1990). Change of personal law under customary law in Nigeria. *International and Comparative Law Quarterly*, *39*, 671–675. https://doi.org/10.1093/iclqaj/39.3.671.
178. O'Neill, K. C., (2002). A new customary law of head of state immunity? Hirohito and Pinochet. *Stanford Journal of International Law*, *38*(2), 289–317. <Go to ISI>://WOS:000176515000004.
179. Orebech, P., Bosselman, F., Bjarup, J., Callies, D., Chanock, M., & Petersen, H., (2005). *The Role of Customary Law in Sustainable Development*. Cambridge University Press.
180. Osman, F., & Baase, M., (2022). The recognition of same-sex customary marriages under South African customary law. *South African Journal on Human Rights*, *38*(1, 2), 1–23. https://doi.org/10.1080/02587203.2022.2128398.
181. Osman, F., & Himonga, C., (2017). The constitutionality of section 7(1) of the Recognition of customary marriages act: Ramuhovhi v president of the republic of South Africa. *Journal of Legal Pluralism*

and Unofficial Law, *49*(2), 166–182. https://doi.org/10.1080/07329113.2017.1344483.

182. Osman, F., (2019). The ascertainment of living customary law: An analysis of the South African constitutional Court's jurisprudence. *Journal of Legal Pluralism and Unofficial Law*, *51*(1), 98–113. https://doi.org/10.1080/07329113.2019.1596013.
183. Ottley, B. L., (2016). Legal dissonance: The interaction of criminal law and customary law in Papua New Guinea. *Asia Pacific Law Review*, *24*(1), 83–86. https://doi.org/10.1080/10192577.2016.1203049.
184. Parisi, F., (2001). *The Formation of Customary Law*. Available at SSRN 262032.
185. Pedersen, O. W., (2014). From abundance to indeterminacy: The precautionary principle and its two camps of custom. *Transnational Environmental Law*, *3*(2), 323–339. https://doi.org/10.1017/s2047102514000132.
186. Pelizzon, A., (2015). Aboriginal customary law: A source of common law title to land. *Griffith Law Review*, *24*(1), 147–150. https://doi.org/10.1080/10383441.2015.1048583.
187. Perreau-Saussine, A., & Murphy, J. B., (2007). *The Nature of Customary Law: Legal, Historical, and Philosophical Perspectives*. Cambridge university press.
188. Petersen, N., (2007). Customary law without custom-rules, principles, and the role of state practice in international norm creation. *Am. U. Int'l L. Rev.*, *23*, 275.
189. Petersen, N., (2017). The international court of justice and the judicial politics of identifying customary international law. *European Journal of International Law*, *28*(2), 357–385. https://doi.org/10.1093/ejil/chx024.
190. Pocar, F., (2016). International criminal justice and the unifying role of customary law. *Uniform Law Review*, *21*(2, 3), 171–176. https://doi.org/10.1093/ulr/unw024.
191. Poespasari, E. D., (2020). The development of inheritance customary legal norm on Minangkabau indigenous society. *Juridical Tribune-Tribuna Juridica*, *10*(2), 328–334. <Go to ISI>://WOS:000546443500010.
192. Polanski, P. P., (2017). Cyberspace: A new branch of international customary law? *Computer Law & Security Review*, *33*(3), 371–381. https://doi.org/10.1016/j.clsr.2017.03.007.

193. Pratiwi, P. F. P., Suprayitno, S., & Triyani, T., (2020). Existence of customary law through comparative education between Dayak Ngaju customary law and national law. *Budapest International Research and Critics Institute-Journal (BIRCI-Journal), 3*(2), 712–717.

194. Qerimi, I., (2020). Special institutes of the kanun of Leke Dukagjini and its application in contemporary time among the Albanians. *Zbornik Pravnog Fakulteta Sveucilista U Rijeci, 41*(2), 591–608. https://doi.org/10.30925/zpfsr.41.2.8.

195. Quane, H., (2013). Legal pluralism and international human rights law: Inherently incompatible, mutually reinforcing or something in between? *Oxford Journal of Legal Studies, 33*(4), 675–702. https://doi.org/10.1093/ojls/gqt018.

196. Rautenbach, C., (2020). The influence of foreign judgments on the development of post-apartheid constitutional law in south Africa: Judicial law-making in action? *Journal of International and Comparative Law, 7*(1), 99–125. <Go to ISI>://WOS:000571381500004.

197. Rose, R., (1989). Casebook on Kenya customary law – Cotran, E. *International and Comparative Law Quarterly, 38*, 238. https://doi.org/10.1093/iclqaj/38.1.238.

198. Rubin, A. P., (1990). Human-rights and humanitarian norms as customary law – Meron, T. *Harvard International Law Journal, 31*(2), 685–694. <Go to ISI>://WOS:A1990EE09000008.

199. Russo, F. V., (1988). Neutrality at sea in transition – state practice in the gulf war as emerging international customary law. *Ocean Development and International Law, 19*(5), 381–399. https://doi.org/10.1080/00908328809545868.

200. Sarbah, J. M., (1904). *Fanti Customary Laws: A Brief Introduction to the Principles of the Native Laws and Customs of the Fanti and Akan Districts of the Gold COAST*. W. Clowes and Sons, limited.

201. Seidman, R. B., (1983). Rules of recognition in the primary courts of Zimbabwe – on lawyers reasonings and customary law. *International and Comparative Law Quarterly, 32*, 871–903. https://doi.org/10.1093/iclqaj/32.4.871.

202. Sheleff, L. S., (2013). *The Future of Tradition: Customary Law, Common Law, and Legal Pluralism*. Routledge.

203. Sheleff, L., (1994). Customary law as common law. *Semiotics and the Human Sciences [Conscience, Consensus and Crossroads in Law:*

Eighth Round Table on Law and Semiotics]. 8th Round Table on Law and Semiotics – Conscience, Consensus, and Crossroads in Law, Penn State Reading, Reading, Pa.

204. Shingleton, B., (1983). UNCLOS-III and the struggle for law – the elusive customary law of seabed mining. *Ocean Development and International Law*, *13*(1), 33–63. https://doi.org/10.1080/00908328309545719.
205. Sibisi, S., (2020). Is the requirement of integration of the bride optional in customary marriages? *De Jure*, *53*, 90–103. https://doi.org/10.17159/2225-7160/2020/v53a6.
206. Siegel, N., (2015). Thinking the boundaries of customary law in south Africa. *South African Journal on Human Rights*, *31*, 357–378. <Go to ISI>://WOS:000367358500006.
207. Sierra, M. T., (1995). Indian rights and customary law in Mexico – a study of the Nahuas in the Sierra de Puebla. *Law & Society Review*, *29*(2), 227–254. https://doi.org/10.2307/3054011.
208. Singer, N. J., (1972). Ethiopian civil code and recognition of customary law. *Houston Law Review*, *9*(3), 460–494. <Go to ISI>://WOS:A1972M057800002.
209. Skomerska-Muchowska, I., (2017). Some remarks on the role of general principles in the interpretation and application of international customary and treaty law. *Polish Yearbook of International Law*, *37*, 255–272. https://doi.org/10.7420/pyil2017m.
210. Snyder, F., (1984). Customary law and the economy. *Journal of African Law*, *28*(1, 2), 34–43.
211. Sprankling, J. G., (2014). The global right to property. *Columbia Journal of Transnational Law*, *52*(2), 464–505. <Go to ISI>://WOS:000333573500003.
212. Sun, J., (2010). The linkage requirement in enforcement immunity. *Chinese Journal of International Law*, *9*(4), 699–716. https://doi.org/10.1093/chinesejil/jmq029.
213. Syaufi, A., & Zahra, A. F., (2021). The existence of customary law: Badamai customary law. *Research Horizon*, *1*(3), 94–99.
214. Tan, C. G. S., (1993). The twilight of Chinese customary law relating to marriage in Malaysia. *International and Comparative Law Quarterly*, *42*, 147–156. https://doi.org/10.1093/iclqaj/42.1.147.

215. Tan, Y. D., (2018). The identification of customary rules in international criminal law. *Utrecht Journal of International and European Law, 34*(2), 92–110. https://doi.org/10.5334/ujiel.434.

216. Tegnan, H., (2015). Legal pluralism and land administration in West Sumatra: The implementation of the regulations of both local and Nagari governments on communal land tenure. *Journal of Legal Pluralism and Unofficial Law, 47*(2), 312–323. https://doi.org/10.1080/07329113.2015.1072386.

217. Thipe, T., & Buthelezi, M., (2014). Discourse and debate. *South African Journal on Human Rights, 30*, 196–205. https://doi.org/10.1080/19962126.2014.11865104.

218. Thirlway, H. W., (1972). *International Customary Law and Codification: An Examination of the Continuing Role of Custom in the Present Period of Codification of International Law*. Martinus Nijhoff Publishers.

219. Thirlway, H., (2015). Human rights in customary law: An attempt to define some of the issues. *Leiden Journal of International Law, 28*(3), 495–506. https://doi.org/10.1017/s0922156515000266.

220. Thirlway, H., (2017). The role of non-state actors: A response to professor Ryngaert. *Netherlands International Law Review, 64*(1), 141–153. https://doi.org/10.1007/s40802-017-0081-6.

221. Tobin, B., (2014). *Indigenous Peoples, Customary Law, and Human Rights-Why Living Law Matters*. Routledge.

222. Tomuschat, C., (2021). The relevance of time in international law. *Polish Yearbook of International Law, 41*, 9–30. https://doi.org/10.24425/pyil.2022.142335.

223. Treasure, W., Fardin, J., Apoh, W., & Wissing, K., (2016). From Mabo to Obuasi: Mining, heritage and customary law in Ghana and Western Australia. *Journal of Energy & Natural Resources Law, 34*(2), 191–211. https://doi.org/10.1080/02646811.2016.1133986.

224. Tripp, A. M., (2004). Women's movements, customary law, and land rights in Africa: The case of Uganda. *African Studies Quarterly, 7*(4), 1–19.

225. Tsai, G. Y. F., (2015). Inheritance dispute resolution in Paiwan tribes. *National Taiwan University Law Review, 10*(2), 289–358. https://doi.org/10.3966/181263242015091002004.

226. Tucker, R. W., (1972). Reprisals and self-defense – customary law. *American Journal of International Law*, *66*(3), 586–596. https://doi.org/10.1017/s0002930000206842.
227. Tucker, R. W., (1972). Reprisals and self-defense: The customary law. *American Journal of International Law*, *66*(3), 586–596.
228. Tunkin, G., (1993). Is general international law customary law only. *Eur. J. Int'l L.*, *4*, 534.
229. Tupper, C. L., (1881). *Punjab Customary Law* (Vol. 1). Office of the superintendent of government printing.
230. Ubink, J. M., (2008). *In the Land of the Chiefs: Customary Law, Land Conflicts, and the Role of the State in Peri-urban Ghana*. Leiden University.
231. Ubink, J., & Weeks, S. M., (2017). Courting custom: Regulating access to justice in Rural South Africa and Malawi. *Law & Society Review*, *51*(4), 825–858. https://doi.org/10.1111/lasr.12298.
232. Ubink, J., (2016). Access vs. justice: Customary courts and political abuse-lessons from Malawi's local courts act. *American Journal of Comparative Law*, *64*(3), 745–784. https://doi.org/10.1093/ajcl/avw009.
233. Utama, T. S. J., (2021). Between Adat law and living law: An illusion of customary law incorporation into Indonesia penal system. *Journal of Legal Pluralism and Unofficial Law*, *53*(2), 269–289. https://doi.org/10.1080/07329113.2021.1945222.
234. Van, C. R. C., (2014). Lex and consuetudo in English lawsuits from the Conquest to Glanvill. *Tijdschrift Voor Rechtsgeschiedenis-Revue D Histoire Du Droit-the Legal History Review*, *82*(1-2), 19–29. https://doi.org/10.1163/15718190-08212p03.
235. Van, E. G., (2021). From indigenous customary law to diasporic cultural heritage: Reappropriations of Adat throughout the history of Moluccan postcolonial migration. *International Journal for the Semiotics of Law-Revue Internationale De Semiotique Juridique*, *34*(3), 695–721. https://doi.org/10.1007/s11196-020-09781-y.
236. Vanboven, T., (1991). Human-rights and humanitarian norms as customary law – Meron, T. *American Journal of International Law*, *85*(1), 212–214. https://doi.org/10.2307/2203582.
237. Vergouwen, J. C., (2013). *The Social Organization and Customary Law of the Toba-Batak of Northern Sumatra* (Vol. 7). Springer Science & Business Media.

238. Vines, P., (2017). Testamentary freedom and customary law: The impact of succession law on the inheritance needs of aboriginal and Torres strait islanders in Australia. *Australian Law Journal, 91*(5), 360–364. <Go to ISI>://WOS:000400901500004.

239. Watson, A., (1984). An approach to customary law. *University of Illinois Law Review,* (3), 561–576. <Go to ISI>://WOS:A1984AAD1500005.

240. Webber, J., (2009). The grammar of customary law. *McGill Law Journal, 54*(4), 579–626.

241. Weinberg, T., (2016). Pushing the boundaries of customary law jurisprudence in Botswana: Social science and the law in the case of Ramantele vs. Mmusi. *Journal of Legal Pluralism and Unofficial Law, 48*(2), 186–207. https://doi.org/10.1080/07329113.2016.1169056.

242. Williams, J., & Klusener, J., (2013). The traditional courts bill: A woman's perspective. *South African Journal on Human Rights, 29*, 276–293. https://doi.org/10.1080/19962126.2013.11865075.

243. Williams, S., (2022). The nature of a beneficiary's interest under a Jersey law trust: Kea Investments v Watson in its historical context. *Trusts & Trustees, 28*(3), 206–212. https://doi.org/10.1093/tandt/ttac010.

244. Willms, J., (2009). Without order, anything goes? The prohibition of forced displacement in non-international armed conflict. *International Review of the Red Cross, 91*(875), 547–565. https://doi.org/10.1017/s1816383109990397.

245. Wilson, G. M., (1961). *Luo Customary Law and Marriage Laws Customs. https://ehrafworldcultures.yale.edu/cultures/fl11/documents/022*

246. Wolff, L. C., (2016). What is a conflict of laws? the case of Chinese customary law in Hong Kong. *Hong Kong Law Journal, 46*, 849–877. <Go to ISI>://WOS:000391084200006.

247. Woodman, G. R., (1969). Some realism about customary law-the West African experience. *Wis. L. Rev.*, 128.

248. Woodman, G. R., (2001). Customary law in common law systems. *IDS Bulletin, 32*(1), 28–34.

249. Woodman, G., (1988). How state courts create customary law in Ghana and Nigeria. *Indigenous Laws and the State*.

250. Worugji, I. N. E., Ndukwe, O. U., & Endeley, I. P., (2019). The dissolution of 'double deck' marriage in Nigeria. *International Journal*

of Law Policy and the Family, *33*(1), 123–138. https://doi.org/10.1093/lawfam/eby020.

251. Wu, C. J., (2018). Rethinking the nature and legal status of illegal structures in Taiwan: A commentary on Taiwan high court judgment case No. 102, Shang Zi, 1188. *National Taiwan University Law Review*, *13*(1), 111–147. https://doi.org/10.3966/181263242018031301003.
252. Young, S., (2019). Consent, custom and international law in South Africa: What Australian lawmakers could learn. *Alternative Law Journal*, *44*(3), 197–202. https://doi.org/10.1177/1037969x19853853.
253. Zamir, N., (2015). Distinction matters: Rethinking the protection of civilian objects in non-international armed conflicts. *Israel Law Review*, *48*(1), 111–132. https://doi.org/10.1017/s0021223714000247.
254. Zarea, R., (2022). Law and culture: Reconceptualization and case studies law and visual jurisprudence LVJ. *International Journal for the Semiotics of Law-Revue Internationale De Semiotique Juridique*, *5, 35*(6), 2527–2531. https://doi.org/10.1007/s11196-022-09938-x.
255. Zenker, O., & Höhne, M. V., (2018). *The State and the Paradox of Customary Law in Africa*. Routledge London.
256. Zerner, C., (1994). Through a green lens – the construction of customary environmental-law and community in Indonesia Maluku Islands. *Law & Society Review*, *28*(5), 1079–1122. https://doi.org/10.2307/3054024.
257. Zilberman, I., (1996). Palestinian customary law in the Jerusalem area. *Catholic University Law Review*, *45*(3), 795–811. <Go to ISI>://WOS:A1996UV01100012.
258. Zitzke, E., (2022). Decolonial comparative law: Thoughts from South Africa. *Rabels Zeitschrift Fur Auslandisches Und Internationales Privatrecht*, *86*(1), 189–225. https://doi.org/10.1628/rabelsz-2022-0008.
259. Zwalve, W. J., (2012). Sola scriptura, An essay in comparative legal history on 'obligacions' in thirteenth century France and England. *Tijdschrift Voor Rechtsgeschiedenis-Revue D Histoire Du Droit-the Legal History Review*, *80*(1, 2), 95–128. https://doi.org/10.1163/157181912x626939.

INDEX

D

U

V

W

X